PHASE2 ADVANTAGE

The Future of Immersive Cybersecurity Education

CERTIFIED

Cyber Security Operations Manager

EXAM PREP GUIDE

Michael I. Kaplan
(Author)

01

C)CSOM Certification Exam Vouchers

Vouchers to purchase the C)CSOM certification exam can be secured via the Phase2 Advantage office. Please see the last page of this exam prep guide for additional information and a **10% discount** off the exam fee when taken separately from a class.

Certified Cyber Security Operations Manager
C)CSOM Exam Prep Guide

Phase2 Advantage
P.O. Box 14071
Savannah, GA 31416
(912) 335-2217

Phase2 Advantage textbooks and study guides may be purchased at discounted rates for educational, business or governmental use when bulk orders are required. For information, please contact Michael I. Kaplan at info@phase2advantage.com.

ISBN-13: 978-1734064056

COURSE DESCRIPTION

Organizations face ongoing threats to their information technology infrastructure on a daily basis. These security struggles need to be approached with modern techniques, a holistic view of security, and a diverse body of knowledge. With the proper tools and training, managers in the Information Security and Cyber Security fields will be much more capable of finding success within their roles.

The *Certified Cyber Security Operations Manager* certification course brings Cyber Security core competencies to advanced levels with new concepts and traditional best practices. Using 16 detailed learning objects, students will be provided with the knowledge and context needed to successfully manage the security of their technical environments. Focusing on the Information Security concerns of today, students will cover topics such as Cloud Security, Threat Intelligence Collection and Analysis, Vulnerability Management, Biometric Security Systems, Incident Response, Securing Systems with Cryptography, and the NICE Cybersecurity Workforce Framework.

SUGGESTED READING

This practical guide to modern encryption breaks down the concepts at the heart of cryptography without shying away from meaty discussions of how they work. You'll learn about authenticated encryption, secure randomness, hash functions, block ciphers, and public-key techniques such as RSA and elliptic curve cryptography. Each chapter includes a discussion of implementation mistakes using real-world examples and details what could go wrong and how to avoid pitfalls.

Paperback: 312 Pages
Publisher: No Starch Press (November 6, 2017)
ISBN-10: 1593278268
ISBN-13: 978-1593278267

Security Risk Management is the definitive guide for building an information security risk management program. This book teaches practical techniques that will be used on a daily basis, while also explaining the fundamentals so students understand the rationale behind these practices. It explains how to perform assessments for new IT projects, how to efficiently manage daily risk activities, and how to qualify the current risk level for presentation to executive management.

Paperback: 360 Pages
Publisher: Syngress; 1 edition (May 31, 2011)
ISBN-10: 1597496154
ISBN-13: 978-1597496155

ABOUT THE DIRECTOR

Michael I. Kaplan is the Director of Operations for Phase2 Advantage, a cybersecurity training and publishing company based in Savannah, Georgia. He is the Chairman of the Savannah Technical College Cybersecurity Advisory Committee and heavily involved in curriculum design. Michael has written numerous courses and cybersecurity training programs for corporate, academic, and government personnel. He has also developed training programs for Law Enforcement and Fugitive Task Force Investigators on the topics of Criminal Topology, Forensic Document Analysis, and Investigations. Michael's technical areas of specialization are Incident Handling and Response, Network Forensics, Digital Forensics, and Information Technology Risk Management. He also provides consulting services for government, corporate, and academic organizations both domestically and internationally.

Table of Contents

DOMAIN 01

The NICE Cybersecurity Workforce Framework

NICE Framework Contributors

The *NICE* (National Initiative for Cybersecurity Education) *Cybersecurity Workforce Framework* is a reference document that describes the interdisciplinary nature of the cybersecurity field. The mission of the Framework is to cultivate an integrated cybersecurity workforce that is globally competitive from "hire to retire." The contributors listed below represent a wide range of disciplines that are involved in the cyber security field.

1. *National Initiative for Cybersecurity Education* (NICE)
2. *National Institute of Standards and Technology* (NIST)
3. U.S. Department of Commerce
4. Governmental Organizations
5. Academic Institutions
6. Private Sector Entities

The NICE Framework Mission (Part I)

The NICE Framework mission stems from the concept that an integrated cyber workforce includes technical and nontechnical roles that are staffed with knowledgeable and experienced people. It seeks to accomplish this goal by focusing on the objectives and areas of importance listed below:

1. Build on Existing Programs
2. Facilitate Change and Innovation
3. Increase Leadership and Vision
4. Create an Integrated Cyber Workforce
5. Define Defensive and Offensive Strategies
6. Define Technical and Nontechnical Roles
7. Address the Challenges to Framework Implementation

The NICE Framework Mission (Part II)

NICE promotes national initiatives that increase the number of people with the knowledge, skills, and abilities to perform required tasks. In support of this mission, the Framework addresses a wide range of objectives directed at academic institutions and workforce development programs.

Domain 01: *The NICE Cybersecurity Workforce Framework*

1. Categorize and Describe Cyber Security
2. Identify and Recruit Cyber Talent
3. Develop and Retain Cyber Talent
4. Establish a Comparable and Repeatable Approach
5. Select and Specify Cyber Roles
6. Develop Cyber Security Curricula
7. Anticipate Workforce Needs

NICE Framework Integration

An integrated workforce can address challenges by preparing organizations to implement their missions and business processes. To achieve this level of integration the Framework has established a common and consistent lexicon that serves as a fundamental workforce reference. Although this standardization strengthens the ability of organizations to communicate across disciplines, it is flexible enough to allow organizations to customize it to fit their needs. Listed below are the areas of the Framework that address its integration into academic and workforce missions.

1. Categories, Specialty Areas, and Work Roles
2. Knowledge, Skills, and Abilities
3. Education, Training, and Development

NICE Framework for Employers

The NICE Framework is designed to strengthen an organizations' ability to communicate consistently and clearly about its cybersecurity workforce. Effective communication between hiring managers and Human Resource personnel can potentially lead to better hiring decisions and development of staff. Listed below are the focus areas within the Framework that are directly relevant to employers.

1. Ability to Inventory and Track the Workforce
2. Identify Strengths and Gaps
3. Training and Qualification Requirements
4. Improve Cyber Position Descriptions
5. Improve Vacancy Announcements
6. Identify Relevant Work Roles

NICE Framework Components

The NICE Framework organizes cybersecurity and related work and defines its core components in support of those areas. Listed below is the hierarchical structure of the Framework.

1. Categories (7)
2. Specialty Areas (33)
3. Work Roles (52)
4. Knowledge, Skills, and Abilities (1,180)
5. Tasks (1,007)

NICE Framework Key Terms

1. **Categories**: Categories provide the overarching organizational structure of the NICE Framework. There are seven Categories, and all are composed of Specialty Areas and work roles. This organizational structure is based on extensive job analyses, which group together work and workers that share common major functions, regardless of job titles or other occupational terms.

2. **Specialty Areas**: Categories contain groupings of cybersecurity work, which are called Specialty Areas. Each specialty area represents an area of concentrated work, or function, within cybersecurity and related work. In previous versions of the NICE Framework, tasks and KSA's were associated with each specialty area. KSA's and tasks are now associated with the work roles.

3. **Work Roles**: Work Roles are the most detailed groupings of cybersecurity and related work which include a list of attributes required to perform that role in the form of *knowledge, skills, and abilities* (KSA's) and tasks performed in that role.

4. **Knowledge, Skills, and Abilities**: *Knowledge, Skills, and Abilities* (KSA's) are the attributes required to perform work roles and are generally demonstrated through relevant experience, education, or training.

5. **Tasks**: A Task is a specific defined piece of work that, combined with other identified tasks, composes the work in a specific specialty area or work role.

NICE Framework Categories

Organizations can use the NICE Framework to develop publications or tools that meet their needs and provide guidance on workforce development. The categories and their function are listed below, followed by the specialty areas associated with the category.

1. **ANALYZE**: This category performs highly-specialized review and evaluation of incoming cybersecurity information to determine its usefulness for intelligence.
    - **a.** All-Source Analyst
    - **b.** Mission Assessment Specialist
    - **c.** Exploitation Analyst
    - **d.** Multi-Disciplined Language Analyst
    - **e.** Target Developer
    - **f.** Target Network Analyst
2. **COLLECT AND OPERATE**: This category provides specialized denial and deception operations and collection of cybersecurity information that may be used to develop intelligence.
    - **a.** All Source-Collection Manager
    - **b.** All Source-Collection Requirements Manager
    - **c.** Partner Integration Planner
    - **d.** Cyber Intel Planner
    - **e.** Cyber Ops Planner
    - **f.** Cyber Operator
3. **INVESTIGATE**: This category investigates cybersecurity events or crimes related, but not limited to, information technology (IT) systems, networks, and digital evidence.
    - **a.** Cyber Investigation
    - **b.** Cyber Crime Investigator
    - **c.** Law Enforcement Forensics Analyst
    - **d.** Counterintelligence Forensics Analyst
    - **e.** Cyber Defense Forensics Analyst

4. **OPERATE AND MAINTAIN**: This category provides the support, administration, and maintenance necessary to ensure effective and efficient information technology (IT) system performance and security.
   - **a.** Technical Support Specialist
   - **b.** Database Administrator
   - **c.** Data Analyst
   - **d.** Knowledge Manager
   - **e.** Network Operations Specialist
   - **f.** System Administrator
   - **g.** Systems Security Analyst

5. **OVERSEE AND GOVERN**: This category provides leadership, management, direction, or development and advocacy so the organization may effectively conduct cybersecurity work.
   - **a.** Cybersecurity Management
   - **b.** Executive Cyber Leadership
   - **c.** Legal Advice and Advocacy
   - **d.** Program Management and Acquisition
   - **e.** Strategic Planning and Policy
   - **f.** Training, Education, and Awareness

6. **PROTECT AND DEFEND**: This category identifies analyzes and mitigates threats to internal information technology (IT) systems and/or networks.
   - **a.** Cyber Defense Analyst
   - **b.** Cyber Defense Infrastructure Support
   - **c.** Cyber Defense Incident Responder
   - **d.** Vulnerability Assessment Analyst
   - **e.** Vulnerability Assessment Manager

7. **SECURELY PROVISION**: This category conceptualizes, designs, procures, and/or builds secure information technology (IT) systems, with responsibility for aspects of system and/or network development.
   - **a.** Risk Management
   - **b.** Software Development
   - **c.** Systems Architecture
   - **d.** Systems Development
   - **e.** Systems Requirements Planning

- **f.** Technology Research and Development
- **g.** Testing and Evaluation

Knowledge, Skills, and Abilities (KSA's)

1. **Knowledge**: A body of information applied directly to the performance of a function.

2. **Skill**: An observable competence to perform a learned psychomotor act.

3. **Ability**: Competence to perform an observable behavior or a behavior that results in an observable product.

Knowledge: Common to All Work Roles

The first six knowledge points listed in the NICE Framework Knowledge Descriptions are common to all cyber security work roles and considered a critical requirement for all positions in the cyber security field. There are a total of 630 knowledge points associated with the NICE Framework work roles.

1. Networking Concepts and Protocols
2. Risk Management Processes
3. Laws, Regulations, and Policies
4. Cyber Security and Privacy Principles
5. Cyber Threats and Vulnerabilities
6. Impacts of Cyber Security Lapses

Skills: Top 6 Observable Competencies

The first six skill points listed in the NICE Framework Skills Descriptions are considered a critical requirement for all positions in the cyber security field. There are a total of 374 skill points associated with the NICE Framework work roles.

1. Conducting Vulnerability Scans
2. Allocating Data Storage Capacity
3. Identifying and Mitigating Malware

4. Analyzing Network Traffic Capacity
5. Applying IT into Proposed Solutions
6. Applying CIA Triad Principles

Ability: Top 6 Observable Behaviors

Ability is defined as competence to perform an observable behavior or a behavior that results in an observable product. The top six ability points listed in the NICE Framework Skills Descriptions are considered a critical requirement for all positions in the cyber security field. There are a total of 176 ability points associated with the NICE Framework work roles.

1. Identify Systemic Security Issues
2. Match Knowledge to Environment
3. Determine the Validity of Trend Data
4. Develop Curricula for Appropriate Audiences
5. Decrypt Digital Data Collections
6. Prepare and Deliver Briefings

Implementing the NICE Framework

One of the challenges in applying the NICE Framework in day-to-day operations is that it must be executed as a bottom-up implementation. Frameworks are typically presented in a top-down, hierarchical manner that serves to make the structure easier to understand for most audiences. Although the Framework is presented in such a manner, successful implementation will require an inverted, bottom-up approach. The proper order for implementation is listed below.

1. Tasks
2. Abilities
3. Skills
4. Knowledge
5. Work Role
6. Specialty Area
7. Category

Creating Work Role Descriptions

Successful implementation of the NICE Framework begins with creating work roles with accurate descriptions and expectations. This tends to be the most time consuming portion of customizing it for day-to-day use within an organization. The steps listed below provide a general overview of creating a work role and assigning it into a relevant category.

1. **Tasks**: Identify the critical tasks to be performed by the personnel in the work role using the 1,007 task descriptions available in the Framework.

2. **Abilities**: Identify the primary abilities expected to be demonstrated by the personnel in the work role using the 176 ability descriptions provided in the Framework.

3. **Skills**: Identify the critical skills that must be possessed by personnel in the work role using the 374 skill descriptions listed in the Framework.

4. **Knowledge**: Identify the important knowledge expected to be exhibited by the personnel in the work role using the 630 knowledge descriptions provided in the Framework.

5. **Work Role Description**: Create a work role description using verbiage from the chosen tasks and KSA's to accurately reflect its requirements and functionality.

6. **Work Role Title**: Create a work role title that both accurately describes the position and aligns with similar title used in the cyber security field.

7. **Assign a Specialty Area**: Assign the work role to one of the 33 specialty areas that most accurately reflects the scope of the position.

8. **Assign a Category**: Assign the work role to one of the seven categories that most accurately reflects the scope of the specialty area.

DOMAIN 01

The NICE Cybersecurity Workforce Framework

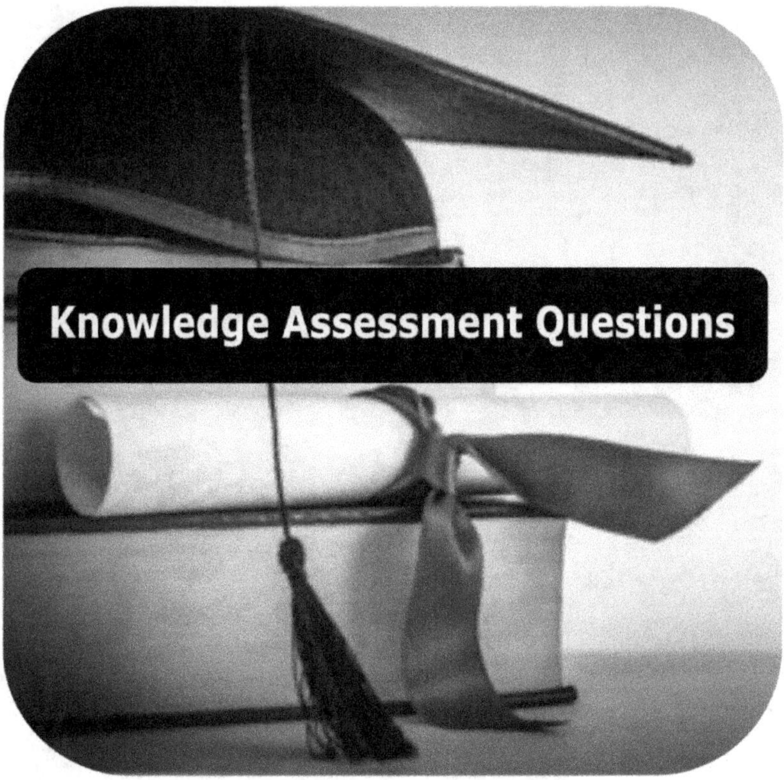

The following knowledge assessment questions are presented as true / false, multiple choice, and fill-in-the-blank. The correct answers are provided in an Answer Key at the end of this text. These questions may or may not be presented on the actual certification exam.

Domain 01: Knowledge Assessment Questions

1. Which of the choices listed below presents a day-to-day challenge for organizations implementing the NICE Framework?

A. Top-Down Implementation

B. Category Training Programs

C. Bottom-Up Implementation

D. Funding for Work Roles

E. None of the Above

2. Each __________ represents an area of concentrated work, or function, within cybersecurity and related work.

A. Work Role

B. Specialty Area

C. Category

D. Knowledge Point

E. None of the Above

3. Select the best choice below for the following definition: "*A specific defined piece of work that, combined with other identified Tasks, composes the work in a specific specialty area or work role*."

A. Skill

B. Ability

C. Knowledge

D. Task

E. None of the Above

4. The __________ Category identifies, analyzes, and mitigates threats to internal information technology (IT) systems and/or networks.

A. Analyze

B. Investigate

C. Protect and Defend

D. Oversee and Govern

E. None of the Above

5. Which choice listed below is one of the first six knowledge points common to all work roles in the NICE Framework?

A. Allocating Data Storage Capacity

B. Determine Validity of Trend Data

C. Conducting Vulnerability Scans

D. Impacts of Cyber Security Lapses

E. None of the Above

6. __________ are the attributes required to perform work roles and are generally demonstrated through relevant experience, education, or training.

A. Work Roles

B. Specialty Areas

C. Knowledge, Skills, and Abilities

D. Categories

E. None of the Above

7. Select the best choice below for the following definition: "*Identifies, analyzes, and mitigates threats to internal information technology (IT) systems and/or networks*."

A. Oversee and Govern

B. Operate and Maintain

C. Protect and Defend

D. Securely Provision

E. None of the Above

8. The __________ Category provides leadership, management, direction, or development and advocacy so the organization may effectively conduct cybersecurity work.

A. Analyze

B. Investigate

C. Protect and Defend

D. Oversee and Govern

E. None of the Above

9. Which choice listed below is one of the six critical observable competencies listed as skill points in the NICE Framework?

A. Analyzing Network Traffic Capacity

B. Laws, Regulations, and Policies

C. Develop Appropriate Curriculum

D. Cyber Security and Privacy Principles

E. None of the Above

10. A __________ is a specific defined piece of work that, combined with other identified Tasks, composes the work in a specific specialty area or work role.

A. Knowledge

B. Skill

C. Ability

D. Task

E. None of the Above

11. Select the best choice below for the following definition: "*Competence to perform an observable behavior or a behavior that results in an observable product*."

A. Skill

B. Ability

C. Knowledge

D. Task

E. None of the Above

12. The __________ Category performs highly-specialized review and evaluation of incoming cybersecurity information to determine its usefulness for intelligence.

A. Analyze

B. Investigate

C. Protect and Defend

D. Oversee and Govern

E. None of the Above

13. NICE is committed to cultivating an integrated cybersecurity workforce that is globally competitive from "hire to retire."

1. True
2. False

14. An integrated cyber workforce consists of only technical roles that are staffed with knowledgeable and experienced people.

1. True
2. False

15. NICE promotes national initiatives that increase the number of people with the knowledge, skills, and abilities to perform required tasks.

1. True
2. False

16. An integrated workforce can address challenges by preparing organizations to implement their policies and vision statements.

1. True
2. False

17. The NICE Framework will strengthen an organizations' ability to communicate consistently and clearly about its cybersecurity workforce.

1. True
2. False

18. The NICE Framework organizes business processes and related work and defines its profit potential in support of those areas.

1. True
2. False

DOMAIN 02

Principles of Identity and Access Management

Authentication Concepts

Authentication, *authorization*, and *accounting* (AAA) work together with identification to provide a comprehensive access management system. For this system to work, two entities must know the credentials being utilized. Listed below are the general components of the authentication process.

1. **Identification**: A person or a system makes a specific claim of identity.

2. **Authentication**: The claim made by the person or system is confirmed to be valid or invalid.

3. **Authorization**: Once the claim of identity has be verified, a determination is made regarding access to resources.

4. **Accounting**: The actions and behaviors of entities are monitored and logged.

Authentication Factors

Authentication factors are typically grouped into the five general categories listed below. One factor may be implemented for basic authentication, two factors for more security, and multiple factors for maximum security.

1. Something You **Know**: A Password or PIN
2. Something You **Have**: A Token or Smart Card
3. Something You **Are**: Biometric Identifiers
4. Somewhere You **Are**: Geolocation or IP Address
5. Something You **Do**: Behaviors Interacting with Network

Password Complexity

A strong password has enough length, does not include words found in a dictionary or name, and combines four types of characters (upper case, lower case, numbers, and symbols). A complex password is not necessarily a strong password; it must also be of sufficient length (typically 14 or more characters).

Longer passwords are stronger and generate stronger encryption keys. The password examples listed below are constructed from lower case letters and are followed by the number of possible permutations of the characters.

1. 6 Characters = (26^6) = 308 Million Permutations
2. 10 Characters = (26^{10}) = 141 Trillion Permutations

The number of permutations may seem large at first glance, but modern computers using the proper software can execute 20 billion computations per second. A 10-character password created with lower case letters only can be cracked in under two hours. If the password is created using all four types of characters (upper case, lower case, numbers, and symbols) the permutations increase significantly and the passwords become difficult to crack.

3. 6 Characters = (94^6) = 689 Billion Permutations
4. 10 Characters = (94^{10}) = 53 Quintillion Permutations

Training Password Users

It is important to provide adequate training to users on password security if they use passwords within the organizations. This holds especially true when user passwords are used to generate encryption keys. Listed below are five general topics that should be presented to password users in training and awareness programs.

1. Password Behaviors
2. Password Expiration Dates
3. Password Recovery Procedures
4. Password History
5. Password Reuse Policies

Implementing Password Policies

Password policies typically start as a written document that identifies the organizations' security goals related to passwords. It then becomes the responsibility of security management to disseminate and enforce the policies. The six components listed below should be included in password policies.

1. **Password History**: Users should not be allowed to reuse passwords or create new passwords that change by only a few characters.

2. **Maximum Password Age**: A maximum password age should be established that forces users to change their passwords on a regular basis.

3. **Minimum Password Age**: A minimum password age should be established that prevents users from creating new passwords in rapid succession and return to using the original password.

4. **Minimum Password Length**: A minimum password length should be established to enhance the security of the credential.

5. **Complexity Requirements**: Complexity requirements should be established to prevent users from creating passwords such as "123456" or "qwerty."

CAC's and PIV's

Common Access Cards (CAC's) and *Personal Identity Verification* cards (PIV's) are specialized smart cards used by DoD and federal agencies. They are typically used to access secure facilities. Several characteristics of CAC's and PIV's are listed below.

1. Includes Photo of the User
2. Provides CIAA and Non-Repudiation
3. Supports Multifactor Authentication
4. Includes Embedded Certificates

PIV Credentials in Facility Access

The *Homeland Security Presidential Directive 12* (HSPD-12) addresses secure facility access for employees and contractors. It establishes a standard identity infrastructure using a non-transferable credential that enhances trust in the system. These guidelines identify three risk-based designations that dictate the level of authentication to be used.

1. **Controlled**: 1 Factor of Authentication
2. **Limited**: 2 Factors of Authentication
3. **Exclusion**: 3 Factors of Authentication

Token / Key FOB

Tokens are small programmable devices that provide a "something you have" factor for authentication. They display a number that changes periodically (usually every 60 seconds) on a liquid crystal display. The token is synched with the authentication server and provides the user with a one-time rolling password. Authentication typically occurs via a web interface using the generated number, username, and a password.

HMAC-Based One-Time Password (HOTP)

HMAC-Based One-Time Password (HOTP) is a one-time password algorithm based on *Hash-Based Message Authentication Code* (HMAC). It is an open standard for creating one-time passwords using a secret key and an incrementing counter. The algorithm uses HMAC to hash the result which is then converted into a HOTP value which remains valid until it is used. The risk associated with this method is the password exists indefinitely until used and has the potential to be compromised if discovered by an attacker.

Time-Based One-Time Password (TOTP)

A *Time-Based One-Time Password* (TOTP) is a temporary passcode that uses the current time of day as one of its authentication factors. It is an open standard for creating one-time passwords using a timestamp and an incrementing counter. The algorithm uses HMAC to hash the result which is then converted into a HOTP value which remains valid for 30 seconds. The risk associated with this method is that clock drift can skew the implementation.

Biometric Methods

Biometric methods are the strongest form of authentication as they are the most difficult for a malicious actor to falsify. The risk associated with these methods exists in the potential for *False Acceptance Rates* (FAR) and *False Rejection Rates* (FRR) which will be discussed in detail in Domain 03 (*Biometric Identification and Security Systems*). Listed below are six of the more popular biometric technologies currently used within the information security industry,

1. Fingerprint and Palm Scanners
2. Retina Scanner
3. Iris Scanners
4. Voice Recognition
5. Facial Recognition
6. Behavioral Recognition

Geolocation Methods

Geolocation consists of a group of technologies used to identify a users' location and is widely used in identity and access management programs. The authentication method uses the IP address to locate the user machine by country, region, state, city, and even zip code. The risk associated with these methods exists in the potential for malicious actors to mask their IP address, making it appear to the authentication server they are in a different country. Using a MAC in addition to an IP address can enhance the security process by blocking network access to unrecognized devices.

Windows Group Policy

Windows domains use *Group Policy* to manage multiple users and computers within an organizations' domain. The administrator can create a *Group Policy Object* (GPO)—and selection of settings—and apply those settings to groups of users or devices. The benefit of the GPO is it can be configured once and then applied to numerous groups, reducing the need for setting individual permissions. The GPO's are implemented on domain controllers.

Kerberos

Kerberos is an authentication protocol that uses tickets to allow communication over a network to prove identity in a secure manner. It was originally developed at MIT for UNIX systems but was then expanded to include other operating systems. The *Key Distribution Center* (KDC) is the core component of the protocol. *Ticket-Granting-Tickets* (TGT's) are issued to users with credentials that are embedded within the ticket. The ticket provides the user with authentication to access devices on the network. To facilitate this process, *Kerberos* requires strict time standardization on the network and a subject / user database.

Microsoft NTLM

New Technology LAN Manager (NTLM) is a suite of protocols providing authentication, integrity, and confidentiality within Windows systems. It is considered to be weak and generally discouraged, but it is still implemented in situations where backward compatibility is required. It is a challenge-response authentication process that is governed by Group Policy. Listed below are the three challenge-response messages that are used to authenticate the user.

1. NEGOTIATE_MESSAGE
2. CHALLENGE_MESSAGE
3. AUTHENTICATE_MESSAGE

LDAP / LDAPS

Lightweight Directory Access Protocol (LDAP) specifies formats and methods to query directories (databases of objects). It provides system administrators with a central access point to manage users, computers, and objects. Microsoft's Active Directory is based on LDAP and identifies objects using strings of code. *Lightweight Directory Access Protocol Secure* (LDAPS) introduces security to the LDAP protocol using *Transport Layer Security* (TLS) that encrypts the data prior to transmission.

Active Directory

Active Directory (AD) is a directory service for Windows domain networks that is included in most Windows Server operating systems. It provides directory-based identity services using a domain controller (AD DS Server). It is responsible for the management and storage of data, certificate services, and the managed rights for all users of the system. Listed below are the three core functions provided by Active Directory.

1. Assigns and Enforces Security Policies
2. Authenticates and Authorizes All Users
3. Installs and/or Updates Software

SSO

Single Sign-On (SSO) refers to the ability of a user to log on or access multiple systems by providing credentials only once. In addition to overall security, it is much more convenient for users of the system. It is founded on a relationship based on the transitive trust model: LinkedIn trusts a user, LinkedIn trusts Facebook, and therefore Facebook trusts the user. The risk associated with this method is a compromise of all associated accounts of a user if the authentication is not exceptionally strong. *Single Sign-On* should not be confused with *Same Sign-On*. Using *Single Sign-On*, the user signs on once and can access numerous domains. Using *Same Sign-On*, the user must reenter credentials for each domain but can use the same credentials locally.

SAML Overview

Security Assertion Markup Language (SAML) is an open standard for exchanging data between an identity provider and a service provider. It is an *Extensible Markup Language* (XML) used for security assertions, primarily with the use of Single Sign-On. The management of security assertions is easy within a security domain but becomes increasingly difficult to manage between different security domains. SAML addresses this by creating a web browser SSO profile (see the next section) that has been standardized for interoperability.

SAML Implementation

A *Security Assertion Markup Language* (SAML) profile describes in detail how assertions, protocols, and bindings combine to support a use case. The SAML specification defines three roles that comprise the access control decision process.

1. **Principle**: Initiates the Service Request
2. **Service Provider**: Responsible for Authentication
3. **Identity Provider**: Processes the Security Assertion

OAuth

OAuth is an open standard for authorization that many organizations use to provide third parties secure access to protected resources. It is designed to work with HTTPS to provide authorization (not *authentication*) services. Users grant access to their information—but are not required to provide passwords—and then websites grant third-party permissions based on a system of secured delegated access.

OpenID Connect

Open ID Connect (OIDC) serves as an authentication layer positioned on top of the OAuth 2 authorization framework. Clients (typically a website) verify the end users' identity but are not required to manage their credentials. The authentication is processed by an authorization server which obtains the users' profile information. The provides a very streamlined experience for the users of the system.

Managing Accounts

Account management is concerned with the creation, management, disablement, and termination of user and system accounts. It is governed by the industry best practices of least privilege, need to know, and credential management. The five categories of accounts listed below are typically the focus of account management programs.

1. End-User Accounts
2. Privileged Accounts
3. Guest Accounts
4. Service Accounts
5. Dual-Purpose Accounts

Access Control Models

Access Control Models (ACM) ensure only authenticated and authorized individuals with proper permissions can access system resources. Listed below are the five primary access controls models used within the information security field.

1. Role-Based Access Control
2. Rule-Based Access Control
3. Attribute-Based Access Control
4. Discretionary Access Control
5. Mandatory Access Control

Role-Based Access Control

Role-Based Access Control (RBAC) is a policy-neutral access-control model defined around user roles and privileges. Roles are created by an administrator for specific units with the same job functions and then assigned rights and permissions. There are four broad categories of roles within an organization.

1. Administrators
2. Executives
3. Managers
4. Team Members

Rule-Based Access Control

Rule-Based Access Control (RBAC) ensures access is allowed or denied to resources based on a set of rules defined by a system administrator. The rules are associated with resources or objects and stored in an *Access Control List* (ACL). The ACL validates the user against the rules and confirms or denies access to the resource. Advanced implementations of rules—such as network access by time of day—are typically dynamic. Many administrators use this method for firewalls and intrusion detection systems.

Attribute-Based Access Control

Attribute-Based Access Control (ABAC) evaluates attributes and grants access based on the value of the established attributes. This method uses policy to evaluate attributes; if a policy match exists access is granted. Policies are typically based on three attributes:

1. User Characteristics
2. Environmental Characteristics
3. Resource Characteristics

Discretionary Access Control

Discretionary Access Control (DAC) ensures every resource object has an owner responsible for establishing access rules for the object. It is a highly flexible model used by Windows and UNIX systems. Every resource includes a *Discretionary Access Control List* (DACL) containing *Access Control Entries* (ACE) describing the rights of a security identifier. The access to the user is granted if the ACE in the DCAL validates the permissions align with the users' *Security Identifiers* (SID).

Mandatory Access Control

Mandatory Access Control (MAC) uses object labels to determine access levels and is the strictest of all control models. This model is a hierarchical control of resources used primary by the military and government organizations. The system administrator defines settings and assigns security labels to each resource based on classification and category. The users' permissions must match those assigned to both classification and category or access will not be granted.

1. **Classification**: Top Secret / Secret / Confidential
2. **Category**: Management Role / Specific Project

DOMAIN 02

Principles of Identity and Access Management

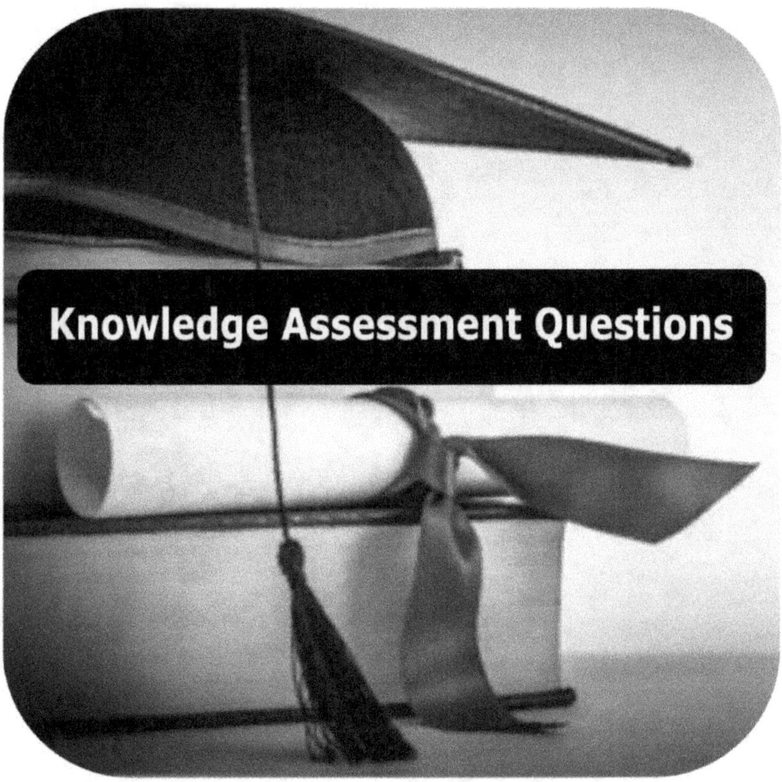

The following knowledge assessment questions are presented as true / false, multiple choice, and fill-in-the-blank. The correct answers are provided in an Answer Key at the end of this text. These questions may or may not be presented on the actual certification exam.

Domain 02: Knowledge Assessment Questions

1. Which choice below is a function and/or characteristic typically associated with physical tokens used for two-factor authentication?

A. Includes Photo of the User

B. Includes Embedded Certificates

C. Synchronized with Server

D. System Recognizes VPN IP

E. None of the Above

2. __________ is a suite of protocols that provides authentication, integrity, and confidentiality within Windows systems.

A. Single Sign-On

B. Lightweight Directory Access Protocol

C. Active Directory

D. New Technology LAN Manager

E. None of the Above

3. Select the best choice below for the following definition: "*An authentication protocol that uses tickets to allow communication over a network to prove identity in a secure manner.*"

A. Common Access Cards

B. HMAC-Based One-Time Password

C. Windows Group Policy

D. Kerberos

E. None of the Above

4. __________ is a directory service for Windows domain networks that is included in most Windows Server operating systems.

A. Single Sign-On

B. Lightweight Directory Access Protocol

C. Active Directory

D. New Technology LAN Manager

E. None of the Above

5. Which choice below is a message used by Microsoft New Technology LAN Manager in its challenge / response process of authentication?

A. NEGOTIATE_MESSAGE

B. CONFIRM_MESSAGE

C. VALIDATE_MESSAGE

D. SYNCHRONIZE_MESSAGE

E. None of the Above

6. __________ specifies formats and methods to query a directories (databases of objects).

A. Single Sign-On

B. Lightweight Directory Access Protocol

C. Active Directory

D. New Technology LAN Manager

E. None of the Above

7. Select the best choice below for the following definition: "*Uses object labels to determine access levels and is the strictest of all control models.*"

A. Role-Based Access Control

B. Mandatory Access Control

C. Attribute-Based Access Control

D. Discretionary Access Control

E. None of the Above

8. __________ refers to the ability of a user to log on or access multiple systems by providing credentials only once.

A. Single Sign-On

B. Lightweight Directory Access Protocol

C. Active Directory

D. New Technology LAN Manager

E. None of the Above

9. Which choice below is a function and/or characteristic typically associated with geolocation technologies used to identify users?

A. Implemented on Domain Controllers

B. Provides a Central Access Point

C. Uses IP and/or MAC Addresses

D. Time Synchronization Required

E. None of the Above

10. __________ serves as an authentication layer positioned on top of the OAuth 2 authorization framework.

A. Single Sign-On

B. OpenID Connect

C. OAuth

D. Active Directory

E. None of the Above

11. Select the best choice below for the following definition: *"Ensures only authenticated and authorized individuals with proper permissions can access system resources."*

A. Biometric Technology

B. Security Assertion Markup Language

C. Geolocation Technology

D. Access Control Model

E. None of the Above

12. __________ ensures access is allowed or denied to resources based on a set of rules defined by a system administrator.

A. Role-Based Access Control

B. Attribute-Based Access Control

C. Rule-Based Access Control

D. Discretionary Access Control

E. None of the Above

13. Authentication, authorization, and accounting (AAA) work together with prioritization to provide a comprehensive access management system.

1. True
2. False

14. Multiple factors may be implemented for basic authentication, two factors for more security, and one factor for maximum security.

1. True
2. False

15. A strong password has enough length, does not include words found in a dictionary or name, and combines four types of characters.

1. True
2. False

16. It is important to provide adequate training to users on password security if they use passwords within the organizations.

1. True
2. False

17. Password policies typically start as a verbal directive that identifies the organizations' security goals related to passwords.

1. True
2. False

18. A Time-Based One-Time Password (TOTP) is a persistent passcode that uses the current time of day as one of its identification factors.

1. True
2. False

DOMAIN 03

Biometric Identification and Security Systems

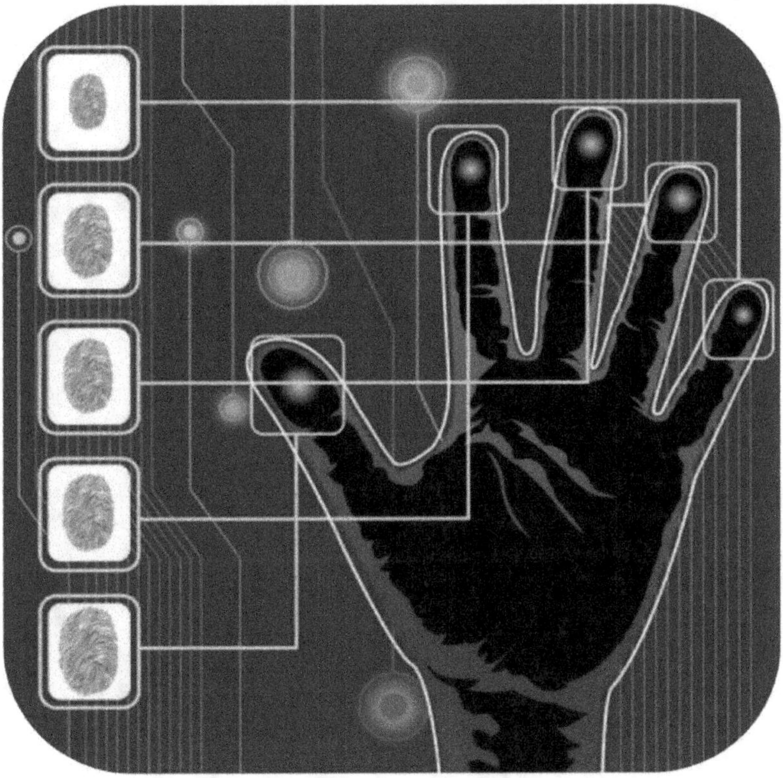

Introduction to Biometrics

Biometrics is the measurement and statistical analysis of peoples' unique physical and behavioral characteristics. In the context of identity and access management it is more reliable than security tokens and knowledge-based credentials. Biometrics can be separated into two categories: *physical* and *behavioral*. Physical biometrics include elements of body composition, and behavioral biometrics address learned behaviors which are measurable. The risk associated with biometric methods is the tendency to raise privacy concerns with the general public.

Biometric Functionality

The selection of a specific biometric for use in a specific application involves consideration of several factors. Listed below are the seven characteristics and capabilities a biometric system should possess to be effective.

1. **Universality**: Everyone has the Measurable Trait
2. **Uniqueness**: The Traits are Sufficiently Different
3. **Permanence**: Trait Variations are Limited Over Time
4. **Measurability**: Trait Measurements are Collectable
5. **Performance**: The Method is Technologically Accurate
6. **Acceptability**: The Public Accepts the Technology
7. **Circumvention**: Inability to Imitate Measured Traits

Biometric Implementation (Part I)

Certain biometrics will be better than others based on the required levels of convenience, security, and acceptance. The effectiveness will be based on the mode of the method: *authentication mode* (verification) or *identification mode*. Identification mode is the most common use; systems test for "positive recognition" to prevent the misuse of identities. Listed below are the three phases of biometric identification.

1. A Subject Reference Model is Generated
2. A Biometric Sample is Matched to the Reference Model
3. A Positive Result is Tested with Authentication

Biometric Implementation (Part II)

No single biometric method (referred to as a *unimodal* system) will meet all the requirements for every possible application. An example of a limitation would include attempting to establish the identity of an unknown person denying the claim of identity. A sample taken from a subject and matched against an existing template in a one-to-many comparison may not generate results. Listed below are the two categories associated with biometric identification.

1. **Positive Recognition**: The sample taken from the subject is matched against a biometric reference template to verify a claim of identity.

2. **Negative Recognition**: The sample taken from the subject is matched against a biometric reference template to disprove an implicit or explicit denial of identity.

Biometric Enrollment

The first time a person uses a biometric system is called *enrollment*, at which time biometric information is captured and stored. It is critical that the retrieval and storage systems remain secure to maintain the integrity of identities. A *vector* (or image) is used to create a *template* (synthesis of characteristics) that will identify the subject in the future. The process of collection consists of four *blocks* (steps):

1. **System Interface**: In block one, the user physically engages with the biometric device.

2. **Pre-Processing / Sanitizing**: In block two, several data points are extracted from the same data source and then aggregated.

3. **Feature Extraction**: In block 3, data points that represent individual features are selected to be stored in a template.

4. **Disposal**: In block 4, unused data points are discarded to protect the identity of the subject.

Multimodal Biometric Systems

Multimodal biometric systems use multiple sensors or biometrics to overcome the limitations of unimodal biometric systems. Fingerprint recognition can be compromised by skin damage, and iris recognition can be compromised with age. In a multimodal method, multiple data points are taken from either the same marker or different biometric measurements. The method then fuses unimodal system data into a multimodal template using sequential, parallel or hierarchical processes.

Biometric Performance

Multimodal and unimodal biometric systems utilize several performance metrics to establish acceptable baselines and detect anomalies. Listed below are seven common key performance indicators used to measure biometric performance.

1. (**FAR**) False Acceptance Rate
2. (**FRR**) False Rejection Rate
3. (**ROC**) Relative Operating Characteristic
4. (**CER**) Crossover Error Rate
5. (**FER**) Failure to Enroll Rate
6. (**FTC**) Failure to Capture Rate
7. (**TSC**) Template Storage Capacity

Soft Biometric Traits

Soft biometric traits are physical, behavioral, or adhered characteristics that are derived from the way humans distinguish their peers. Although these traits lack permanence and distinctiveness, they are easily collected and are useful when supplementing identity information. The risk of this method is the traits are strongly culturally based and have the potential to be used for categorization and profiling. Listed below are examples of soft biometric traits.

1. Race
2. Gender
3. Height

Fingerprint Recognition Systems

Fingerprints are the traces of an impression from the friction ridges (epidermal ridges) of any part of a human hand. They are detailed, unique, durable, and suitable as long-term biometric markers. Fingerprints are easily deposited on suitable surfaces as a result of sweat from the eccrine gland. A print deposited unintentionally on any surface is referred to as a "chanced impression."

Fingerprint Classification

Manual fingerprint classification systems are based on the general friction ridge patterns of several (or all) fingers. The *Henry System*, used by English-speaking countries, consists of three basic patterns: Arches, Loops, and Whorls.

Fingerprint Sensors

A *fingerprint sensor* is an electronic device used to capture a digital image of a fingerprint pattern. The sample image, called a "live scan," creates a digitally-processed template using extracted biometric features. Listed below are three prominent technologies used by fingerprint sensors.

1. Optical Imaging
2. Ultrasonic Imaging
3. Capacitive Imaging

Optical Fingerprint Imaging

Optical fingerprint imaging involves using specialized electronic devices to capture a digital image of the print using visible light. The finger is placed on the *touch surface* (top sensor) and the phosphor layer below illuminates the finger. The light is reflected to a template of solid-state pixels which captures the visual print image with a specialized digital camera. The risk of this method is the potential to have the image affected by either the quality of the skin or the scanning surface.

Ultrasonic Fingerprint Imaging

Ultrasonic fingerprint imaging uses medical ultrasonography principles to create visual images of the fingerprint. High-frequency sound waves created by piezoelectric transducers are passed through the dermal layer of the finger. The reflected energy is measured and the resulting wave measurements form an image. Because the waves are interacting with the dermal layer (under the epidermal layer) of the finger, the need for a clean finger or clean scanning surface is no longer needed.

Capacitive Fingerprint Imaging

Capacitance is the ability of electrical conductors and insulators to store an electric charge when a potential difference in voltage exists. This method uses sensor array pixels, the epidermal layer of the skin, and the dermal layer of the skin to form an image. A small electric charge is emitted which the dermal layer—which is electrically conductive—absorbs. The epidermal later—which is not conductive—serves as the dielectric. The capacitance between ridges and valleys varies and the dielectric forms an air gap in the areas of variation. The measured capacitance forms an image which is then stored on a biometric template.

Facial Recognition Systems

A *facial recognition system* is an application capable of identifying or verifying a person from a digital image or video frame image. The system extracts landmarks to identify features and an algorithm analyzes the relative position of the landmarks against a gallery of normalized facial images. The collected facial data is compressed into useful markers and the rest is discarded. To verify identify the subject in the future, a probe image is compared to facial data to determine a match.

Three-Dimensional Facial Recognition

A newly-emerging trend in biometric identification, claimed to achieve improved accuracy, is referred to as *three-dimensional facial recognition*. Sensors map the shape of facial contours such as the eye socket, chin and nose. Three tracking cameras are typically used to map the face from several viewing angles. This method is not affected by changes in lighting and multiple cameras may be used to conduct facial recognition in real time even when the subjects are unaware of the scan.

Facial Recognition Weaknesses

Facial recognition systems and their supporting algorithms are far from perfect and continue to struggle to perform under certain conditions. Listed below are several shortcomings associated with this method of biometric identification which often cause them to misidentify people.

1. Difficulty with Identifying Minorities
2. Affected by Poor Lighting, Glasses, and Makeup
3. Affected by Low Resolution Images
4. Less Effective with Facial Expressions
5. Reliance on Inconsistent Research Datasets

Iris Recognition Systems

Iris recognition systems are based on a process of using visible and near-infrared light to take a high-contrast photograph of a persons' iris. This method of automated biometric identification uses mathematical pattern-recognition to analyze a video image of the iris. The complex patterns of the iris are unique, stable, and this biometric method is effective at a distance and in real time even when the subjects are unaware of the scan.

Iris Recognition: Advantages

The iris of the eye has been described as the ideal part of the human body for biometric identification for several reasons. Listed below are several advantages of using iris recognition as a biometric identification method.

1. A Well-Protected Internal Organ

2. Flat with Predictable Geometry
3. Textures Have Multiple Unique Factors
4. Both Eyes of Individuals have Different Textures
5. The Chance of False Matches is Low
6. No Need to Touch Equipment
7. Works with Contact Lenses and Glasses

Iris Recognition: Disadvantages

Iris recognition is a relatively new technology and is incompatible with the substantial investments made in fingerprint recognition systems. It also has several disadvantage which are listed below.

1. Recognition is Defeated by High-Quality Images
2. Scanners are Difficult to Adjust
3. Scanners are Bothersome with Different Heights
4. Affected by Lighting Changes
5. Significantly More Expensive than Other Methods
6. Difficult to Perform at a Distance
7. Susceptible to Poor Image Quality

Retinal Imaging Systems (Part I)

Retinal imaging is a biometric scanning technique that uses the unique patterns of a persons' blood vessels in the retina. Each persons' retina, which is comprised of a complex structure of capillaries, is unique. The structure is not entirely genetically determined so even identical twins have different structures. The retina typically remains unchanged for life but can be altered by diseases such as diabetes or glaucoma. It is considered to be the most precise biometric method with an error rate in one in 10,000,000.

Retinal Imaging Systems (Part II)

Retinal imaging is not to be confused with a similar ocular-based technology, iris imaging, which is commonly called "iris scanning." In this biometric process, a subject looks through an eyepiece and a beam of low-energy infrared light traces a standardized path on the retina. As blood vessels absorb light readily the reflections vary during the scan. The pattern variations are digitized and the collected data is stored in a database.

Retinal Imaging: Disadvantages

Although retinal imaging systems provide high rates of accuracy and several advantages, the technology does suffer from some drawbacks. Listed below are six disadvantages associated with retinal imaging systems.

1. Accuracy is Affected by Eye Disease
2. Procedure is Perceived as Invasive
3. Procedure is not User-Friendly
4. Subject Must be Close to Optical Lens
5. Significantly High Equipment Cost
6. Eye Damage with Prolonged Use

Keystroke Dynamics

Keystroke dynamics is the detailed timing information which describes when each key was pressed and when it was released. This method is considered to be a "behavioral biometric" that measures an individuals' manner and rhythm of typing and uses the data to create a template of the unique typing pattern. The *dwell time* (amount of time the key is pressed) and the *flight time* (the time between keys being pressed) are processed by neural algorithms to create a template. The *vibration information* (the pressure associated with *dwell time*) can also be measured and used as the basis for authentication.

Keystroke Biometric Data

The techniques used for keystroke dynamics vary widely in power and sophistication, from statistical approaches to AI neural networks. Listed below are areas that are measured when creating a keystroke dynamics template.

1. Raw Speed Uncorrected for Errors

2. Seek-Times and Hold-Times
3. Characteristics of Letter Sequences
4. Characteristics of Common Errors
5. Substitutions, Reversals, and Drop-Outs

Keystroke Dynamics: Authentication

Behavioral biometrics—which rely on what is referred to as a "*confidence measurement*"—are considered to be less reliable than physical biometrics which rely on a "*pass/fail*" measurement. However, there are many benefits to this method. Risk mitigation can be explicitly defined and thresholds adjusted at the level of an individual. Additionally, keystroke dynamic data points can be collected continuously. Listed below are two examples of how this method could be effectively implemented.

1. **Example #01**: An executive is forced to access a sensitive system at gunpoint and then steps away so the malicious actor can operate. Although the executive logged in the biometrics would indicate a different actors' involvement afterward.

2. **Example #02**: An administrator does not sign out of the system when leaving and an unauthorized actor accesses the computer. In another scenario, a privileged user signs on and allows a non-privileged user to access the system. Both scenarios may be considered violations of policy.

Keystroke Dynamics: Disadvantages

A major vulnerability associated with keystroke dynamics is that a persons' typing varies substantially during the day and between days. Listed below are several disadvantages of this method.

1. Susceptible to Temporal Changes
2. Individuals can Become Fatigued
3. Affected by a Change in Emotions
4. Individuals can Switch Computers
5. Affected by Cut-and-Paste / Voice-to-Text
6. Affected by Pauses to Read or Speak

7. Affected by Extra / Missed Doses of Medications

Voice Recognition Systems

Voice recognition is the ability of an electronic security device to recognize the voice of an individual (which is as unique as a fingerprint). This method is used for both identification and authentication. When a known speaker claims an identity, the system requires a 1:1 match. When identifying an unknown speaker, the system requires a 1:N match. In both cases, recognition is based on a "voice print." This technology has many implementations is both covert operations and forensic disciplines.

Voice Recognition Technology

Technologies used to store and process voice prints include frequency estimation, pattern-matching algorithms, and neural networks. This method uses a traditional and comfortable technology that is perceived as non-invasive by most people. It is often integrated with two-factor authentication systems. Voice recognition technology does have a number of disadvantages, several of which have been listed below.

1. Affected by Ambient Noise Levels
2. Affected by Changes in Behavioral / Emotional Attributes
3. Affected by Cross-Channel Systems

DOMAIN 03

Biometric Identification and Security Systems

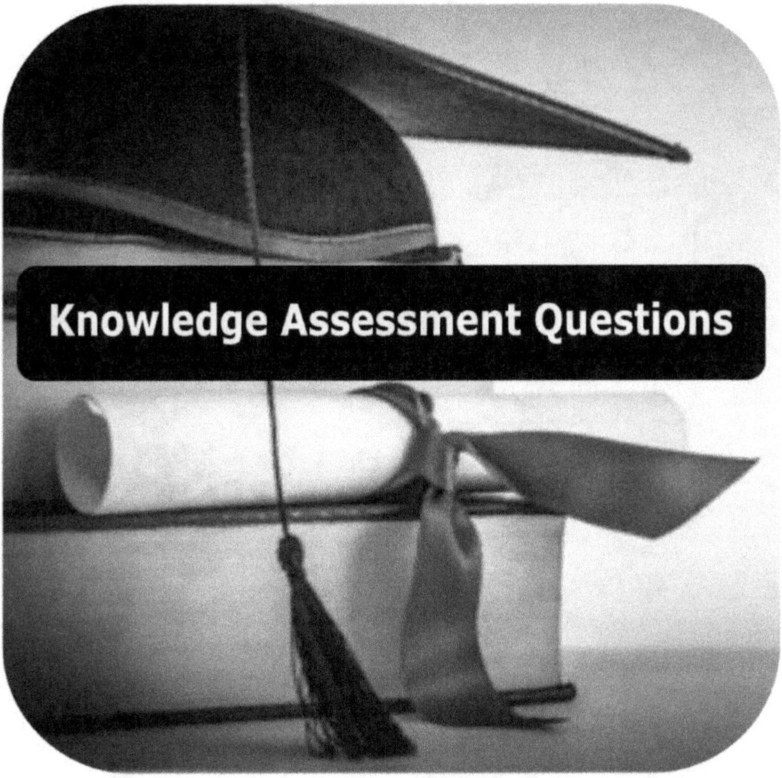

The following knowledge assessment questions are presented as true / false, multiple choice, and fill-in-the-blank. The correct answers are provided in an Answer Key at the end of this text. These questions may or may not be presented on the actual certification exam.

Domain 03: Knowledge Assessment Questions

1. Which choice below is a factor to be considered when selecting a specific biometric technology with a specific application?

A. Supported by Vendors

B. Accepted by the Public

C. Proven in Court

D. Subjected to Peer-Review

E. None of the Above

2. Technologies used to store and process voice prints typically include frequency estimation, pattern-matching algorithms, and __________.

A. Capacitive Imaging

B. Ocular Imaging

C. Behavioral Biometrics

D. Neural Networks

E. None of the Above

3. Select the best choice below for the following definition: "*The traces of an impression from the friction ridges of any part of a human hand.*"

A. Chance Impressions

B. Epidermal Ridges

C. Fingerprints

D. Manual Classification

E. None of the Above

4. Iris recognition is a relatively new technology and is incompatible with the substantial investments made in __________ recognition systems.

A. Vocal

B. Retinal

C. Fingerprint

D. Digital

E. None of the Above

5. Which choice below is a system of manual fingerprint classification that was created in India and based on three basic fingerprint patterns?

A. Haque

B. Bertillon

C. Natal

D. Henry

E. None of the Above

6. A(n) __________ recognition system is an application capable of identifying or verifying a person from a digital image or video frame image.

A. Vocal

B. Facial

C. Fingerprint

D. Optical

E. None of the Above

7. Select the best choice below for the following definition: "*A biometric scanning technique that uses the unique patterns of a persons' blood vessels in the retina.*"

A. Retinal Imaging

B. Multimodal Imaging

C. Ultrasonic Imaging

D. Ocular Imaging

E. None of the Above

8. __________ is the ability of electrical conductors and insulators to store an electric charge when a potential difference in voltage exists.

A. Capacitance

B. Scanning

C. Ultrasound

D. Imaging

E. None of the Above

9. Which choice below is a reason the iris of the eye has been described as the ideal part of the human body for biometric identification?

A. Transparency of the Cornea

B. Well-Protected Internal Organ

C. Color Sensitivity Rating

D. Unpredictable Geometry

E. None of the Above

10. __________ classification systems are based on the general friction ridge patterns of several (or all) fingers.

A. Digital

B. Unimodal

C. Multimodal

D. Manual

E. None of the Above

11. Select the best choice below for the following definition: "*The ability of an electronic security device to recognize the voice (as unique as a fingerprint) of an individual.*"

A. Frequency Estimation

B. Pattern-Matching

C. Voice Recognition

D. Temporal Imaging

E. None of the Above

12. Soft biometric traits are defined as __________, behavioral, or adhered characteristics that are derived from the way humans distinguish their peers.

A. Emotional

B. Psychological

C. Physical

D. Conditional

E. None of the Above

13. The first time a person uses a biometric system is called registration, at which time biometric information is captured and stored.

1. True
2. False

14. Unimodal biometric systems use multiple sensors or biometrics to overcome the limitations of multimodal biometric systems.

1. True
2. False

15. Soft biometric traits are physical, behavioral, or adhered characteristics that are derived from the way humans distinguish their peers.

1. True
2. False

16. Ultrasonic fingerprint imaging involves using specialized electronic devices to capture a digital image of the print using visible light.

1. True
2. False

17. A facial recognition system is an application capable of identifying or verifying a person from a digital image or video frame image.

1. True
2. False

18. Keystroke dynamics is the detailed timing information which describes when each key was pressed and when it was released.

1. True
2. False

DOMAIN 04

Securing Systems and Data Using Cryptography

Key Definitions

Cryptography:

The science of hiding the meaning of communication.

Cipher:

Something that transforms characters or bits into an unreadable format.

Cryptographic Algorithm:

A complex mathematical formula that converts readable data into an unreadable format.

Cryptanalysis:

The science of analyzing and breaking encryption mechanisms.

Cryptosystem:

The required components for encryption and decryption operations (software, protocols, algorithms, keys).

Plaintext:

Readable text (decrypted).

Ciphertext:

Unreadable text (encrypted).

Work Factor:

The time, effort, and resources necessary to break a cryptosystem.

Cryptography: Core Concepts

Cryptography has several important core concepts that allow it to be a viable solution when securing devices and communications.

1. **Integrity**: Hashing
2. **Confidentiality**: Encryption
3. **Authentication**: Digital Signatures
4. **Accountability**: Non-Repudiation

Providing Integrity with Hashing

Hashing is an algorithm performed on data to produce a number called a hash (also referred to as a *checksum*). It validates data has not been modified or corrupted as the same data will always generate the same hash value. A hash is always created twice: first when the hash is created, and next when the hash values are compared. A few examples of hashing algorithms are listed below.

1. **MD5** (Message Digest 5)
2. **SHA-2** (Secure Hash Algorithm)
3. **HMAC** (Hash-Based Message Authentication Code)

Message Digest 5 (MD5)

Message Digest 5 (MD5) produces a 128-bit hash displayed as 32 characters in hexadecimal format. Hexadecimal characters are composed of four bits and use the numbers "0-9" and the characters "a-f." Experts discourage the use of this algorithm due to vulnerabilities that were discovered in 2004 but it is still widely accepted and used for email, forensic, and executable integrity.

Secure Hash Algorithm (SHA)

Secure Hash Algorithm (SHA) is a hashing algorithm that comes in several variations and grouped into four families (-0, -1, -2, -3). SHA-2 is the most widely used implementation of the algorithm. It can be used to create 224-, 256-, 384-, and 512-bit hashes. Like all hashing algorithms, SHA does not provide confidentiality.

Hash-Based Message Authentication Code (HMAC)

Hash-Based Message Authentication Code (HMAC) is a fixed-length string of bits like other hashing algorithms such as MD5 and SHA-1 (HMAC-MD5 and HMAC-SHA1). HMAC adds additional randomness to the algorithm by incorporating a secret key shared by the sender and receiver into its calculation. The message is hashed using MD5 and the secret key then further randomizes the hash value. The MD5 provides integrity of the message, and the shared secret key provides authenticity of the sender and receiver.

Key Stretching

Attackers will often attempt to discover passwords by calculating a guessed hash and then comparing it to the hash of the stored password. *Key stretching* is a process designed to increase the strength of stored passwords by adding additional bits after the original hash has been calculated. This process, known as "salting the hash," is effective in defeating brute force and rainbow table password attacks.

Important Encryption Terms

Understanding key encryption terms makes it easier to understand many of the more advanced cryptography concepts. The terms listed below will be discussed at length throughout this domain.

1. **Random / Pseudo-Random Numbers**: These numbers are generated by a *Pseudo-Random Number Generator* (PRNG), an algorithm that uses mathematical formulas to produce sequences of numbers approximating the properties of random numbers.

2. **Initialization Vector (IV)**: A fixed-size input to a cryptographic primitive that is typically required to be random or pseudorandom.

3. **Nonce (Number Used Once)**: An arbitrary number that can be used just once in a cryptographic communication.

4. **Exclusive OR (XOR)**: A Boolean logic operation that is widely used in cryptography as well as in generating parity bits for error checking and fault tolerance.

5. **Confusion / Diffusion**: Two properties of the operation of a secure cipher that work to thwart the application of statistics and other methods of cryptanalysis.

6. **Deprecated Algorithm**: An algorithm that is available and allowed but, due to recognized weaknesses and failings, is not recommended for use.

7. **High Resiliency**: A characteristic of a cryptographic algorithm that allows it to remain secure after some of its components have been compromised.

Exclusive OR (XOR)

The *Exclusive OR* (XOR) operation is implemented extensively because it can be used to encrypt or decrypt easily and quickly. It is a logical "either/or" operation in which only one value can be true. The Key Value and the Plaintext Value are combined; if the bits are the same value the result is "0," and if the bits are a different value the result is "1." The XOR then creates a cipher value based on the results. This function is widely used in stream ciphers when encryption must happen quickly.

Key Space (Key Length)

The *Key Space* (or the length of the key) represents all possible values that can be used to generate a cryptographic key. The larger the key size is ($2^{64} < 2^{128} < 2^{256} < 2^{512}$) the larger the key space will be. Larger key spaces create larger work factors making the key more difficult to break. Each bit added to the key space doubles the key length as shown in the examples below.

1. 1 Bit = 2 Options (0,1)
2. 2 Bits = 4 Options (2^2)
3. 3 Bits = 8 Options (2^3)

Symmetric Encryption Characteristics

Symmetric Encryption is an encryption methodology that uses a single key to encrypt (encode) and decrypt (decode) data. The sender and receiver use the same key (shared key). Protection depends on maintaining key secrecy and the key exchange must take place "out-of-band." The same process and initialization vector is used to encrypt and decrypt messages. This type of encryption provides confidentiality for the users and larger keys are difficult to break.

Symmetric Key Management Issues

Although symmetric encryption has many benefits, there are several key management issues that can make its implementation impractical. It does not provide authenticity or non-repudiation and it does not scale well in enterprise environments. This can be seen below using the key formula [n • (n-1) / 2], where "n" is the number of keys required for users.

1. 3 Users: 3 Keys
2. 10 Users: 45 Keys
3. 1,000 Users: 499,500 Keys

Encryption / Decryption Methods

The two methods used for encryption and decryption, regardless of the degree of algorithmic complexity, are *substitution* and *transposition*. In substitution, the process substitutes one bit for another using either new or existing bits. In transposition, the process rearranges bits in the bitstream using only existing bits.

Block Ciphers

A *Block Cipher* encrypts data in blocks of specific sizes, such as 64-bit or 128-bit blocks. Large messages are divided into blocks which are then encrypted individually. This method is good when the size of the data is known such as in database fields and software applications.

Stream Ciphers

A *Stream Cipher* encrypts data as a stream of bits or bytes rather than dividing the data into blocks of specific sizes. The algorithm incorporates a keystream generator to combine keystream bits with message bits using an efficient XOR operation. Stream ciphers are more complex than block ciphers. This method is good when the size of the data is unknown such as in hardware implementations or when data is being streamed.

Advanced Encryption Standard (AES)

The *Advanced Encryption Standard* (AES) is a strong symmetric block cipher that encrypts data in blocks of specific sizes. Based on the Rijndael algorithm, it uses 128-, 192-, and 256-bit encryption. It was adopted by NIST in 2001 and serves as the government standard for "Sensitive / Unclassified" information. Listed below are the three primary benefits of AES.

1. **Fast**: Only 1 Encryption Pass is Required
2. **Efficient**: Works Well on Smaller Devices
3. **Strong**: Provides a High Level of Confidentiality

Asymmetric Encryption Characteristics

Asymmetric Encryption (also known as *Public Key Cryptography*) uses a paired public and private key algorithm for secure data communication. This method uses a public and private key pair that is mathematically related, but the private key cannot be derived from the public key. Public and private keys can both be used to encrypt and decrypt messages if the sender and receiver both have the corresponding keys.

Asymmetric Encryption: Advantages

Asymmetric encryption has advantages over symmetric encryption that should be considered when choosing an implementation. It is easily scaled and only requires one key pair; 1,000 users require 2,000 keys. No out-of-band key exchange is required; the public key is freely distributed and requires no protection. Finally, it provides both the sender and receiver with true authentication and non-repudiation.

Asymmetric Encryption: Disadvantages

Asymmetric encryption tends to offer more benefits than symmetric encryption, but it does have distinct disadvantages. Due to the complexity of the algorithmic process, it is 1,000 times slower than symmetric encryption. Encryption capability is limited by the key length so it can only be used to encrypt smaller amounts of data. Finally, both a key management and key validation system are required to support the public and private key pairs.

Diffie-Hellman Key Exchange

The *Diffie-Hellman Key Exchange Protocol* was created in 1976 as a method for two users to generate a shared private key with which they can then exchange information securely. This method requires no prior relationship between the parties. A symmetric session key is responsible for encryption and the key agreement is conducted in a secure manner. Although the session keys are encrypted the data itself is not encrypted. Additionally, there are no digital signatures generated to provide authentication.

RSA Encryption Algorithm

RSA is made up of the initial letters of Ron **R**ivest, Adi **S**hamir, and Leonard **A**dleman, who first publicly described the algorithm in 1977. The algorithm provides digital signatures, secure key distribution, and encryption services. It is a one-way function based on the difficulty of factoring large numbers to their original primes.

Elliptic Curve Cryptography

Elliptic Curve Cryptography (ECC) is an asymmetric encryption based on the algebraic structure of elliptic curves over finite fields.

The creators of ECC, Victor Miller and Neal Koblitz, chose not to use the same mathematics as RSA and instead based their algorithm on three points located along an elliptic curve (P,Q,R). The general principle is if you know the mathematics of the curve and two known points, determining the third point is easy.

If you do not know the mathematics of the curve and know only a single point, reverse engineering the process to discover the two unknown points is impossible. ECC uses a small key with high resiliency: a 256-bit ECC key is equal to a 3,072-bit RSA key. Due to its smaller key size, it works well with smaller devices with less processing power. Despite its benefits, ECC certificates are not widely accepted or used.

Email: Using Cryptographic Protocols

Many implementations use a combination of symmetric and asymmetric encryption methods to create strong hybrid security solutions. In both cases below, symmetric encryption is used to secure the message.

1. **Digital Signatures**: The senders' private key encrypts digital signatures, and their public key decrypts them.

2. **Email Encryption**: The recipients' public key encrypts the messages, and their private key decrypts them.

Email: Digital Signatures

Digital Signatures are like handwritten signatures on printed documents that identify individuals, but they provide more security benefits. They are typically created with the *Digital Signature Algorithm* (DSA), a Federal Information Processing Standard, using an encrypted hash of the message. They are encrypted with the senders' private key and decrypted with the senders' public key. Digital signatures provide integrity, authentication, and non-repudiation.

Signed and Secured Messages

When referring to digitally signed and secured messages using hybrid cryptography, the "session key" is also known as the "symmetric key." The sender and the receiver follow the process listed below to send and receive signed and secured messages.

1. **Sender**: The senders' message is passed through a hashing algorithm and a *message digest* (MD) is generated. The message digest is encrypted with the senders' private key and the symmetric key is encrypted with the receivers' public key.

2. **Receiver**: The receiver decrypts the message digest with the senders' public key, decrypts the symmetric key with receivers' private key, and decrypts the message with the shared symmetric key.

SPF Authentication

Sender Policy Framework (SPF) is an authentication system designed to prevent email spoofing by verifying that domain IP addresses are valid. The SPF record includes IP addresses and is configured on the outgoing mail server. The IP address will pass authentication if it has an "A" record in the zone file or an "MX" host listed in the DNS. It will "soft fail" if it is unrecognized by the system. SPF can increase the delivery of legitimate emails as they are less likely to be marked as spam.

DKIM Authentication

DomainKeys Identified Mail (DKIM) is an authentication process that verifies a message was sent from a legitimate user of an email address. It was jointly created by Yahoo! and Cisco in 2005 to provide authentication within a domain. Most email providers use DKIM by default and is commonly implemented with SPF to provide authentication within a domain. Because the receiving server must support DKIM, and due to the complexity associated with the technology, there is less implementation of DKIM than SPF.

DMARC Authentication

Domain-Based Message Authentication, Reporting and Conformance (DMARC) ensures legitimate email is authenticated by DKIM and SPF standards. The technology focuses on two key values as the basis for its authentication decisions: *alignment* and *reporting*. The email must pass either the SPF values (*Header From + Envelope From*) or the DKIM values (*Header From + Domain Name*) to be authenticated. If either SPF or DKIM alignment checks pass, then the DMARC alignment test passes. If not, authentication fails, and the email is rejected or quarantined.

Proper Key Management and Oversight

Public Key Cryptography (asymmetric encryption) requires that digital keys be effectively managed and safeguarded during their life cycle. The life cycle of the key is referred to as the *crypto-period*. Listed below are the five primary areas of key oversight.

1. Secure Key Creation
2. Secure Key Distribution
3. Secure Key Storage
4. Secure Key Recovery
5. Secure Key Destruction

Safeguarding Cryptographic Keys

The best practices associated with properly safeguarding cryptographic keys are based on widely accepted information security protocols. In addition to the security objectives, the proper level of protection helps to reduce the opportunity for wasted resources. Listed below are several best practices that are implemented for key protection.

1. Require "Split Knowledge" for Dual Control
2. Ensure the Key is of Proper Length
3. Based the Key Life Cycle on Data Sensitivity
4. Never Present the Key in Plaintext
5. Create a Key Back-Up and/or Key Escrow

Digital Certificates

There is more information and common elements contained in a digital certificate than just the public key itself. Listed below are common elements typically contained in digital certificates.

1. Serial Number
2. Issuer
3. Validity Dates
4. Subject (Owner)
5. Usage Rights
6. Public Key

Certificate Authority (CA)

A *Certificate Authority* (CA) has the responsibility to issue, manage, validate, and revoke digital certificates. It can be large and public (such as Symantec or Comodo) or small and private (such as a corporate network). A commercial Certificate Authority generates revenues by selling digital certificates and must be trusted by the public to be effective. The certificate binds the users' identity to the public key (referred to as *key pinning*). Certificate Authorities are currently issuing X509 v3 certificates.

Certificate Chaining

Certificate Chaining combines all the issued certificates from the root CA down to the certificate issued to the end user. The first certificate created by the CA, referred to as a *root*, is kept in a *trusted root store* (a collection of root certificates). The Certificate Authorities negotiate with web and browser developers to accept their certificates, which will then be trusted by the entities that use the websites and browsers. This process makes certificate chaining a hierarchical and centralized trust model. The three levels of certificates included in a chain are *root*, *child*, and *end-user*.

Registration Authority (RA)

Users and systems request certificates from the Certificate Authority using a *Registration Authority* to facilitate the process.

The user initiates the process by creating a public / private key pair and submitting a *Certificate Signing Request* (CSR) to the Registration Authority via a web form. The CSR contains information about the keys' purpose, the public key, and the requesting end-user. Once the end-users' identity has been validated—typically with a copy of an official ID—the certificate is issued with the public key.

Certificate Directory

The *Certificate Directory* is a function of the Certificate Authority that is responsible for storing and safeguarding issued certificates. It manages and maintains all digital certificates during their validity dates. Certificate Directories are typically accessible to the public and can be accessed by end-users and systems.

Certificate Revocation List (CRL)

There are some instances when a Certificate Authority will revoke an issued certificate before its expiration date and place it on a *Certificate Revocation List* (CRL). Listed below are several circumstances in which revocation may occur.

1. Compromise of a Key
2. Compromise of the Certificate Authority
3. Change of Organizational Affiliation
4. The Certificate is Superseded
5. The Business Ceases Operation
6. A Hold is Placed on the Certificate
7. A User or Business Changes Names

Cryptography Security Threats

Becoming complacent in the use of encryption methods and implementations, in the face of emerging cybercrime activity, will usually not end well. Listed below are five categories of cryptography security threats that present security managers with unique and difficult challenges.

1. Ciphertext-Only Attacks (COA)
2. Known-Plaintext Attacks (KPA)
3. Chosen-Plaintext Attacks (CPA)
4. Chosen-Ciphertext Attacks (CCA)
5. Downgrade Attacks

Ciphertext-Only Attacks (COA)

A *Ciphertext-Only* attacker has access to ciphertexts but does not know the associated plaintexts, or how the plaintexts were selected. Although the plaintext is unknown some information can be derived, such as the language of the message originator. Expected statistical distribution can then be utilized to decrypt or derive the key. In the event the key cannot be decrypted, this method may still prove useful for side-channel analysis objectives.

Frequency Analysis (Expected Statistical Distribution)

Using *Expected Statistical Distribution*, patterns in ciphertext are matched with plaintext messages allowing the attacker to reverse-engineer the encryption process.

Known-Plaintext Attacks (KPA)

A *Known-Plaintext* attacker has access to both ciphertext and plaintext forms of a message and employs analysis to determine the key. It is effective against simple ciphers such as substitution ciphers and is typically used with other decryption methods. The KPA is a passive attack model.

Chosen-Plaintext Attacks (CPA)

A *Chosen-Plaintext* attacker can perform encryption queries for selected plaintext messages and observe the resulting ciphertext. The attacker obtains "n" plaintexts which are then sent to the *encryption oracle* (a central system containing information about other systems). The oracle encrypts the plaintext and returns the ciphertext. The plaintext and ciphertext are compared and the attacker attempts to extract the key.

Chosen-Ciphertext Attacks (CCA)

A *Chosen-Ciphertext* attacker can perform both encryption queries and decryption queries for accessed plaintext and ciphertext messages. The attacker obtains ciphertext and uses it to create and encrypt a message that is sent to a receiving victim. The receiver decrypts the message and returns an encrypted response. The attacker then compares the ciphertext and plaintext message values and attempts to derive the key.

Downgrade Attacks

A *Downgrade Attack* forces a target system to downgrade its security and allow an attacker to exploit the lesser level of security control. It is associated with weak implementations such as *Secure Socket Layer* (SSL). Despite the known vulnerabilities associated with SSL it is still routinely installed on servers in addition to *Transport Layer Security* (TLS).

Many servers typically include SSL 2, SSL 3, TLS 1.0, TLS 1.2, and TLS 1.3. The attacker disables TLS functionality on their system, communicates with the victim system, and attempts to force it to downgrade from TLS to SSL. The attacker can then take advantage of known vulnerabilities. This threat can be easily mitigated by disabling SSL 2 and SSL 3.

DOMAIN 04

Securing Systems and Data Using Cryptography

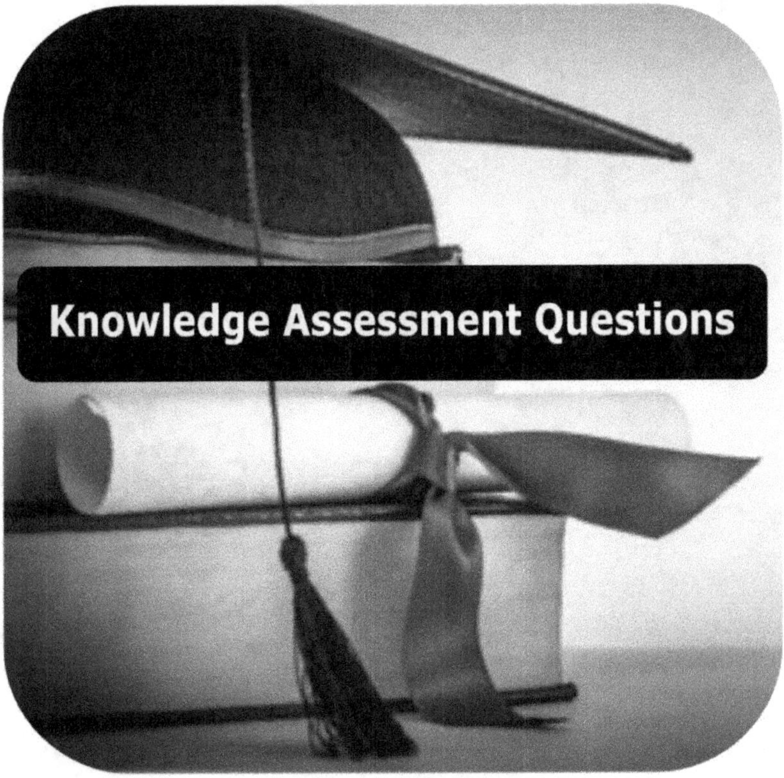

The following knowledge assessment questions are presented as true / false, multiple choice, and fill-in-the-blank. The correct answers are provided in an Answer Key at the end of this text. These questions may or may not be presented on the actual certification exam.

Domain 04: Knowledge Assessment Questions

1. Which choice below is one of the several key management issues associated with symmetric key encryption that can make implementation impractical?

A. Protection Depends on Key Secrecy

B. Same Process to Encrypt / Decrypt

C. Sender / Receiver Use Same Key

D. Does not Scale Well

E. None of the Above

2. Hexadecimal characters are composed of __________ bits and use the numbers "0-9" and the characters "a-f."

A. Eight

B. Four

C. Twelve

D. Sixteen

E. None of the Above

3. Select the best choice below for the following definition: "*The required components for encryption and decryption operations (software, protocols, algorithms, keys).*"

A. Cryptography

B. Cryptanalysis

C. Cryptosystem

D. Ciphertext

E. None of the Above

4. A(n) __________ is a fixed-length string of bits like other hashing algorithms such as MD5 and SHA-1 (HMAC-MD5 and HMAC-SHA1).

A. Secure Hash Algorithm

B. RSA Encryption Algorithm

C. Hash-Based Message Authentication Code

D. Pseudo-Random Number

E. None of the Above

5. Which choice below is one of the advantages associated with asymmetric encryption that cannot be provided by symmetric encryption?

A. Substitutes One Bit for Another

B. No "Out-of-Band" Key Exchange

C. Blocks are Encrypted Individually

D. Algorithm has a Keystream Generator

E. None of the Above

6. __________ is an encryption methodology that uses a single key to encrypt (encode) and decrypt (decode) data.

A. Asymmetric Encryption

B. Public Key Encryption

C. Cipher Block-Chaining

D. Symmetric Encryption

E. None of the Above

7. Select the best choice below for the following definition: "*An attacker can perform both encryption queries and decryption queries for accessed plaintext and ciphertext messages.*"

A. Chosen-Ciphertext Attack

B. Known-Plaintext Attack

C. Ciphertext-Only Attack

D. Chosen-Plaintext Attack

E. None of the Above

8. The two methods used for encryption and decryption, regardless of the degree of algorithmic complexity, are __________ and transposition.

A. Substitution

B. Obfuscation

C. Hashing

D. Key Stretching

E. None of the Above

9. Which choice below is one of the advantages associated with the symmetric encryption method known as "Diffie-Hellman Key Exchange"?

A. Provides Strong Data Encryption

B. Generates a Shared Public Key

C. Provides Digital Signatures

D. No Prior Relationship Required

E. None of the Above

10. A __________ encrypts data as a stream of bits or bytes rather than dividing the data into blocks of specific sizes.

A. Caesar Cipher

B. Stream Cipher

C. Vigenére Cipher

D. Scytale Cipher

E. None of the Above

11. Select the best choice below for the following definition: "*An authentication process that verifies a message was sent from a legitimate user of an email address.*"

A. Sender Policy Framework

B. Secure Hash Algorithm

C. DomainKeys Identified Mail

D. Advanced Encryption Standard

E. None of the Above

12. __________ is an authentication system designed to prevent email spoofing by verifying that domain IP addresses are valid.

A. DomainKeys Identified Mail

B. Public Key Cryptography

C. Sender Policy Framework

D. Advanced Encryption Standard

E. None of the Above

13. A Chosen-Ciphertext Attack forces a target system to downgrade its security and allow an attacker to exploit the lesser level of security control.

1. True
2. False

14. Hashing is an algorithm performed on data to produce a number called a hash (also referred to as a checksum).

1. True
2. False

15. The Certificate Directory is a function of the Certificate Authority that is responsible for storing and safeguarding issued certificates.

1. True
2. False

16. The *Inclusive AND* operation is used extensively because it can be used to encrypt or decrypt easily and quickly.

1. True
2. False

17. A Known-Plaintext attacker has access to both ciphertext and plaintext forms of a message and employs analysis to determine the key.

1. True
2. False

18. Key Stretching (or the length of the key) represents all possible values that can be used to generate a cryptographic key.

1. True
2. False

DOMAIN 05

Secure Network Architecture for Non-Architects

Introduction to Secure Architecture

In order to understand what secure architecture is, it is important to understand its origin and subsequent evolution. In the early days the focus was on network security, protecting the perimeter from external threats. As networks became more secure attacks on infrastructure became more prevalent and the focus shifted to infrastructure security. As infrastructure has become more secure attack methodologies changed again which shifted the focus to application security. Listed below are several frameworks that have contributed to the evolution of network security.

1. Zachman Framework (1987)
2. NIST Framework (1989)
3. TOGAF Framework (1995)
4. SABSA Framework (2007)

Zachman Framework

The *Zachman Framework* is an enterprise ontology that provides a fundamental and formalized structure for enterprise architecture. It presents a two-dimensional classification system that organizes and analyzes data based on two schemata. The first schema addresses general interrogatives: who, what, when, where, and why. The second schema addresses the concepts of *reification* (the process of treating an immaterial idea as a material thing) and *instantiation* (providing an instance or material evidence in support of a concept). The framework considers users of data and issues with data but does not imply a specific technical methodology.

TOGAF Framework

The *Open Group Architecture Framework* (TOGAF) is a framework that provides an approach for developing an enterprise architecture. It is intended to serve as a high-level approach to design. The framework defines system components, provides recommended standards, and establishes a common vocabulary. It addresses four architectural domains (business, information, application, and technology) referred to as *TOGAF Pillars*. Its high-level approach can make it difficult to implement.

SABSA Framework

The *Sherwood Applied Business Security Architecture* (SABSA) is a framework for security architecture and service management. It is both a model and methodology for developing risk-driven architectures and infrastructure security solutions. It was founded on business analysis principles to support critical business functions. It is not widely accepted and has little relevance outside of network security.

Reference Security Architecture

A *reference security architecture* is a document which provides recommended integrations of products and services to form a solution. The reference architecture embodies industry best practices, typically suggesting the optimal delivery method for specific technologies. Listed below are several focus areas addressed in the document.

1. Border Protection
2. Detection Services
3. Content Control Services
4. Configuration Management
5. Identity and Access Management
6. Application Security
7. Software Development Life Cycle
8. Physical Security Technology
9. Cryptographic Security
10. Auditing Processes

Border Protection

Border protection is typically thought of as the component technological devices that provide security at the network layer. Listed below are several focus areas that should be considered when addressing network border protection.

1. Network Zoning
2. The Testing and Development Environment
3. The *Quality Assurance* (QA) and Mirror Environment

4. The Production Environment
5. The Desktop Environment
6. Internal and External *Demilitarized Zones* (DMZ's)
7. *Bring Your Own Device* (BYOD) Integration

Detection Services

Detection services are those capabilities put in place with the specific focus of attempting to detect incidents in the process of occurring. Listed below are several focus areas that should be considered when addressing network detection services.

1. *IDS* and NIDS (Intrusion Detection Systems)
2. *IPS* and NIPS (Intrusion Protection Systems)
3. Firewalls and Routers
4. *Network Access Controls* (NAC's)
5. Event Monitoring
6. Dashboards and *GRC* Platforms (Governance, Risk, and Compliance)

Content Control Services

Content control services are those capabilities put in place to monitor and control the internal and external data flow within a network. Listed below are several focus areas that should be considered when addressing content control services.

1. *Data Loss Prevention* (DLP)
2. Whitelisting and Blacklisting
3. Content Filtering
4. Web Activity Monitoring
5. Anti-Virus Services
6. Anti-Spam Services
7. File Transfers (FTP and SFTP)

Configuration Management

Configuration management is implemented to ensure that a solution remains in the configuration for which is was originally intended. Listed below are several focus areas that should be considered when addressing network configuration management.

1. Hardening
2. Golden Images
3. Virtualization
4. Patch Management
5. Vulnerability Assessment
6. *Group Policy Objects* (GPO's)

Identity and Access Management

Identity and access management (IAM) consists of policies and technologies to ensure the proper people have the appropriate access to resources. Listed below are several focus areas that should be considered when addressing identity and access management.

1. Provisioning
2. Credentials
3. Access Management
4. Data Repositories
5. Federation

Software Development Life Cycle (SDLC)

The *application layer* is where most vulnerabilities are presented and the greatest effort in reducing vulnerabilities is expended. The *Software Development Life Cycle* (SDLC) is a process used by the software industry to design, develop and test applications. Listed below are the six phases of the SDLC.

1. Planning and Analysis
2. Design and Development
3. Testing and Evaluation
4. Deployment
5. Monitoring and Maintenance
6. Decommission and Disposal

Physical Security Technology

Physical security has become increasingly reliant on technology to function and plays an important role in security architecture. Listed below are several focus areas that should be considered when addressing physical security technology.

1. Physical Access Control
2. Video Surveillance
3. Physical Intrusion Detection
4. Visitor Management
5. Communication Systems
6. Central Management Systems
7. Environmental Controls

Cryptographic Services

Cryptographic services are complex technological components of security architecture that are crucial for the protection of information assets. Listed below are several focus areas that should be considered when addressing cryptographic services.

1. Data at Rest
2. Data in Motion
3. Certificate Authority
4. Certificate Validation
5. *Certificate Revocation Lists* (CRL's)
6. High Security Models
7. Tokenization

Auditing Services

Although *auditing* is not technical by nature it must take into consideration technology standards an organization is required to meet. Listed below are several focus areas that should be considered when addressing auditing services.

1. Risk Registers (Security)
2. Risk Registers (Architectural)
3. Compliance Scanning

4. Industry Standards
5. Security Certifications

Architecture Design Document (ADD)

The *architecture design document* (ADD) details the projects' end state and the steps required for the solution to be implemented successfully. It is typically segmented into four categories based on the *TOGAF Pillars* listed below.

1. Business Architecture
2. Information Architecture
3. Application Architecture
4. Technology Architecture

Business Architecture

The *business architecture* identifies and defines the organizations' strategy, governance, structure, goals, and key business processes. The objective is to create a governance model that is in alignment with the organization. Regardless of the aspects of the business included in this document, the four areas of focus listed below should be included.

1. Entire Cost and Impact
2. Process Flows
3. RACI Chart Components
4. Change Management and Updates

Information Architecture

Information architecture describes the structure of an organizations' logical and physical data assets and data management resources. This document generally addresses the focus areas listed below.

1. Solution Information
2. Structure of the Data
3. Structure of the Database

4. System Information
5. Criticality of the Data
6. Classification of the Data
7. *CRUD* Matrix of Permissions (Create, Read, Update, and Delete)

Application Architecture

Application architecture documents solution deployments, system interactions, and their relationships to core business processes. This document generally addresses the focus areas listed below.

1. *COTS* Applications (Commercial Off-the-Shelf)
2. Custom Applications
3. Hybrid Applications
4. Web Application Firewalls
5. Input Validation
6. Session Considerations
7. Exception Handling

Technology Architecture

Technology architecture describes the hardware, software, and network infrastructure needed to support the deployment of a solution. Several common components of this document are listed below.

1. Network Components
2. Server Components
3. Database Components
4. Application Server Components
5. System Management Tools
6. Back-Up Components
7. Endpoint Components

Zero Trust Networks: Assertions

Modern networks and usage patterns no longer resemble those that made traditional perimeter defense a practical solution years ago. The *Zero Trust Model* rejects the concept of perimeter defense and instead embraces the idea that no perimeter exists, and all components of the network must be equally defended. It always assumes the network is hostile, threats are both internal and external, and threats are always active. Due to these assertions locality cannot decide the level of trust for actors in the network. Every person and device must be authenticated and always authorized. The model uses multisource and dynamic policies to accomplish these objectives.

Zero Trust Network Flows

The perimeter model attempts to build a wall between trusted and untrusted sources; the Zero Trust model assumes all actors are threats. Given that assumption, network flows are scrutinized at all times. The following is a general overview of the network flow process.

The user and the device are authenticated based on temporal, geographical, and behavioral attributes. A *trust score* is computed, and the results are bonded to form an *agent*. The *control plane* (security policy) signals the *data plane* (network resources) that the network flow will be allowed to take place. The control plane verifies the device and application are using proper encryption protocols and the network flow is authorized and logged.

If at any time during this process the trust score fails to meet a predefined threshold, the control plane will prevent the network flow from occurring and the failed attempt will be logged.

Zero Trust Network Agents

It is insufficient to treat the user and device separately because policy often needs to consider the two together to enforce behavior. A network agent is the term given to known data regarding network actors such as users, devices, and applications. While information regarding network actors is maintained in persistent storage, the agent is formed "on demand." When a request is made it evaluates the known data, variable attributes, and trust score against the security policy to make an authorization decision.

Unlike a typical perimeter-based system in which trust is granted users and devices based on roles and rules, trust scores in a Zero Trust network are dynamic and volatile. The flexibility of a variable trust system allows enforcement policies to be implemented when encountering unique and unknown threats.

Zero Trust Privilege Considerations

By considering all details of an access attempt, the determination of authorization is more granular than a simple binary response. The level of privilege granted on a Zero Trust network is highly dynamic, changing in direct proportion to trust scores and circumstances.

The static privilege of a traditional network can be risky. It can be too rigid and defined to adequately address network threats. It can be too loosely defined for security policies to be adequately asserted. Finally, it can become accumulated without proper controls and management.

In addition to considering the assigned privilege of users and devices on the network, this model also evaluates the attributes listed in the examples below.

1. **Temporal Attributes**: The time of day a user or device is attempting to access the network.

2. **Geographical Attributes**: The location from which the user or device is attempting to access the network.

3. **Behavioral Attributes**: The assets and resources the user or device is attempting to access on the network.

Trust Agent Data Fields (Part I)

The granularity of data stored within a trust agent can vary based on the needs of the organization and maturity of the system. Listed below are several data fields that may be used to evaluate users of a network.

1. Agent Trust Score
2. User Trust Score
3. User Role and Group Role
4. User Place of Residence
5. User Authentication Method

Trust Agent Data Fields (Part II)

Device data populated during the procurement process is more trusted than device data reported back from an agent running on it. As a result, trust scores for devices vary as well. Listed below are a number of data fields that may be used to evaluate devices on a network.

1. Device Trust Score
2. Device Manufacturer
3. TPM Manufacturer and Version
4. Current Device Location
5. IP Address

Zero Trust Networks: Disadvantages

There are several potential shortcomings, risks, and attack vectors associated with a Zero Trust network that can undermine its utility. The examples listed below can potentially compromise zero trust networks due to their lack of focus on perimeter security.

1. Identity Theft
2. Endpoint Enumeration
3. Untrusted Computing Platform
4. Social Engineering
5. Physical Coercion
6. Invalidation (No Longer Authorized)
7. Control Plane Security

DOMAIN 05

Secure Network Architecture for Non-Architects

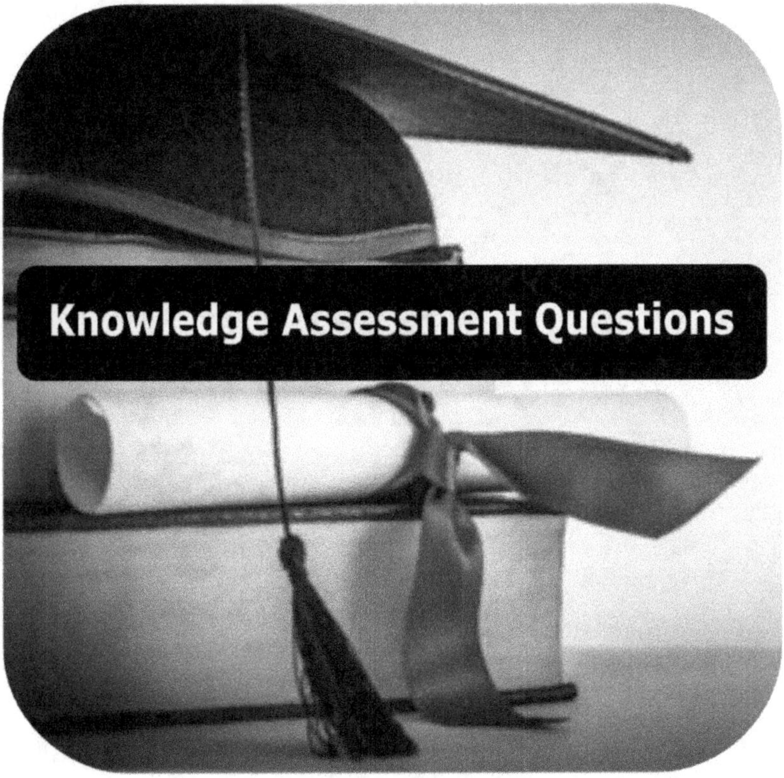

The following knowledge assessment questions are presented as true / false, multiple choice, and fill-in-the-blank. The correct answers are provided in an Answer Key at the end of this text. These questions may or may not be presented on the actual certification exam.

Domain 05: Knowledge Assessment Questions

1. Which choice below is a characteristic of *The Open Group Architecture Framework* that provides an approach for developing enterprise architecture?

A. Mid-Level Design Approach

B. Provides a Unique Vocabulary

C. Created by John Zachman

D. Defines System Components

E. None of the Above

2. Modern networks and usage patterns no longer resemble those that made traditional __________ a practical solution years ago.

A. Perimeter Defense

B. Compensating Controls

C. Logging Reports

D. Alerting Systems

E. None of the Above

3. Select the best choice below for the following definition: "*An enterprise ontology that provides a fundamental and formalized structure for enterprise architecture.*"

A. COBIT Framework

B. TOGAF Framework

C. Zachman Framework

D. ITIL Framework

E. None of the Above

4. The __________ identifies and defines the organizations' strategy, governance, structure, goals, and key business processes.

A. Data Architecture

B. Business Architecture

C. Technology Architecture

D. Application Architecture

E. None of the Above

5. Which choice below is a potential risk and/or attack vector associated with Zero Trust Networks that can undermine its utility?

A. Data Plane Security

B. Control Plane Security

C. Server Enumeration

D. Trusted Computing Platform

E. None of the Above

6. __________ is/are complex technological components of security architecture that are crucial for the protection of information assets.

A. Physical Security

B. Content Control Services

C. Cryptographic Services

D. Detection Services

E. None of the Above

7. Select the best choice below for the following definition: *"Describes the hardware, software, and network infrastructure needed to support the deployment of a solution."*

A. Technology Architecture

B. Business Architecture

C. Data Architecture

D. Application Architecture

E. None of the Above

8. The __________ is where most vulnerabilities are presented and the greatest effort in reducing vulnerabilities is expended.

A. Network Layer

B. Session Layer

C. Data Link Layer

D. Application Layer

E. None of the Above

9. Which choice below is one of the six phases comprising the Software Development Life Cycle (SDLC)?

A. Purchasing

B. Operating

C. Securing

D. Planning

E. None of the Above

10. A(n) __________ is a document which provides recommended integrations of products and services to form a solution.

A. Reference Security Architecture

B. Software Architecture Document

C. Enterprise Architecture Document

D. Architecture Design Document

E. None of the Above

11. Select the best choice below for the following definition: "*Complex technological components of security architecture that are crucial for the protection of information assets.*"

A. Identity and Access Management

B. Content Control Services

C. Cryptographic Services

D. Configuration Management

E. None of the Above

12. The __________ documents solution deployments, system interactions, and their relationships to core business processes.

A. Data Architecture

B. Business Architecture

C. Technology Architecture

D. Application Architecture

E. None of the Above

13. The TOGAF Framework is an enterprise ontology that provides a fundamental and formalized structure for enterprise architecture.

1. True
2. False

14. The granularity of data stored within a trust agent can vary based on the needs of the organization and maturity of the system.

1. True
2. False

15. Border protection is typically thought of as the component technological devices that provide security at the transport layer.

1. True
2. False

16. Technology architecture describes the hardware, software, and network infrastructure needed to support the deployment of a solution.

1. True
2. False

17. Identity management is implemented to ensure that a solution remains in the configuration for which is was originally intended.

1. True
2. False

18. The perimeter model attempts to build a wall between trusted and untrusted sources; zero trust assumes all actors are malicious.

1. True
2. False

DOMAIN 06

Identifying Network Baselines and Anomalies

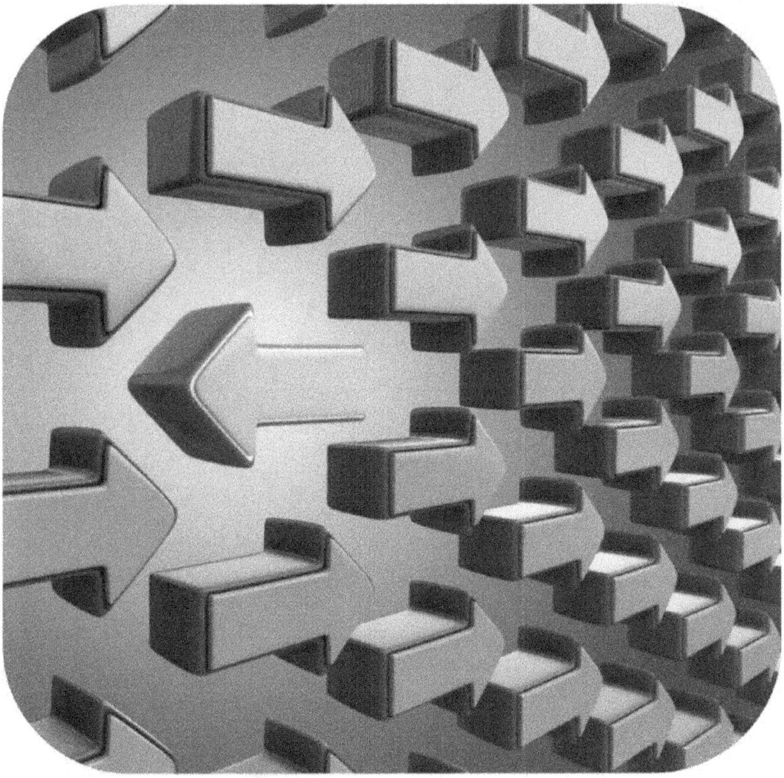

Baseline Measuring Objectives

Baselining is the practice of establishing performance, usage, and behavioral norms for systems and networks. As demonstrated with the examples listed below, data can be derived from many sources to facilitate the baselining process.

1. Processor Utilization
2. Memory Utilization
3. Storage Input and Output Rates
4. Wired Resource Utilization
5. Wireless Resource Utilization

Networks are Highly Complex

There are potentially thousands of data points to monitor on a network, and it is critical to be able to access information at any given time from each of them. The data points listed below are typically present in enterprise network environments.

1. The Internet
2. *Local Area Networks* (LAN's)
3. *Wide Area Networks* (WAN's)
4. *Virtual LAN's* (VLAN's)
5. All Network Devices
6. All Network Storage
7. All Network Applications

Length of Monitoring Time

By setting a baseline, administrators can define what is normal for enterprise networks and identify patterns that indicate signs of trouble. A seven-day monitoring window will usually be enough time to reveal performance trends.

It is important to consider the context of the timing; cyclical usage patterns exist and analysis is sensitive to these patterns. Business cycles must also be considered as baselines may vary significantly during these cyclical periods.

Identifying Usage Patterns

Network maintenance includes configuration management, fault management, performance, security, and account management. Administrators take this into account when establishing baselines. Identifying usage patterns will help to identify network issues and validate or invalidate issues that have been discovered. Listed below are examples of times when usage patterns may vary.

1. Peak Operational Usage Hours
2. After Hours and Weekends
3. Holidays and Seasonal Spikes

Setting Up a Network Monitoring System

Intrusion Detection System (IDS) platforms cannot reliably perform both intrusion detection and network surveillance duties simultaneously. When an IDS platform is configured for full-packet capture its effectiveness as a network sensor diminishes. As a result, sensor deployment requires planning and preparation. Listed below are factors that may affect a monitoring system.

1. Network Architecture
2. Network Bandwidth
3. Segment Utilization
4. Non-Technical Influences

Network Sensor Deployment (Part I)

The placement of the network sensor is possibly the most important factor in setting up an effective monitoring system. A solid understanding of the network is essential to executes this task successfully. Listed below are several questions administrators should be asked during the planning phase.

1. What are the Locations of Network Egress Points?
2. Are There Specific Routes for Internal Traffic?
3. Are There Specific Routes for External Traffic?
4. What are the "Choke Point" and/or Boundary Locations?
5. How is Endpoint Traffic Encapsulated?

6. Are There NAT Devices and/or Web Proxies in Use?

Network Sensor Deployment (Part II)

The configuration and security of the network sensors is relevant to the potential evidence it may capture during the monitoring process. It is critical that the sensor be placed in a secure location and protected from unauthorized access.

The chain of custody requirement will dictate the level of the control implemented. Prior to deployment the patch management system should be updated and validated. As with all important tasks, every aspect of sensor deployment and monitoring should well-documented.

Statistical Monitoring (Part I)

Statistical monitoring focuses on the high-level view of what flows, or connections, are traversing the network. It is very useful when there is an incomplete visibility of endpoints or when limited information is available regarding ongoing network activity. The process involves capture packets to parse protocol headers and interpret both the timing and structure of the packets. The data generated is suitable for further NetFlow analysis.

Statistical Monitoring (Part II)

NetFlow and *ARGUS* are tools utilized to recognize patterns in data streams. These data streams contain a count of the number of bytes and packets for each "flow," or session, observed by a device. They are used to answer specific questions and identify suspicious communications. Several examples of these types of communication are listed below.

1. Characteristics of Beaconing
2. Suspected Malicious Communications
3. Unauthorized and/or External Port Scans
4. Information Flows in Opposite Directions

Header and Full Packet Logging (Part I)

In many cases, the decision on how to handle network data depends on the subject(s) being monitored, and for what reason. Header and full packet logging typically serve two distinct purposes:

1. **Collect Transferred System Data**: This data helps the team to generate signatures and better monitor network activity.

2. **Identify Potentially Stolen Data**: This can assist in providing evidence for internal investigations and to support legal matters.

Header and Full Packet Logging (Part II)

The means by which the header and packet capture is performed is also affected by the purposes of the investigation. Two popular choices for this task are a *Network Intrusion Detection System* (NIDS) and the Wireshark packet analyzer.

1. **NIDS**: A NIDS is typically used to retain an entire session. It can gather malware quickly, identify stolen data, and identify interactive login sessions.

2. **Wireshark**: Wireshark is typically used for targeted collections. Raw packets are collected from the network in real-time that represent actual conversations (not logged events).

Network Monitoring Evaluation

Improper sensor placement, poorly written signatures, and faulty analysis will provide inaccurate and misleading baseline measurements. Listed below are a number of actions which can be taken to ensure network monitoring is being implemented properly.

1. Verify the Operation of the Sensors

2. Verify Traffic is Routed Through Proper Gateways
3. Create Test Signatures to Generate Known Alerts
4. Closely Monitor Sensor Statistics
5. Log Sensor Performance Metrics
6. Check Relevant Drivers and Hardware
7. Analyze Data Volume and Packet Arrival Rates

Indicators of Compromise (IOC's)

Definition:

Indicators of Compromise (IOC's) serve as forensic evidence of potential intrusions on a host system or network. These artifacts enable information security professionals and system administrators to detect intrusion attempts or other malicious activities.

Potential Signs of Compromise

Normally, the investigation team immediately reports any suspicious findings to the appropriate individual(s) within the organization that have the authority to make decisions and act. The individual(s) must weigh the risk of acting without an understanding of the situation versus the risk of additional investigative activities. Listed below are several suspicious findings that may warrant further investigation and/or action.

1. Unusual Outbound Network Traffic
2. Anomalies in Privileged Account Activity
3. Geographical Usage Irregularities
4. Swells in Database Read Volume
5. Mismatched Port-Application Traffic
6. Suspicious System File Changes
7. Irregular Spikes in CPU Usage
8. DNS Request Anomalies
9. Unexpected Patching of Systems
10. Mobile Device Profile Changes
11. Bundles of Data in the Wrong Places
12. Web Traffic with Non-Human Behavior
13. Signs Of DDoS Activity

The Need for Network Monitoring

In some situations, data captured by a network sensor or other network device is the only evidence that actions were taken by an attacker. Although some administrators may be reluctant to implement network monitoring for privacy or secrecy concerns, it does have the potential to yield beneficial findings and results.

1. Generate Potentially Actionable Information
2. Turn Gathered Intelligence into Signatures
3. Confirm or Dispel Suspicions
4. Accumulate Evidence and/or Indicators
5. Verify the Scope of the Compromise
6. Identify Additional Parties Involved
7. Generate a Timeline of Events

Iterative Lead Gathering Process

Gathering leads during a network investigation is a structured and well-organized process. It is important to avoid malware fixation when gathering leads; an attackers' goal is rarely to install malware. Once credentials are compromised, malware becomes secondary. The process of gathering leads typically involves the steps listed below.

1. Gather the Initial Leads
2. Begin the Indicator of Compromise (IOC) Creation Process
3. Deploy and Refine the Created IOC's
4. Identify any Systems of Interest
5. Collect any Relevant Evidence
6. Analyze the Data for New Leads

Defining Leads of Value

Sorting the good leads from the bad is important, especially when the organization has a limited team with limited time and resources. The leads must be relevant, actionable, and have sufficient detail. All gathered data must be clarified to verify the leads veracity and determine its context. Once this has occurred, the lead can be converted into intelligence with value.

Turning Leads into Indicators

Leads gathered during network monitoring can result in host-based indicators, network-based indicators, or a combination of both. Leads have detectable characteristics that may signal malicious actions and are primarily used to scope the incident. Indicators are grouped into one of two categories:

1. **Property-Based Indicators**: These can be associated with a particular Registry Key or identified by hashing.

2. **Methodology-Based Indicators**: These can be identified by their implementation or function, such as an unexpected executable file.

Indicator of Compromise (IOC) Creation

*Indicator of Compromis*e (IOC) creation is the process of documenting the characteristics and the artifacts of an incident in a structured manner. It is an iterative process with a goal of creating robust, sustainable signatures to generate reliable information. Listed below are focus areas typically associated with IOC creation.

1. Working Directory Names
2. Output File Names
3. Login Events
4. Persistence Mechanisms
5. IP Addresses
6. Domain Names
7. Malware Protocol Signatures

Indicator of Compromise Deployment

Deploying IOC's manually within a network for enterprise-level incident response platform would be exceptionally difficult; automation is the only practical method. Most network-based IOC solutions support Snort rules. While there are free and open-source tools available they do not scale well at the enterprise level. There are no free enterprise solutions for host-based IOC's and there are currently no standards guiding their implementation. Security personnel interested in host-based IOC's should consider *YARA*, Mitre's *CybOX*, and FireEye's *OpenIOC* solutions as options.

IOC: Identifying Systems of Interest

Prioritization during IOC investigations is based on numerous factors, not just the criticality of data and/or the business processes affected. When an IOC is first created it will generate a series of "hits" why may (or may not) be relevant. An initial triage is performed to validate the results for reliability. Once validated, the results are categorized by activity (i.e., stages of the Attack Life Cycle) and then prioritized based on relevance to the event.

Indicator of Compromise Verification (Part I)

Ensure that the properties of a new indicator do not identify the malware or activity *solely* at a specific point in the lifecycle. Consider the real-world scenario described below:

> An email is sent as part of a phishing campaign containing a malicious file—a Word document with a "dropper"—and a second-stage executable file. The user opens the document unaware it is malicious, and the second-stage malware is executed, removing the "dropper" as part of the process.

If the IOC signature alerts on the "dropper" and security personnel are fixated on that alert they may miss the second-stage malware entirely. They may also waste valuable time attempting to locate, isolate, and mitigate the "dropper" which no longer exists.

Indicator of Compromise Verification (Part II)

Ensure the process identifies data relevant to the indicator and how the data changes over time in the indicator itself. Examine the payload completely and validate all components of the malicious payload have been identified. Understanding the phases of the Attack Life Cycle and the functionality of the components of the payload, a determination can be made regarding the purpose of the component in question. A determination can also be made as to whether additional components of the malicious payload may exist as well. Listed below are several locations which should be considered for investigation once the executable file has been discovered and identified.

1. File Entries in the Prefetch Directory
2. File Names in the MRU Registry Key
3. API Calls Logged in the Browser History
4. DNS Cache Entries for the Hosting Site
5. Second-Stage Malware File Metadata

Event-Based Alert Monitoring (Part I)

Event-based alerting is the form of monitoring to which most Information Security and Incident Response personnel are accustomed. There are free and commercial platforms available with the potential to monitor the entire enterprise network easily. The alerts are generated by rules and thresholds which are established prior to placing the sensor.

The traditional method of event-based alerting is via a *Network Intrusion Detection System* (NIDS) and/or specialized software monitoring traffic patterns on the network. In many cases, Snort or Suricata will be the standardized tools for this process. Events of interest will then trigger alerts and the iterative process for gathering leads will begin and/or continue.

Event-Based Alert Monitoring (Part II)

Event-based alert monitoring relies on indicators (or signatures) matched against traffic observed by the network sensor. Snort, one of the most widely deployed tools for this purpose, has many output plugins which can be implemented based on the needs of the objective. It is easy to integrate, generates specific and robust indicators, and is unlikely to return false alerts. Listed below are examples of Snort functionalities which can be implemented for network monitoring and alerting.

1. Matches on TCP / IP Headers
2. Serial Number Identification
3. Validity Date Identification
4. Issuer Name Identification

Snort and Snort Rules

Snort rules help in differentiating between normal internet activities and malicious activities in real time. Snort is a free open-source *Intrusion Detection System* (IDS) / *Intrusion Protection System* (IPS) solution that operates on a flexible, rule-based language. It is capable of analyzing signatures, protocols, and anomalies to detect malicious network traffic in real-time. It can also use both *Libpcap* and *Winpcap* libraries (like the Wireshark analyzer) to do packet logging and inspections.

DOMAIN 06

Identifying Network Baselines and Anomalies

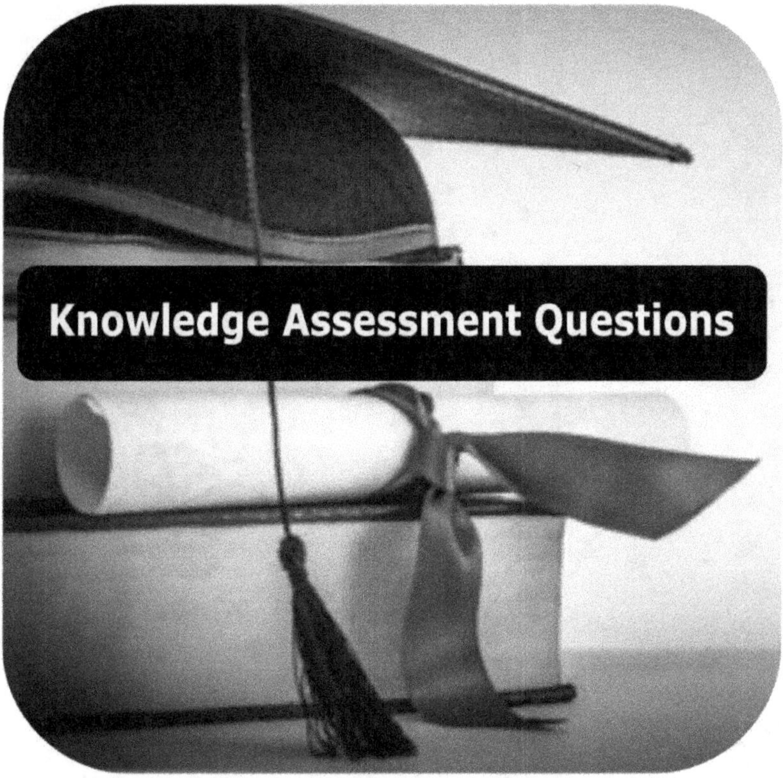

The following knowledge assessment questions are presented as true / false, multiple choice, and fill-in-the-blank. The correct answers are provided in an Answer Key at the end of this text. These questions may or may not be presented on the actual certification exam.

Domain 06: Knowledge Assessment Questions

1. Which choice below is an issue that must be taken into consideration when measuring network baselines?

A. Business Cycles

B. Data Sensitivity

C. Network Segmentation

D. User Roles and Profiles

E. None of the Above

2. Teams interested in __________ IOC's should consider *YARA*, Mitre's *CybOX*, and FireEye's *OpenIOC* solutions as options.

A. Host-Based

B. Server-Based

C. System-Based

D. Network-Based

E. None of the Above

3. Which choice below must be considered due to the affect it may have on the placement of network monitoring sensors?

A. Vendor Support

B. Network Bandwidth

C. Access Management

D. Logging Systems

E. None of the Above

4. __________ focuses on the high-level view of what flows, or connections, are traversing the network.

A. Full Packet Logging

B. Data Loss Prevention

C. Egress Monitoring

D. Statistical Monitoring

E. None of the Above

5. Which choice below is a condition which makes statistical monitoring an optimal approach for incident investigators?

A. Complete Visibility of Endpoints

B. Answering General Questions

C. Characteristics of Beaconing

D. Large Volumes of Information

E. None of the Above

6. The placement of the network __________ is possibly the most important factor in setting up an effective monitoring system.

A. Indicator

B. Sensor

C. Log System

D. Schematic

E. None of the Above

7. Which choice below is **not** an objective to be considered when establishing network baseline measurement objectives?

A. Processor Speed

B. Memory Capacity

C. Storage Capacity

D. Business Capacity

E. None of the Above

8. __________ alerting is the form of monitoring to which most Incident Response and IT personnel are accustomed.

A. Event-Based

B. Host-Based

C. System-Based

D. Perimeter-Based

E. None of the Above

9. Which tool listed below is uniquely useful to Incident Response Teams conducting full packet captures on a network?

A. Retina CS Community

B. Nessus Professional

C. Wireshark Analyzer

D. AlienVault USM

E. None of the Above

10. Indicator generation is a(n) __________ process with a goal of creating robust, sustainable signatures to generate reliable information.

A. Linear

B. Detailed

C. Iterative

D. Finite

E. None of the Above

11. Which choice below considered to be the last phase of the Indicator Generation Life Cycle?

A. Publish

B. Validate

C. Edit

D. Prioritize

E. None of the Above

12. __________ rules help in differentiating between normal internet activities and malicious activities in real time.

A. Synchronized

B. System

C. Security

D. Snort

E. None of the Above

13. Baselining is the practice of establishing performance, usage, and behavioral norms for systems and networks.

1. True
2. False

14. Event-based monitoring relies on alerts (or warnings) matched against traffic observed by the network sensor.

1. True
2. False

15. Network maintenance typically includes configuration management, fault management, performance, security, and account management.

1. True
2. False

16. Ensure that the properties of a new indicator can identify the malware or activity solely at a specific point in the lifecycle.

1. True
2. False

17. Intrusion Detection System platforms cannot reliably perform both intrusion detection services and network surveillance duties simultaneously.

1. True
2. False

18. Prioritization during IOC investigations is based on two specific factors: the criticality of data and the business processes affected.

1. True
2. False

DOMAIN 07

Incident Response and Remediation Strategies

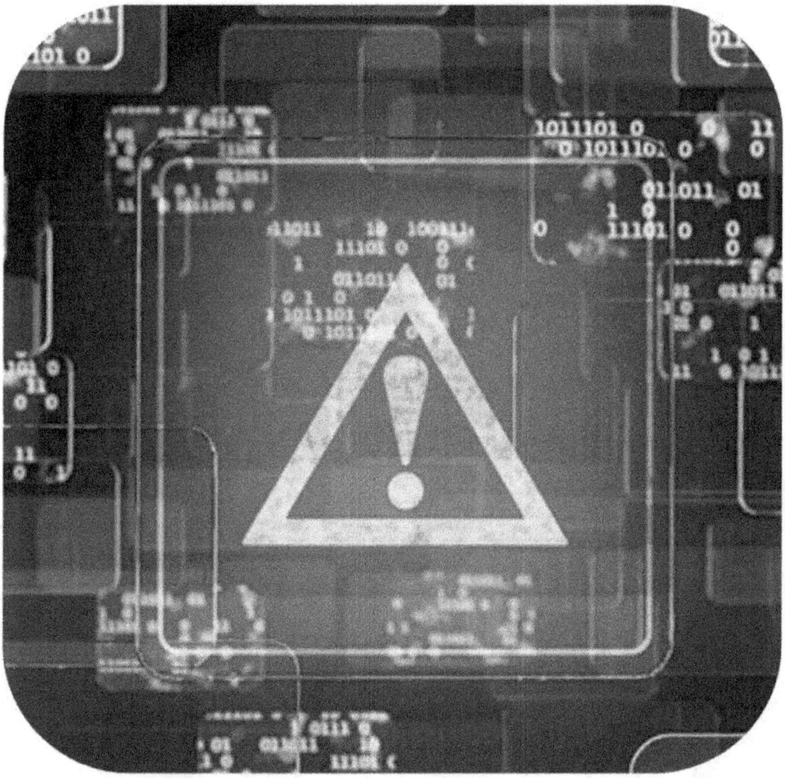

What Constitutes an Incident?

Definition:

> *Any unlawful, unauthorized, or unacceptable action that involves a computer system, cell phone, tablet, and any other electronic device with an operating system, or that operates in a computer network.*

The Incident Response Life Cycle

The *Incident Response Life Cycle* typically consists of seven steps. The process is cyclical, not linear, and the cycle can begin again at any time during a network investigation. The seven steps of the life cycle are listed below.

1. Preparation and Planning
2. Detection and Identification
3. Incident Containment
4. Eradication of Compromise
5. Remediation of Incident
6. Strategic Recommendations
7. Document Lessons Learned

What is Incident Response?

Incident Response is a non-linear, cyclical system whose processes are initiated in parallel execution and iterate continuously. It is a coordinated and structured approach to manage incidents of all severity levels from detection to resolution. Listed below are 12 objectives typically associated with the incident response process.

1. Confirm the Incident Occurrence
2. Rapid Detection and Containment
3. Determine the Scope of the Incident
4. Prevent an Uncoordinated Response
5. Determine Factual Information
6. Minimize any Operational Disruption
7. Minimize Damage of the Compromise
8. Restore Normal Operations
9. Manage Public Perception

10. Allow for Criminal and/or Civil Actions
11. Educate Organizational Leadership
12. Enhance the Future Security Posture

7 Stages of the Attack Life Cycle

Not all seven stages of the *Attack Life Cycle* are always part of an attack, but this model can generally be adapted to fit any incident. Listed below are the seven stages in the order in which they would typically occur during an incident.

1. Initial Compromise
2. Establish a Foothold
3. Escalate Privileges
4. Internal Reconnaissance
5. Move Laterally
6. Maintain a Presence
7. Complete the Mission

Stage #1: Initial Compromise

During this phase the attacker successfully executes malicious code on a victim system. This can be accomplished by exploiting a discovered vulnerability or through the use of social engineering. In the case of code exploitation, Internet-facing systems and third-party applications are usually the targets of choice.

Stage #2: Establish a Foothold

During this phase the attacker will take steps to ensure continued access to the victim system through a remote access capability. The attacker may install a persistent backdoor and/or utilize shellcode or binaries. In most cases, an attempt will be made to compromise legitimate credentials. If any or all of these tactics are successful, the *command and control* (C2) will be established between the attackers' system and the victims' system.

Stage #3: Escalate Privileges

During this phase the attacker will attempt to obtain greater access to the victims' system and/or data. Listed below are several common tactics an attacker may use to escalate privileges.

1. Password Hash and/or Token Dumping
2. Password Cracking
3. Keystroke and/or Credential Logging
4. Lateral Compromise of Multiple Accounts

Stage #4: Internal Reconnaissance

During this phase the attacker will explore the victim environment using a number of tools, tactics, and procedures. Listed below are several objectives an attacker may have during this stage.

1. Enumeration of the Network Topology
2. Identification of Critical Systems and/or Data
3. Identification of Key Roles and/or Responsibilities
4. Conducting an Information Flow Analysis

Stage #5: Move Laterally

During this phase the attacker will attempt to move from system to system within the victim environment. Listed below are several tactics the attacker may employ to accomplish this objective.

1. Access Network Share Servers
2. Compromise the Windows Task Scheduler
3. Access Remote Desktop Computing
4. Access Virtual Network Computing

Stage #6: Maintain a Presence

During this phase the attacker will attempt to ensure continued access without being detected. Listed below are several tactics the attacker may employ to accomplish this objective.

1. Installation of Multiple Backdoor Families
2. Installation of Web Shells and Scripting
3. Use of Legitimate Application Backdoors
4. Accessing Virtual Private Networks

Stage #7: Complete the Mission

During this phase the attacker will accomplish the primary goal. This may be theft of data from the victim system, modification of system information, or both. Once ana attacker has completed the primary mission a persistent access to the victim system will still be maintained. This allows the Attack Life Cycle to be repeated indefinitely if and when the attacker chooses to do so.

Effective Remediation (Part I)

Remediating large incidents is a complex endeavor that requires high-level remediation steps and tactical action types to be successful. Effective Incident Response requires a two-pronged approach: *incident investigation* and *incident remediation*. The goal of combining these various approaches and strategies is to increase the overall security posture of the organization.

Effective Remediation (Part II)

The remediation process begins with the creation of a draft remediation plan that should be completed prior to the eradication event. In the early stages of the incident the document will undergo numerous revisions as the status of the incident is updated. As the remediation plan is developed it is not uncommon to discover the response will be more difficult than originally anticipated.

Although it may be tempting to make wide, sweeping changes to improve the organizations' security posture, is not advisable to do so. Many good options may not be practical to implement during the remediation effort and will need to be reconsidered during the post-incident strategic planning phase.

Effective Remediation (Part III)

Some organizations choose to create a very detailed plan including Microsoft Project workflows, Excel spreadsheets, and other documents. Others choose to use a more informal planning system such as one-page policy statements. The level of detail will vary based on the type of incident and will be written to meet the needs of the remediation owner. Regardless of the structure used, three basic rules apply to all effective plans:

1. Ensure the Final Plan is Comprehensive
2. Ensure the Plan is Implementable
3. Ensure the People Involved are Trusted to Handle Details

Effective Remediation (Part IV)

There is no single strategy to a successful remediation effort; the right strategy depends on several factors specific to the incident. However, every remediation plan typically includes some aspect of the eight high-level steps listed below.

1. Form the Remediation Team
2. Determine the Timing of the Remediation
3. Develop Remediation Posturing Actions
4. Develop Containment Actions
5. Develop the Eradication Plan
6. Determine the Eradication Event Timing
7. Develop Strategic Recommendations
8. Document the Lessons Learned

Effective Remediation (Part V)

Documenting areas for improvement and lessons learned is a critical part of the incident response process. These documents should be stored in a central location which is accessible only to authorized personnel. These documents will help improve the organization over time and make future responses more effective and concise. As lessons learned are considered, implementing a small number of incremental changes is usually more effective than large actions that may be irrelevant to the investigation.

Effective Remediation (Part VI)

Regardless of the incident type, there are typically seven common factors specific to each incident that must be considered. These common factors are:

1. Incident Severity
2. Remediation Timing
3. The Remediation Team
4. Existing Technology
5. Budget and Finances
6. Management Support
7. Public Scrutiny

Assigning a Remediation Owner (Part I)

The *remediation owner* accepts responsibility for the remediation effort and interacts with both technical and non-technical personnel. Selection of this individual is a key component of forming the team. This person must be highly knowledgeable in technical issues but must also have a dep understanding of non-technical issues as well. Listed below are examples of the non-technical areas of proficiency.

1. Organizational Operations
2. Organizational Strategy
3. Human Resources
4. Legal Counsel

Assigning a Remediation Owner (Part II)

A good candidate for this position is a senior technical person with solid non-technical experience as well. This diversity of skills will allow the individual to provide better direction for the team. It is important that the remediation owner has management support and the authority to push difficult actions to completion. This person must also be able to effectively resolve disagreements within the team as they arise. A good project manager may be able to lead a remediation effort if they are surrounded by an effective team of technical and non-technical personnel.

Assigning a Remediation Owner (Part III)

During large incidents, the remediation owner is separate from the other owners involved (incident owner and investigation owner). At other times, a single person has responsibility for the investigation and the remediation, especially with less complex incidents. In all cases, the remediation must posses the five key qualities listed below.

1. An Understanding of IT and Security
2. The Ability to Focus on Execution
3. An Understanding of Internal Politics
4. A Proven Record of Building Support
5. Communications Skills Across Multiple Disciplines

Remediation Posturing Actions (Part I)

Posturing actions are taken during an ongoing incident and are designed to be implemented with minimum impact on the attacker. When implemented effectively, they can enhance the investigation teams' visibility into the incident, add additional sources of evidence, and decrease the amount of time required to be spent during later phases. Listed below are examples of high-level posturing actions.

1. Enhanced Logging: Network-Specific
2. Enhanced Logging: System-Specific
3. Enhanced Logging: Application-Specific

Remediation Posturing Actions (Part II)

Many posturing actions can be supported by simply improving the type of data that is retained by the endpoints and logging systems. Listed below are examples of these types of actions.

1. Centralize Authentication Logs
2. Centralize SIEM Log Files
3. Enhance Event-Based Alerting
4. Patch Third-Party Applications
5. Implement Multifactor Authentication

6. Reduce Critical Data Storage Locations
7. Enhance Native Security Authentication

Remediation Posturing Actions (Part III)

The specific audit events that are logged will depend on the scope of the incident and the goals of the remediation effort. Listed below are examples of auditing actions that may be considered during an ongoing incident.

1. Audit Failed Logon Events
2. Audit Successful Logon Events
3. Audit Account Management
4. Audit Object Access
5. Audit Privilege Use
6. Audit Process Tracking
7. Audit System Events

Remediation Posturing Actions (Part IV)

Another common posturing goal is to increase the security of an application or system without alerting the attacker. The investigation owner should be consulted prior to execution to determine if the actions may adversely affect the investigation or remediation effort. Typical actions include:

1. Strengthen Password Security
2. Patch Commonly Targeted Applications
3. 2F Authentication in Uncompromised Environments
4. Fix Application Flaws Used by the Attacker

Remediation Posturing Actions (Part V)

In some instances, it is acceptable to remove a compromised system from the environment; systems are rebuilt all the time and attackers expect some degree of flux. However, if 25-30 infected machines are taken offline at once, the attacker may assume that they've been discovered. The attacker may change their *tools, tactics, and procedures* (TTP's), making it difficult for the team to re-scope the incident. An alternative would be to issue new accounts to users if they or their devices have been compromised and set alerts for the known compromised accounts.

Implications of Alerting an Attacker

Taking actions that alert attackers that they have been discovered is usually considered detrimental to the investigation as they will likely react in some way to the discovery. The attackers reaction may be benign if they have confidence in their ability to maintain a presence in the environment. They may change *tools, tactics, and procedures* (TTP's) making the investigation difficult. They may become dormant and attempt to obfuscate themselves. In a worst-case scenario, they may become destructive and attempt to overwhelm the victim organization with compromised systems.

Eradication Plan Development (Part I)

Eradication actions are implemented during a short period of time to remove the attacker permanently from the environment. The event is typically executed when the incident has been fully scoped and the victim organization is fully recovered. The eradication involves all compromised systems and accounts; every attack vector is removed, removing the attackers' access permanently. The objective of the eradication event is to restore trust in every system and account.

Eradication Plan Development (Part II)

Eradication plans should be designed with the expectation that the attacker will attempt to regain access to the victim environment. To prevent this occurrence, the seven high-level steps are usually followed.

1. Disconnect the Victim from the Internet
2. Block Known Malicious IP Addresses
3. Blackhole Relevant Domain Names
4. Change User Account Passwords
5. Implement Network Segmentation

6. Mitigate the Original Vulnerabilities
7. Rebuild the Compromised Systems

Eradication Plan Development (Part III)

In many organizations, weekends are a good time to conduct an eradication event as disruption to operations tends to be minimal. Knowing the attackers' working hours will increase the chances of a successful eradication as they may be unaware they have lost access. The victim should be disconnected from the Internet to ensure the attacker has no access to the environment and prevent possible disruptions to the eradication effort. The severity of the incident will dictate the level to which connectivity is discontinued.

Eradication Plan Development (Part IV)

The longer the duration of the eradication event, the greater the chance that the attacker will regain access to the victim environment. In that event, the team will have to investigate and re-contain the compromise. This will re-start the incident response process over from the beginning and limit the teams' actions to remove the attacker. Listed below are actions that can be taken in the event this situation occurs.

1. Rebuild Systems from Known Good Media
2. Implement a Detailed System Cleaning Program
3. Disable and/or Delete Compromised Accounts

Eradication Plan Development (Part V)

An eradication effort that is often difficult to implement is identifying and changing all user and system passwords. Listed below are several examples of password usage that will need to be considered during the event.

1. Windows, Linux, and Mac Accounts
2. Service Accounts
3. Local Administrator and Root Accounts
4. Integrated Credential Database Accounts

5. Application Accounts
6. Networking Device Accounts
7. Database Accounts

Eradication Plan Development (Part VI)

During an eradication effort, response teams should be prepared to develop contingencies for a variety of common complications. Users may be on vacation or traveling for business purposes which may lead to passwords remaining unchanged or not changed in a timely manner. Inactive accounts that have not been disabled will not have a user to change the password and may be overlooked. Finally, systems outside the domain in which the eradication effort takes place will remain unaffected and may lead to a secondary compromise if not addressed.

Plan Timing and Execution (Part I)

The timing of the eradication event is critical. If it is executed too early and the environment has not been completely scoped, the attackers' access may not be completely removed and the remediation effort will fail. If it is executed too late, the attacker may change TTP's and accomplish the desired objective. An ideal time to execute the eradication event is when the team has properly scoped the compromise and implemented posturing actions. This is referred to as the "Strike Zone."

Plan Timing and Execution (Part II)

Determining when the incident response team is in the "strike zone" can be difficult; it is more of an art than a science. The following conditions are good indicators that the timing may be right for the eradication event. Good visibility into the breached area is critical and the attackers' TTP's must be understood. Daily compromises are decreasing daily, and those that remain are known IOC's. In a parallel execution, the remediation effort has been thoroughly planned and approved by the remediation owner.

Plan Timing and Execution (Part III)

The planning process for the eradication event should start as soon as the incident owner has decided upon a remediation approach. The plan is considered "work in progress" and is continually revised based on new information. Early planning will increase the effectiveness of the effort. All process owners must agree on the plan. The date must not be allowed to pass; implementations that are difficult will become virtually impossible to execute.

Plan Timing and Execution (Part IV)

The more planning that is performed in anticipation of the eradication event, the more straightforward the event will be. When the systems are taken offline, the process of changing passwords can begin. Changing passwords before rebuilding the systems will reduce the time of the eradication effort. Changing passwords is the hardest part of any eradication event; it takes the most amount of time and causes the majority of unanticipated issues for the remediation team.

Plan Timing and Execution (Part V)

Once the networking actions have been completed, the system and application administrators can start remediating compromised systems. Attention to detail is crucial to ensure systems are not accidently overlooked, improperly rebuilt, or not rebuilt at all.

Although cleaning systems is easier than rebuilding systems, it is better to take the time and effort to rebuild them. This helps to ensure trace malware is removed completely from all compromised systems. Effective communication is critical during this process to verify all systems have been properly remediated.

DOMAIN 07

Incident Response and Remediation Strategies

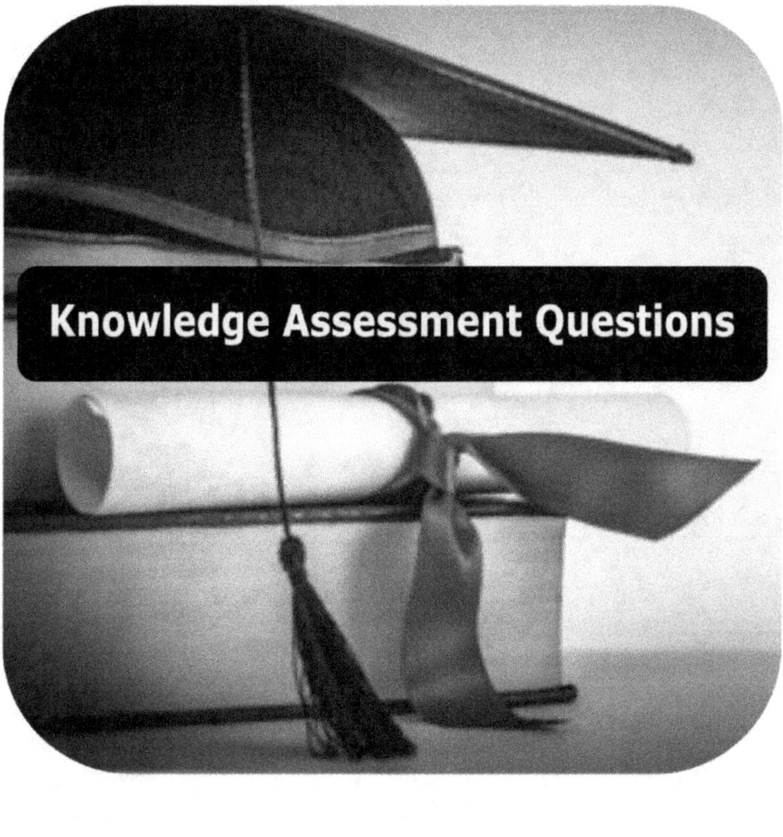

The following knowledge assessment questions are presented as true / false, multiple choice, and fill-in-the-blank. The correct answers are provided in an Answer Key at the end of this text. These questions may or may not be presented on the actual certification exam.

Domain 07: Knowledge Assessment Questions

1. Which choice below is a tactic an attacker may choose to use in Stage 01 of the Attack Life Cycle to execute the initial compromise?

A. Ensure Remote Access

B. Keystroke and Credential Logging

C. Enumerate the Network Topology

D. Social Engineering

E. None of the Above

2. Effective Incident Response requires a two-pronged approach: incident __________ and incident remediation.

A. Recovery

B. Discovery

C. Eradication

D. Investigation

E. None of the Above

3. Which choice below is a tactic an attacker may choose to use in Stage 05 of the Attack Life Cycle to move laterally in the network?

A. Keystroke / Credential Logging

B. Establish C2 with Victim System

C. Access Windows Task Scheduler

D. Modify System Information

E. None of the Above

4. Regardless of the type of incident encountered, there are typically __________ common factors specific to each incident that must be considered.

A. Three

B. Nine

C. Seven

D. Six

E. None of the Above

5. Which choice below is a tactic an attacker may choose to use in Stage 03 of the Attack Life Cycle to escalate acquired privileges?

A. Keystroke / Credential Logging

B. Establish C2 with Victim System

C. Enumerate the Network Topology

D. Move from System to System

E. None of the Above

6. __________ actions are taken during an ongoing incident and are designed to be implemented with minimum impact on the attacker.

A. Investigative

B. Posturing

C. Remediation

D. Eradication

E. None of the Above

7. Which choice below is a tactic an attacker may choose to use in Stage 06 of the Attack Life Cycle to maintain a presence?

A. Information Flow Analysis

B. Access Virtual Private Networks

C. Access Network Shares

D. Password Hash / Token Dumping

E. None of the Above

8. __________ actions are implemented during a short period of time to remove the attacker from the environment.

A. Eradication

B. Posturing

C. Remediation

D. Investigative

E. None of the Above

9. Which choice below is a tactic an attacker may choose to use in Stage 02 of the Attack Life Cycle to establish a foothold?

A. Compromise Multiple Accounts

B. Modify System Information

C. Install a Persistent Backdoor

D. Enumerate Network Topology

E. None of the Above

10. An ideal time to execute the eradication event is when the team has properly __________ the compromise and has implemented posturing actions.

A. Planned

B. Remediated

C. Contained

D. Scoped

E. None of the Above

11. Which choice below is a tactic an attacker may choose to use in Stage 04 of the Attack Life Cycle to conduct internal reconnaissance?

A. Execute Malicious Code

B. Social Engineering

C. Install a Persistent Backdoor

D. Identify Key Responsibilities

E. None of the Above

12. Once the networking actions have been completed, the system and application administrators can start __________ compromised systems.

A. Activating

B. Removing

C. Remediating

D. Investigating

E. None of the Above

13. Incident Response is a linear, sequential system whose processes are initiated in parallel execution and iterate occasionally.

1. True
2. False

14. Although it may be tempting to make wide, sweeping changes to improve the organizations' security posture, is not advisable to do so.

1. True
2. False

15. Incident Response is a coordinated and structured approach to manage incidents from detection to resolution.

1. True
2. False

16. The remediation owner delegates responsibility for the remediation effort and interacts exclusively with technical personnel.

1. True
2. False

17. The planning process for the eradication event should start as soon as executive management has decided upon a remediation approach.

1. True
2. False

18. Taking actions that alert attackers that they have been discovered is usually considered detrimental to the investigation.

1. True
2. False

DOMAIN 08

Network and Host Data Collection Methods

Network Forensics vs. Digital Forensics

Network Forensics	**Digital Forensics**
Volatile / Dynamic Information	Data at Rest
Critical Dependency on Logs	Medium Dependency on Logs
Live Acquisition	Post-Mortem Images
Reactive and Preemptive	Primarily Reactive
External Time Considerations	Internal Time Considerations
Networked Devices	Independent Devices

General Process for Performing Analysis

As a manager in the field of Information Security, Computer Forensics, or Incident Response, it is hard to deny the importance of science. Listed below are the steps typically followed when performing scientific analysis.

1. Define and Understand the Objectives
2. Obtain Relevant Data
3. Inspect the Data Content
4. Perform Conversion and/or Normalization
5. Select an Analysis Method
6. Perform the Analysis
7. Evaluate the Results

Define and Understand the Objectives

Defining and understanding objectives is not a difficult task. However, defining good objectives that are realistic can be very challenging. Knowledge of the technology involved and the scope of the situation makes defining good objectives easier. Listed below are questions to ask when defining objectives.

1. What is Trying to be Determined?
2. Can Conclusions be Drawn from Available Facts?
3. How Much Time will be Involved?
4. What Resources will be Required?
5. Who is Interested in the Results?

6. What is the Outcome of the Results?

Know the Data

Before analysis can be performed, the team needs to explore possible sources of data and understand how to use them. The data collected will be used to perform analysis and answer investigative questions, so investigators must attempt to collect only that data which is relevant and useful to the investigation. Knowing the existing data sources can indicate what type of data they may provide. This guides the team in knowing what data to collect.

Where is the Data Stored?

In this context, "data" is used in a broad sense: operating system files, applications, databases, and user data. Listed below are examples of data sources which should be considered during the investigation.

1. Desktops, Laptops, and Tablets
2. Servers
3. Mobile Devices
4. Storage Solutions and External Media
5. System and Network Devices
6. Cloud Storage Solutions
7. Back-Ups and Data Recovery Media

Available Data Sources

From a general analysis standpoint, four high-level categories of evidence may exist in the seven locations previously listed.

1. Operating Systems (Windows Registry, Unix Syslog, OS X)
2. Applications (Cache, Files, Logs, Preferences)
3. User Data (Centralized Locations for Each User)
4. Network Services and/or Devices

Access to Data Sources

Once data has been obtained to analyze, one of the first challenges likely to be encountered is determining how to access it. The data may not be in an "accessible state." Listed below are examples of challenges faced when accessing data.

1. Data may be Encrypted
2. Data may be Encoded
3. Data may be Compressed
4. Data may be Custom Formatted
5. Data may Exist on Various Hard Drives and Images
6. Data may be Damaged or Destroyed

The Host Device Power State

Maintaining the power state of the device being secured is critical for capturing all available data and not modifying the device itself. Powered systems contain volatile data that may be lost if the system is powered down. Malware may exist solely in memory that will be lost. Additionally, the power cycle may modify the device itself, changing the hash value of the imaged drive. A hash value that is changed indicates contamination and/or compromise. To avoid these issues data should be collected in order of volatility.

1. CPU Cache and Process Registers
2. Memory, Routing Tables, and ARP Cache
3. Temporary File Systems
4. Disks and Drives
5. Remote Logging and Monitoring Data
6. Configuration and Network Topology
7. Archival and/or Back-Up Media

File Systems

From an investigative standpoint, the file system is the place where the "fingerprints" of the system users will be found when collecting data. They are created by the operating system to perform the functions listed below.

1. Effectively Manage Storage Space
2. Provide Efficient Access with Indexing
3. Provide a Standard Naming Format
4. Link Filenames to Actual Data
5. Copy and Delete Files from the Disk
6. Create a Record of Data Storage and Allocations

New Technology File System (NTFS)

NTFS is a popular Windows file system that was introduced in Windows NT 3.1 in 1993. It replaced the *File Allocation Table* (FAT) system. Compared to FAT it is much more stable and secure, performs at much higher speeds, and greatly reduces slack space. It is exclusive to Windows; it is not compatible with other operating systems. By default, most security features are not enabled as users tend to implement third-party security solutions.

Locating Endpoint Data (Part I)

A bit-level copy (forensic image) of the original endpoint hard drive is needed prior to investigating any data residing in the file system. Listed below are locations in the file system that should be considered when performing data collection.

1. Root User Folder
2. Desktop Folder
3. Recycle Bin Folder
4. "My Documents" Folder
5. File Metadata
6. System Restore Points

Locating Endpoint Data (Part II)

Forensic copies of hard drives consider all system data, including areas the operating system does not recognize but can still be used. It is important to copy (forensic image) all system data prior to analyzing artifacts, identifying malicious behavior, or looking for indicators of compromise. Listed below are file system folders that should be considered when performing data collection.

1. Printer Spooler Folder
2. Application Data Folder
3. Start Menu Folder
4. "Send To" Folder
5. Program Files Folder
6. Pinned Files / Jump List Folder
7. Favorite Data Folder
8. Swap Files Folder
9. Cookies Folder
10. "Most Recent" Folder
11. Thumbs Cache Folder
12. Registry Folder

The Windows Registry

The *Windows Registry* is essentially a database that records virtually every action and activity performed in the operating system. Listed below are the five root keys of the Registry that are the most relevant for collecting data during investigations.

1. HKEY_LOCAL_MACHINE
2. HKEY_CURRENT_CONFIG
3. HKEY_CLASSES_ROOT
4. HKEY_USERS
5. HKEY_CURRENT_USERS

Deleted Files

When a file is deleted on a Windows operating system, many actions take place simultaneously contingent upon the file system being used. The IN_USE flag is cleared in the *Master File Table* (MFT) and the entry in the Parent Directory is cleared. The file directory is resorted and the data clusters are marked as "unallocated." The data may still be fully or partially recoverable as it remains available until it is overwritten.

Windows Recycle Bin

From a technical viewpoint, the Recycle Bin works by moving deleted files into two special directories: INFO and INFO2. When the file entry is deleted from the directory the INFO and INFO2 directories are updated. These are hidden file directories not visible in explorer and cannot be accessed without special tools, making them impossible to access by standard users.

The directories contain valuable information: the file path, time and date of deletion, and the *Security Identifier* (SID) of the user deleting the file. This information allows investigators to confirm files were intentionally deleted by a specific user. This information can be located on Windows systems at C:\$Recycle.Bin\%SID%\.

Slack Space

Slack space is leftover storage that can be found on a hard drive when the system does not need all the space being allocated for the file. Slack is not recognized as free space by the operating system. It can be used by other programs, making it an attractive target for malware. Free space and slack can be distinguished by their composition: free space will have zeros at the end of a file, slack space with have zeros between files. Slack space may contain valuable data which can be accessed using specialized tools such as *WinHex*.

The Importance of IoT Devices

Many *Internet of Things* (IoT) companies are new to networking and tend to focus on the production of products versus dealing with vulnerabilities. These devices are known to lack secure development and therefore presents both challenges and benefits. These devices provide information on user behavior that may be valuable during an investigation.

1. **Doorbell with Video Monitoring**: These video devices activate when a doorbell is pressed, capturing an image of the person ringing the bell. The video provides positive proof of an individuals' location at a given time.

2. **Internet-Enabled Thermostat**: These devices activate when an individual enters a building and deactivate when they leave. They are typically controlled by the individuals'

mobile phone. The thermostat may provide positive proof of an individuals' location at a given time.

When to Perform a Live Response

Listed below are five important factors to consider when deciding if a live response (LR) is appropriate when investigating a network incident.

Question #01:

Is there a reason to believe volatile data contains information critical to the investigation that is not present elsewhere?

Question #02:

Can the live response be executed in an ideal manner, minimizing any changes to the target system?

Question #03:

Is the number of affected systems large, making it infeasible to perform forensic duplication on all of them?

Question #04:

Is there a risk that forensic duplications will take an excessive amount of time, or potentially fail altogether?

Question #05:

Are there legal or other special considerations that make it a wise choice to preserve as much data as possible?

Live Response Challenges

There are serious potential challenges to performing a live response; the process may crash the system and/or destroy evidence. Listed below are several questions to consider before assuming the risks associated with performing a live response.

1. Has the Process been Tested on a Similar System?
2. Is the System Sensitive to Performance?
3. What is the Impact of a System Crash?
4. Have all Stakeholders been Informed?
5. Has Written / Formal Approval been Received?

Selecting a Live Response Tool

As techniques in live data acquisition and forensics evolve, available industry tools and procedures must be continually evaluated. Listed below are several factors to consider when selecting a tool for live data acquisition.

1. Is the Tool Accepted in the Forensic Community?
2. Does the Tool Address Common Operating Systems?
3. Does the Tool Collect the Right Type of Data?
4. Is the Data Collection Time Acceptable?
5. Are the Tools' Procedures and/or Processes Configurable?
6. Is the Analysis Output is Easily Understood?

Data Collection Considerations

Throughout an investigation, continuously evaluate what data to collect based on how quickly and effectively critical questions are answered. Based on the considers listed below, the focus and the priorities of the investigation may be subject to change.

1. Current Running System State
2. Network Connections and/or Processes
3. Contents of the System Memory
4. File Listings and/or System Logs
5. Application-Specific Data

Common Live Response Data (Part I)

Although every operating system has unique and proprietary sources of evidence, many areas of commonality exist between all of them. Listed below is data common to all operating systems,

1. Time, Date, and Time Zone
2. Operating System Version Information
3. General System Information
4. Boot-Up Services and Programs
5. Tasks Scheduled to Automatically Run
6. Local Users and/or Group Members Accounts

Common Live Response Data (Part II)

Some data is proprietary and inherent to the specific operating system, and some data comes from common sources such as logging. Listed below are sources of information that should be available regardless of the operating system version.

1. NIC Details (IP and MAC Addresses)
2. Routing / ARP Table and DNS Cache
3. Network Connections and Processes
4. Currently Loaded Drivers and/or Modules
5. Files and/or Open Handles
6. Running Processes (PID's and Runtimes)

Common Live Response Data (Part III)

It's important to note that operating system settings can greatly affect the available evidence, leaving some questions unanswered. Listed below are examples of evidence that may be affected.

1. System Configuration Data
2. User Login History (Identifiers)
3. Standard System Log Data
4. List of Installed Software
5. Relevant Application Log Data
6. Full File System Listing

Live Collection Best Practices

As with most tools, it is very important to learn the correct way to use them. Live response tools are no exception to this rule. The user must prepare for the collection by testing on multiple systems with the goal of minimizing interaction time. It is also beneficial to create simulated problems such as the examples listed below.

1. Broken USB Ports
2. Non-Functional Network Cards
3. Locked Device Screens

Live Collection Best Practices Checklist

Best Practice #01:

Document exactly what you do and when you do it. Note the difference between actual and system time. Do not forget to include time zones in notes.

Best Practice #02:

Treat the suspect system as "contaminated" - do not interact with it unless you have an established plan. Get on and off the system as quickly as possible.

Best Practice #03:

Use tools that minimize the impact on the target system. Avoid GUI-based collection tools; choose tools with a minimal memory profile and do not make excessive changes to the target system.

Best Practice #04:

Use tools that keep a log and use cryptographic checksums of their output as the output is created (not after the fact).

Best Practice #05:

Fully automate the collection process if possible, perhaps eliminating the need for a human to interact with the suspect system.

Best Practice #06:

Make every effort to collect data in the order of volatility and take all measures to protect this type of data wherever possible.

Best Practice #07:

Treat all the data collected as evidence; be sure to follow data preservation procedures, including the creation of an evidence tag and chain of custody. Compute MD5 checksums of evidence.

Best Practice #08:

Consider files on media you connect to the suspect system as lost to the attacker. Do not keep notes, indicators, documents, or reports on the media from which the live response will run.

Best Practice #09:

Consider any credentials you use as compromised. Use an account other than your primary, and change passwords frequently. Use two- factor authentication whenever possible.

Best Practice #10:

Do not take actions that will cause unnecessary modifications to the suspect system unless there is no other option. Doing so may destroy valuable evidence. Use external media / shares if possible.

Best Practice #11:

> Do not use the suspect system to perform analysis; this can make the discernment of attacker activity from responder activity difficult. It can also make system changes and destroy potential evidence.

Live Response: When Things Go Wrong

Thinking through worst-case scenarios in advance and testing alternate solutions will help prepare the team for when things go wrong. Investigators will likely encounter situations such as the inability to connect removable media to the target system, data that has been encrypted, and operating systems not compatible with the available data collection toolkit.

Preparation for these scenarios can be made in several ways. The team should have DVD's or CD-ROM's to run their toolkits if they cannot be run on the target system. They should possess encrypted network streaming tools such as *Cryptcat* or *Stunnel* to overcome the challenge of encrypted data. Finally, the team should be trained and prepared to execute automated functions manually (when feasible and practical) should issues arise with the tools themselves.

DOMAIN 08

Network and Host Data Collection Methods

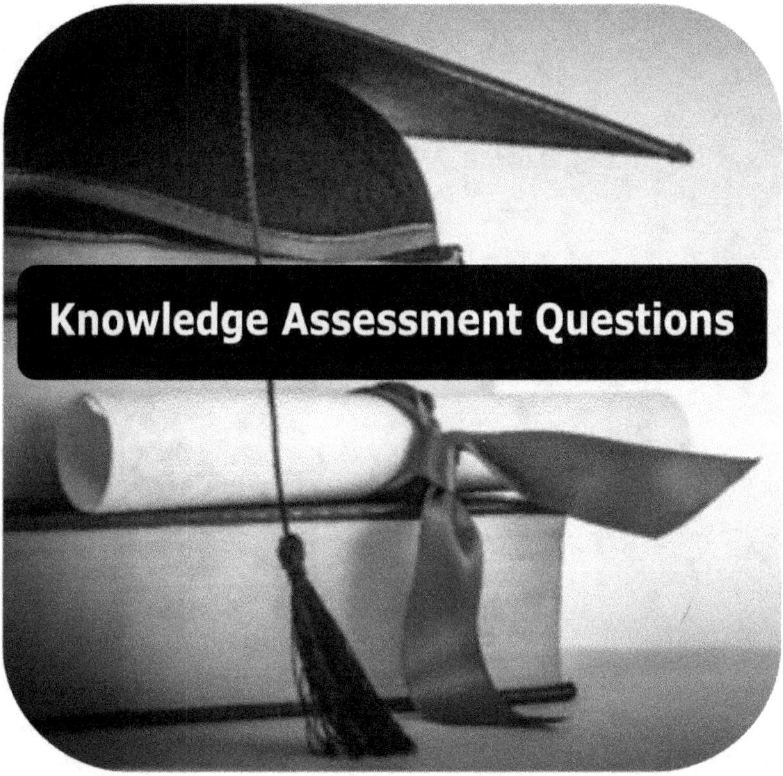

The following knowledge assessment questions are presented as true / false, multiple choice, and fill-in-the-blank. The correct answers are provided in an Answer Key at the end of this text. These questions may or may not be presented on the actual certification exam.

Domain 08: Knowledge Assessment Questions

1. Which choice below presents a challenge to system and network administrators attempting to access data that has been collected?

A. Data may be Private

B. Data may be Privileged

C. Data may be Proprietary

D. Data may be Encoded

E. None of the Above

2. It is important to note that operating system settings can greatly affect the ___________, leaving questions unanswered.

A. Perimeter Defense

B. Windows Registry

C. Available Evidence

D. Production Server

E. None of the Above

3. Select the best choice below for the following definition: "*Leftover storage that can be found on a hard drive when the system does not need all the space being allocated for the file.*"

A. Slack Space

B. Memory

C. CPU Cache

D. File Table

E. None of the Above

4. Maintaining the ___________ of the device being secured is critical for capturing all available data and not modifying the device itself.

A. Location

B. Power State

C. Documentation

D. Position

E. None of the Above

5. Which choice below is a location of potentially volatile data that should be collected as quickly as possible during an investigation?

A. Monitoring Data

B. Process Register

C. Archival Media

D. Hard Disk

E. None of the Above

6. From an investigative standpoint, the file system is the place where the __________ of the system users will be found.

A. "Fingerprints"

B. Identities

C. Job Roles

D. Passwords

E. None of the Above

7. Which choice below is a component of the Windows Registry that should be considered as a potential source of digital evidence?

A. HKEY_PREVIOUS_CONFIG

B. HKEY_REMOTE_MACHINE

C. HKEY_CLASSES_ROOT

D. HKEY_PREVIOUS_USERS

E. None of the Above

8. A(n) __________ copy of the original endpoint hard drive is needed prior to investigating any data in the file system.

A. Byte-Level

B. Duplicate

C. Authorized

D. Bit-Level

E. None of the Above

9. Which choice below is a characteristic of Microsoft's New Technology File System (NTFS) that presents evidence collection challenges?

A. Increased Memory

B. Less Expensive Solution

C. Compatible with Other O/S's

D. Reduces Slack Space

E. None of the Above

10. Many IoT companies are new to networking and tend to focus on the production of products versus dealing with __________.

A. Development

B. Threats

C. Vulnerabilities

D. Risks

E. None of the Above

11. What is the first action that should be taken prior to analyzing artifacts, identifying malicious behavior, or looking for indicators of compromise?

A. Copy all System Data

B. Document all Devices

C. Photograph all Evidence

D. Secure all Log Files

E. None of the Above

12. Forensic copies of __________ consider all system data, including areas the operating system does not recognize but can still be used.

A. Malware

B. Thin Clients

C. Software

D. Hard Drives

E. None of the Above

13. Before analysis can be performed, the team needs to explore possible sources of data and understand how to use them.

1. True
2. False

14. The Domain Controller is essentially a database that records virtually every action and activity performed in the operating system.

1. True
2. False

15. From a technical viewpoint, the Recycle Bin works by moving deleted files into two special directories: RECYCLE and RECYCLE2.

1. True
2. False

16. Once data has been obtained to analyze, one of the first challenges likely to be encountered is determining how to access it.

1. True
2. False

17. Persistent data is potentially valuable to the incident investigation and can be lost when the device being secured is powered off.

1. True
2. False

18. Although every operating system has unique and proprietary sources of evidence, many areas of commonality exist between all of them.

1. True
2. False

DOMAIN 09

Investigations, Evidence and Chain of Custody

Understanding Elements of Proof

Every case type and investigation have its own considerations—whether the goal is litigation or developing a stronger security posture. *Elements of proof* define the elements of the asserted claim. During the initial investigation the driving claims are few and broad. Greater detail develops as the investigation progresses based on the needs of the primary consumer of the results.

Most investigations are led by legal teams with the responsibility of proving or disproving a case. However, investigations involving legal teams will generate a higher degree of scrutiny for members of the investigative team.

The Purpose of Investigations

An investigation is a systematic inquiry and/or examination, typically conducted for the purpose of identifying and/or verifying facts. Listed below are the general interrogatives addressed in an investigation.

1. **WHO**: All Persons Involved
2. **WHERE**: All Relevant Locations
3. **WHAT**: Description of the Factual Elements
4. **WHEN**: Time of all Related Events
5. **WHY**: Motivation for all Actions Taken
6. **HOW**: Details of Execution Methods

Investigative Interview Strategies

In most investigations, interviews are the main tool investigators use to find out what happened and/or verify physical and technical evidence. However, a good investigation interview is only as good as the person conducting it, regardless of the nature of the investigation itself. Listed below are 14 best practices to employ when conducting interview during an investigation.

1. Create a Comprehensive Question List
2. Select a Non-Threatening Location
3. Maintain an Open and Objective Mind
4. Ask Open-Ended Questions
5. Start with the Easy Questions First
6. Keep Your Opinions to Yourself
7. Focus Solely on the Facts
8. Ask About Additional Witnesses
9. Ask About Additional Evidence
10. Ask About Apparent Contradictions
11. Do not Retaliate Against the Interviewee
12. Request a Future Contact for More Information
13. Keep the Interview Confidential
14. Document or Record all Interviews

Nonverbal Communication

We respond to thousands of nonverbal cues and behaviors including postures, facial expression, eye gaze, gestures, and tone of voice. Listed below are examples of nonverbal communication which should be observed and notated during the interview.

1. Facial Expressions
2. Body Movements and/or Hand Gestures
3. Body Posture
4. Eye Contact
5. Paralanguage (Tone of Voice)
6. Physiological Changes
7. Incongruent Communication

Documenting Interviews

Preparation is the key to so many endeavors in life and interviewing potential targets and witnesses during investigations is no exception. Listed below are several best practices that should be implemented when documenting interviews.

1. **Prepare a List of Interview Questions**: Interviews are structured, formal events that require careful preparation and planning. Write out questions in advance that must be answered and/or addressed.

2. **Leave Ample Space Between Questions**: Leave space for writing answers. If answers are documented in more than one location, they may be overlooked later.

3. **Divide Notation Space into Two Sections**: One section will be for answers to the questions, the second space with be for notes regarding nonverbal cues when the questions are asked and answered.

4. **Balance Notes and Active Listening**: Notes are a critical part of the interview process and active listening shows the interviewee you are paying attention to what it said. Both are equally important and must be balanced.

5. **Limit Notes to Most Important Phrases**: To balance note taking and active listening, limit the notes to the most important phrases and words. In the event more detail is required, consider recording the interview.

6. **Devise an Efficient Note-Taking System**: The best method of taking notes is the way that works for you. A system that works will be developed over time.

7. **Notate Answers Requiring Follow-Up**: Create a special symbol or notation to place next to answers that require a follow-up with the interviewee. Using the words "follow-up" may blend in with the notes and be overlooked later.

Time Zones and Investigative Timelines

Time poses many challenges during an investigation, especially when correlating events and timelines. Time zones and daylight savings time can vary from region to region. It is better to choose one time standard such as *Universal Coordinated Time* (UTC) to use during all investigations. Using a single time standard like UTC may seem difficult at first, but once established, it can benefit investigations in numerous ways.

Investigative Report Writing

The Golden Rule of report writing is, "*if it is not documented it did not happen*." Professional reports must be accurate, complete, readable, and address the questions at hand. Reports must be completed in a timely manner and meeting minimum reporting and formatting standards. This is the most vital component of the investigative process, but it tends to pose the most challenges for investigators. When the day of judgment arrives involving a report you wrote, you should sleep well knowing the report will stand up to scrutiny.

Why Write Reports? (Part I)

Drafting a report is recommended any time you investigate an incident or analyze evidence, no matter how large or small. It may be required due to a legal or policy requirement, or it may be a directive from leadership. It is always a core component of the investigation as the questions it answers tend to originate from some type of legal process. The investigator must ensure the answers provided in the report are correct as it may have a significant impact on peoples' lives. Additionally, there are many circumstances in which failing to write a report may be considered negligent.

Why Write Reports? (Part II)

Whenever the investigation involves legal staff, be sure to discuss reporting guidelines and deliverables prior to starting any work as the report will undoubtedly face a high degree of scrutiny. If the report does not involve legal staff its content can have multiple uses such as those listed below.

1. Forces Thoughts Regarding Actions
2. Helps Identify Factual Connections
3. Helps the Investigator to Uncover Mistakes

4. Used to Provide Input and/or Status Updates
5. Used to Transfer Specific and/or Unique Knowledge
6. Can be Utilized to Perform Training

Reporting Standards

Because it is rare that the preliminary stages of an investigation will uncover every relevant fact, label any interim reports created as "DRAFT." When the final version of the report is produced, it should adhere to the standards listed below:

1. Focused (Avoid Off-Topic Discussions)
2. Understandable (Keep the Audience in Mind)
3. Factual (Unambiguous and Correct)
4. Timely (Complete in Reasonable Amount of Time)
5. Reproducible (By a Third Party)

Report Style and Formatting (Part I)

An investigative report is a factual document of findings, with any opinions clearly identified and supported by facts included in the report. Professional reports also follow accepted style and formatting guidelines. Writing in "active voice" tends to be clearer and more succinct. Write concise sentences using the past tense and be as specific as possible. Finally, focus on what was done as opposed to what could not be done. Focusing on the latter may be interpreted as incompetence.

Report Style and Formatting (Part II)

Style guidelines are not meant to be rules that cannot be broken or changed; the intent is to increase the readability of the report. Listed below are style guidelines typically incorporated into professional reports.

1. Use Content Transitions
2. Use Acronyms Correctly
3. Avoid Jargon and/or Ambiguous Words
4. Use Names Consistently

5. Avoid Informal Language
6. Clearly Identify Opinion
7. Support Opinions with Reported Facts

Content Formatting Standards

Formatting standards apply to the presentation aspects of a report, such as fonts, dates, charts, figures, and tables. These standards are designed to make the presentation of the report content more readable and give it a professional appearance. Listed below are several formatting standards that are accepted as best practices.

1. Use Consistent Fonts and Spacing
2. Use Consistent Date and Time Formats
3. Standardize Metadata Reporting
4. Use Captions and References
5. Use Tables and Figures Appropriately
6. Use Bulleted and/or Numbered Lists

Report Content and Organization (Part I)

A report template should be developed for each type of incident investigation the Security Manager is tasked with undertaking. However, there must be a justification for multiple templates as minor differences in investigation types can be addressed in the investigative notes. Although not all will be used for every event, the three templates listed below will typically be used for incidents.

1. Overall Incident Template
2. General Analysis Template
3. Malware Analysis Template

Report Content and Organization (Part II)

The *overall investigation template* is for a report on the entire event and includes all analysis and other reports generated during that time. Listed below is the organizational structure these types of templates generally follow.

1. Title Page and Table of Contents
2. Background Information
3. Investigation Goals and Findings
4. Professional Recommendations
5. Mid-Level Content Sections
6. Individual Analysis Reports
7. Appendices and Glossaries

Quality Assurance (QA) for Investigative Reports

No matter how confident we are as investigators that we have drafted a good report, a *quality assurance* (QA) review always reveals issues. The QA process is designed to prevent investigators from delivering substandard reports. Reports should not be reviewed by the individual who generated it; the process of "peer review" should be implemented as it is an industry standard. Listed below are the objectives of the quality assurance review process.

1. Review for Compliance with Style
2. Review for Compliance with Formatting
3. Review for Factual Content Accuracy
4. Review for Technical Accuracy

Incident Scene Management

Incident scene management, and evidence management as a part of that, must be learned and incorporated into the investigators' toolkit. Listed below are the high-level steps that are typically followed during incident scene management.

1. Approach and Secure the Incident Scene
2. Survey to Determine the Scene Boundaries
3. Evaluate Physical Evidence Possibilities
4. Take Preliminary Photographs and/or Video
5. Conduct a Detailed Search of the Scene
6. Collect and Record all Evidence Types
7. Conduct a Final Survey and Release the Scene

Field Investigation Toolkits

Regardless of the type of investigation being conducted—physical or digital—standard items should be a part of the investigative toolkit. These standardized items include, but are not limited to:

1. Consent and Authorization Forms
2. Digital Camera, Memory, and Batteries
3. Notebooks, Pens, and Markers
4. Evidence Collection Containers
5. Evidence Labels, Identifiers, and Seals
6. Photographic Ruler (ABFO Scales*)
7. Personal Protective Equipment (PPE)

   * *American Board of Forensic Odontology*

Locard's Principle of Exchange

Locard's Principle of Exchange states, "*When a person or object comes into contact with another person or object, a cross-transfer of materials occurs.*" It was developed by Dr. Edmond Locard, a pioneer in forensic science. It applies to fragmentary and/or trace evidence and mandates that all evidence at a scene must be collected. Although its primary focus is typing criminals to crime scenes, it can also reveal investigators in crime scenes as well.

Evidence Dynamics

Evidence dynamics refers to any influence that changes, obscures, adds, contaminates, or obliterates evidence regardless of intent. It helps investigators understand the behavior of evidence and plays a key role in incident scene reconstruction. While it was originally intended to apply to physical evidence it can be equally applied to digital evidence. It can be used to describe both execution mechanisms and "CRUD" (**C**reate, **R**ead, **U**pdate, and **D**elete) operations that occur during network investigations.

Chain of Custody (Part I)

Chain of custody refers to the documentation of acquisition, control, analysis, and disposition of physical and digital evidence.

It applies to all individuals responsible for handling evidence collected at an incident scene. Listed below are the high-level areas of focus addressed by chain of custody protocols.

1. Processes and Procedures Performed
2. Time and Date of Evidence Acquisition
3. Original Location of Collected Evidence
4. Methods of Evidence Collection
5. Methods of Examination and Analysis
6. Reason for Evidence Collection

Chain of Custody (Part II)

Intentional (tampering) or unintentional (accidental) changes to digital and physical evidence presents risks in any investigation. Listed below are examples of evidence that need to be protected using chain of custody protocols.

1. Photographs
2. Reports
3. Lab Information
4. Notebooks
5. Checklists
6. Log Files
7. Videos and Screen Captures

Maintaining Case Notes

From the moment of initial detection and notification to the final report and disclosure documents, keeping case notes is critical. These notes are typically informal documentation used to keep the investigative team focused. They allow others to pick up tasks and third parties to reproduce efforts.

Case notes address the higher-level actions and results of investigative team members, not the actions of malicious actors. Even though case notes are informal, they must be kept professional as they are considered discoverable evidence.

Legal Challenges in Digital Investigations

Evolving privacy and data protection regulations across diverse geographies may add to the complexity of gathering digital evidence. While the need to conduct investigations is important it cannot be done to the detriment of an individuals' rights. Listed below are legal standards that may present serious challenges during digital investigations.

1. *Electronic Communications Privacy Act* (ECPA)
2. The Fourth Amendment
3. The Fifth Amendment
4. International Jurisdictions
5. *Nulla Poena Sine Lege*

Electronic Communications Privacy Act

The *Electronic Communications Privacy Act* (ECPA) was passed in 1986 to expand and revise wiretapping and electronic eavesdropping provisions. This Act consisted of three significant initiatives. It added amendments to the *Wiretap Act*, it updated the *Stored Communications Act*, and it created the *Pen Register Act*.

It bars electronic eavesdropping which may hinder some network investigations using sensors for full-header and packet capturing. It bans the disclosure of illegally obtained data which may poses problems between jurisdictions with laws that lack parity for the term "illegally obtained." It prohibits investigators from unlawfully accessing data at rest which may create gray areas in which many organizations will fear to tread. Finally, it prohibits the use of pen register and trace devices which may serve to complicate both network and mobile investigations.

The Fourth Amendment

The *Fourth Amendment* limits the legal authority of government—or its agents—to search and seize evidence without a warrant. The text of this Amendment is listed below for review:

The Fourth Amendment:

> *The right of the people to be secure in their persons, houses, papers, and effects, against unreasonable searches and seizures, shall not be violated, and no Warrants shall issue, but upon probable cause, supported by Oath or affirmation, and particularly describing the place to be searched, and the persons or things to be seized.*

It only applies to government agencies and guarantees a reasonable expectation of privacy but can be waived due to exigent circumstances in times of emergency. It is also the foundation for the *Apparent Authority* principle which grants the right to third parties to reveal information by virtue of the shared authority of a relationship (employer/employee, domestic co-habitants).

This Amendment has proven especially problematic for investigations involving mobile devices as the courts have established that in modern times, phones now hold the "privacies of life." As with any regulation, an individuals' consent is the most relevant exception to this rule.

The Fifth Amendment

The *Fifth Amendment* protects people from self-incrimination, meaning giving a statement that might expose oneself to a crime. The text of this Amendment is listed below for review:

The Fifth Amendment:

> *No person shall be held to answer for a capital, or otherwise infamous crime, unless on a presentment or indictment of a Grand Jury, except in cases arising in the land or naval forces, or in the Militia, when in actual service in time of War or public danger; nor shall any person be subject for the same offence to be twice put in jeopardy of life or limb; nor shall be compelled in any criminal case to be a witness against himself, nor be deprived of life, liberty, or property, without due process of law; nor shall private property be taken for public use, without just compensation.*

The focus of this Amendment is protection against self-incrimination and establishing the fact that silence does not indicate guilt. This has proved to be problematic for investigations involving devices with access codes and/or encryption, as courts have ruled that compelling an individual to unlock or decrypt a device would be a violation of their rights. Biometric data (such as thumbprints and facial recognition) are exceptions to this rule. As with any regulation, an individuals' consent is the most relevant exception to this rule.

Nulla Poena Sine Lege

Nulla poena sine lege is a universal legal principle, requiring that one cannot be punished for doing something that is not prohibited by law. It is a basic requirement for the rule of law in all civilized nations. This legal concept can be divided into four categories.

1. *Nulla Poena Sine Lege* ***Praevia*** (Prior): The law must exist prior to the offense; it cannot be written during or after an offense and used against an individual. This poses challenges as technology always out-paces law.

2. *Nulla Poena Sine Lege* ***Scripta*** (Written): The law must be written; it cannot be oral or customary. This poses challenges when dealing with individuals who commit offenses living in nations with no written law to address the offense.

3. *Nulla Poena Sine Lege* ***Certa*** (Clear): The law must be well-defined such that a citizen would reasonably know when an offense was being committed. This poses challenges in international courts where the language of the law between countries lacks parity.

4. *Nulla Poena Sine Lege* ***Stricta*** (Exact): The law must be exact; this prohibits the application of analogy in criminal cases. This poses challenges for cases in which the offense in question is not specifically addressed in the law because the law did not anticipate its existence.

DOMAIN 09

Investigations, Evidence and Chain of Custody

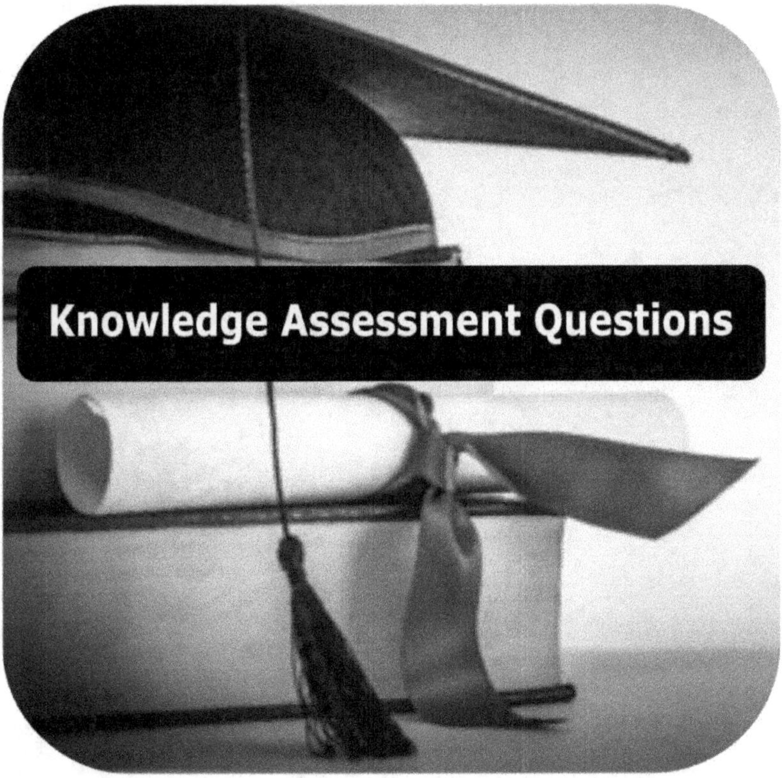

The following knowledge assessment questions are presented as true / false, multiple choice, and fill-in-the-blank. The correct answers are provided in an Answer Key at the end of this text. These questions may or may not be presented on the actual certification exam.

Domain 09: Knowledge Assessment Questions

1. Select the best choice below for the following definition: "*A factual document of findings, with any opinions clearly identified and supported by facts included in the report.*"

A. Investigative Report

B. Case Notes

C. Analysis Summary

D. Forensic Evidence

E. None of the Above

2. __________ define(s) the elements of a claim and are typically driven by the primary consumer of the investigative report.

A. Chain of Custody

B. Probable Cause

C. Elements of Proof

D. Reasonable Doubt

E. None of the Above

3. Which choice below refers to any influence that changes, obscures, adds, contaminates, or obliterates evidence regardless of intent?

A. Scene Management

B. Chain of Custody

C. Evidence Dynamics

D. Evidence Management

E. None of the Above

4. A(n) __________ is a systematic inquiry and/or examination, typically conducted for the purpose of identifying and/or verifying facts.

A. Negotiation

B. Consultation

C. Interrogation

D. Investigation

E. None of the Above

5. The non-verbal cue referred to as __________ can be defined as, "*A pattern in which the sender gives conflicting messages on verbal and nonverbal levels*."

A. Paralinguistic Communication

B. Incongruent Communication

C. Haptic Communication

D. Proxemic Communication

E. None of the Above

6. Which choice below refers to the documentation of acquisition, control, analysis, and disposition of physical and digital evidence?

A. Evidence Dynamics

B. Evidence Management

C. Scene Management

D. Chain of Custody

E. None of the Above

7. The __________ protects people from self-incrimination, meaning giving a statement that might expose oneself to a crime.

A. Fifth Amendment

B. First Amendment

C. Fourth Amendment

D. US Constitution

E. None of the Above

8. Select the best choice below for the following definition: "*A systematic inquiry and/or examination, typically conducted for the purpose of identifying and/or verifying facts.*"

A. Interview

B. Investigation

C. Analysis

D. Forensics

E. None of the Above

9. Select the best choice below for the following definition: "*When a person or object comes into contact with another person or object, a cross-transfer of materials occurs.*"

A. Cultural Transmission Theory

B. Symbolic Interaction Theory

C. Locard's Principle of Exchange

D. Social Construction Theory

E. None of the Above

10. Regardless of the type of investigation being conducted—physical or digital—__________ items should be a part of the investigative toolkit.

A. Operational

B. Technical

C. Standard

D. Personal

E. None of the Above

11. What choice below is the primary purpose and importance of evidence dynamics in incident response investigations?

A. Reconstruction of the Incident

B. Remediation of the Incident

C. Mitigation of the Incident

D. Eradication of the Incident

E. None of the Above

12. The non-verbal cue referred to as __________ can be defined as, "*The non-lexical component of communication such as intonation, pitch and speed of speaking*."

A. Paralanguage

B. Incongruence

C. Haptics

D. Proxemics

E. None of the Above

13. All case types and investigations have the same considerations—whether the goal is litigation or developing a stronger security posture.

1. True
2. False

14. Regardless of the type of investigation being conducted—physical or digital—standard items should be a part of the investigative toolkit.

1. True
2. False

15. In most investigations, interviews are the primary tool investigators use to find out what happened and/or verify physical and technical evidence.

1. True
2. False

16. We respond to thousands of verbal cues and behaviors including postures, facial expression, eye gaze, gestures, and tone of voice.

1. True
2. False

17. *Nulla poena sine lege* is a universal legal principle, requiring that one cannot be punished for doing something that is not prohibited by law.

1. True
2. False

18. An investigation is a systematic inquiry and/or examination, typically conducted for the purpose of identifying and/or verifying assumptions.

1. True
2. False

DOMAIN 10

Risk Management Frameworks and Implementations

Risk Management: Key Definitions

Risk:

A measurement of potential impact or damage from a threat occurring that combines the severity of outcomes with the likelihood of occurrence.

Threat:

An event with the capacity to cause damage, disruption, liability, injury, loss, or other negative outcomes.

Vulnerability:

A gap or weakness in a process, policy, control, asset, system or configuration that increases the likelihood or impact of the occurrence of a threat.

Risk Sensitivity:

A relative measurement of a resources' tolerance for risk exposures, independent of any threat or vulnerability.

Risk Assessment:

The process of identification, analysis, and potential mitigation of risks to an organization, business processes, assets, individuals, brand, image, or reputation.

Risk Management:

The program or process an organization uses to manage risk by setting the context of risk-related activities, setting tolerances for risk, identifying risk, assessing risk and mitigating risk.

Risk Appetite:

The level of risk that an organization is prepared to accept in pursuit of its objectives, and before action is deemed necessary to reduce the risk.

Residual Risk:

The amount of risk or danger associated with an action or event remaining after natural or inherent risks have been mitigated by risk controls.

The Threat Landscape

Understanding the wide range of potential threats is important if one is to identify and mitigate those threats. Additionally, the complexity of the *Internet of Things* (IoT) is increasing the attack surface and poses a wide variety of unique risks for security managers. Listed below are examples of common threats security personal must be prepared for on a daily basis.

1. Physical and Natural Events
2. Loss of Essential Services
3. Compromise of Information
4. Unauthorized Actions
5. Compromise of Functions
6. Manufactured Threats

The Key Attributes of Risk

Each of the attributes listed below influence both risk and each other simultaneously.

1. Predictability
2. Scope
3. Warning
4. Capability
5. Likelihood
6. Impact
7. Day of Week
8. Time of Day

The 5 Layers of Risk

Remember the influences of the attributes of risk listed previously. Mentally layering risk and applying that to a top-down risk hierarchy such as the one listed below can help prioritize solutions.

1. External Risk
2. Facility-Wide Risk
3. Data Systems Risk
4. Unit and Department Risk
5. Proximity Risk

Risk Management Program Development

Information Security personnel developing risk management programs should focus on critical details and procedures of implementation. Listed below are six high-level objectives that must be considered when developing a risk management program.

1. Context and Purpose of the Program
2. Scope, Charter, and Methodology
3. Authority, Structure, and Reporting
4. Asset Identification and Classification
5. Risk Management Objectives
6. Creation of the Implementation Team

Risk Management Process

There are numerous frameworks available to Information Security managers for assessing risk that are widely accepted in the industry. Listed below are six high-level objectives that must be considered when establishing a risk management process.

1. Understand the Potential Threats
2. Determine the Existing Vulnerabilities
3. Determine if Risk Levels are Acceptable
4. Assess the Risk Mitigation Options
5. Review Control Effectiveness

Risk Management Procedure

The *risk management procedure* utilized by security managers is a continual and ongoing process that is always evolving. Listed below are the high-level steps associated with risk management procedure.

1. Identify Information Assets and Value
2. Perform a Risk Assessment
3. Determine the Risk Treatment and Response
4. Accept or Reject the Residual Risk
5. Monitor Risk and Communicate Results

Conducting an Asset Inventory

An *asset inventory* is a critical component of effective risk management and is typically kept in both the *Business Continuity Plan* (BCP) and the asset location. Listed below are examples of the type of information typically included in an asset inventory.

1. System Type and Version
2. Installed Software (Including Version)
3. Name and Title of Resource Owner
4. Physical and Logical Location
5. Logical Network Addressing
6. Vendor Support Information

Creating an Asset Resource Profile

The *resource profile* is supporting confidential information for risk mitigation and should be documented in the asset inventory. Listed below are examples of the type of information typically included in a asset inventory.

1. General System Description
2. Functions and Features
3. Information and/or Data Classification
4. Criticality to the Organization
5. Applicable Compliance Regulations
6. Identified User Community

Asset Valuation

The basic considerations when determining the value of a specific asset include both *quantifiable* (tangible) and *qualifiable* (intangible) costs. Listed below are factors to consider when determining the value of an asset.

1. Criticality and/or Sensitivity
2. Cost to Replace or Repair
3. Loss of Current and/or Future Revenue
4. Legal and/or Regulatory Sanctions
5. Brand Image and/or Reputational Value

Risk Management Frameworks

Adapt and utilize established risk management reference models based on organizational culture, program objectives, and specific needs. The frameworks and standards listed below are widely accepted in the risk management industry.

1. COBIT 5
2. ISO 31000
3. IEC 31010
4. NIST SP 800-39
5. ISO / IEC 27005

Risk Analysis Methodologies

The risk analysis methodologies listed below can be applied in both technical and non-technical frameworks. Each will be discussed in greater detail in the following pages.

1. **OCTAVE Allegro**: Operationally Critical Threat, Asset, and Vulnerability Evaluation

2. **FRAAP**: Facilitated Risk Analysis and Assessment Process

3. **FAIR**: Factor Analysis of Information Risk

4. **NIST RMF**: NIST Risk Management Framework

OCTAVE Allegro

The *Operationally Critical Threat, Asset, and Vulnerability Evaluation* (OCTAVE) methodology is a three-phased approach developed to build asset-based threat profiles. It is utilized to identify vulnerabilities, evaluate risks, and develop methodologies and strategies for mitigation using highly-detailed questionnaires. It is best suited for smaller projects and one-time assessments.

FRAAP

The *Facilitated Risk Analysis and Assessment Process* (FRAAP) is a streamlined approach that relies on the input of subject matter experts to address issues of risk during project-level assessments. The format encourages collaboration between highly-skilled staff and can be very effective the facilitator dedicates time to the pre-planning phase. This format is also easily adaptable to other analysis methods.

FAIR

The *Factor Analysis of Information Risk* (FAIR) method considers two primary factors to measure risk: *Loss Event Frequency* (LEF) and *Probable Loss Magnitude* (PLM). It analyzes the frequency and capability of the event, factors the data against existing control strength, and utilizes the outcome to create a six-level risk exposure table. This is a detailed and probabilistic analysis method that is best suited for well-developed risk management programs.

NIST RMF

The *National Institute of Standards and Technology Risk Management Framework* (NIST RMF) is a six-step, high-level approach to risk analysis and also serves as a *certification and accreditation* (CA) mechanism in many government institutions. Its objective is real-time risk management using automated tools to conduct continuous monitoring to inform risk-based decisions. It is designed to be integrated with architectural design and the *Secure Development Life Cycle* (SDLC). It also sets standards for the implementation and accountability of controls. Listed below are the six steps of the NIST RMF and their stated objectives.

1. CATEGORIZE:	Define the System and Data
2. SELECT:	Baseline Security Controls
3. IMPLEMENT:	Apply the Security Controls
4. ASSESS:	Review the Security Controls
5. AUTHORIZE:	Use of the System
6. MONITOR:	Assess the System in Use

Vulnerability Assessment ≠ Risk Assessment

A *vulnerability assessment* tends to be a useful tool to identify system weaknesses that may be visible to potential threat sources. It identifies potential system weaknesses based on programmed rules and known exploits. Not all vulnerabilities present risks, and one vulnerability may present many risks. It is one of several components of the risk assessment process.

Risk Assessment ≠ Vulnerability Assessment

A *risk assessment* is based on the category of information and data being analyzed. Unlike a vulnerability assessment, it provides a multi-dimensional view of the environment. It accounts for system architecture, all existing controls, and generates an output based on capability, likelihood, and impact. When conducting a risk assessment, ensure that the risk evaluation and proposed mitigation aligns with business and organizational needs.

Identifying Manufactured Risks

Identify *manufactured risks* whenever possible and be aware of their potential impacts even if they cannot be controlled or mitigated. These are external risks that may go unnoticed during a risk assessment but have the potential to seriously impact the organization. Listed below are examples of manufactured risks.

1. Industrial Sites: Close Proximity to Toxic Chemical Tanks
2. Airports: Organizations' Assets in a Flight Path

3. Fires: Water Damage and Suppression Impacts
4. Pipelines: Combustible Gas and/or Fuels
5. Infrastructure: Fragility and/or Critical Dependencies

Third-Party Service Providers

Security managers should be involved in all phases of the *Service Level Agreement* (SLA) process and ensure supporting providers have adequate security controls. The contract should specify expected security levels, risk assessment and analysis to be performed, and all post-relationship processes to be followed. Outsourced contracts provide many benefits but also tend to increase risk and make managing regulatory requirements more difficult.

Third-Party Risk Considerations

Not all third-party service providers can be audited but, for those that can, the audit requirement should be negotiated into the SLA. Listed below are a number of steps that can be taken to reduce the risks associated with third-party providers that should be written into any contract and/or SLA.

1. Right to Source Code (Escrow)
2. Vendors' Obligation to Remain Compliant
3. Right to Audit the Vendor Processes
4. Insistence on *Standard Operating Procedures* (SOP's)
5. Right to Assess the Assigned Contractors' Skillsets

Overview: Qualitative Analysis

Most *qualitative analysis* approaches use a relative scale to rate risk exposures based on a set of predefined criteria for each level. This type of analysis relies on the knowledge of the individual conducting the assessment and, as a result, may be subjective and prone to inaccuracies. The scale used for the analysis is based on descriptive criteria (as opposed to numerical criteria) and maps to an endpoint risk exposure value. The criteria are less prone to error if they are written in greater detail.

Defining Severity

The *risk severity rating* is meant to describe the scope of the assets' risk exposure, not list all the potential consequences of an impact. The level of severity is asset agnostic and is contingent upon the impact on *confidentiality*, *integrity*, *availability*, and *accountability* (CIAA). It is rated on the degree of disruption caused by the exploitation of a weakness. The rating also considers the scope and amount of time the resources are affected. The risk severity rating is typically presented in three levels: low, medium, and high.

Data Availability Severity

Data availability severity measures the impact on external services, internal processes, and the overall degradation of performance. It combines these metrics with the length of the disruption to establish clear criteria for each level of severity. The distinctions between each level should be clearly visible and easy to recognize. If not, the scale can be revised to improve clarity.

Data Integrity Severity

Integrity severity concerns will focus primarily on unauthorized or unintended access to **c**reate, **r**ead, **u**pdate, or **d**elete data ("CRUD"). It considers the varying degrees of unauthorized access and uses that criteria to create a relative scale such as the example listed below.

1. **LOW**: May Indirectly Contribute to CRUD

2. **MEDIUM**: May Allow Limited Access for CRUD

3. **HIGH**: May Allow Unrestricted Access for CRUD

Questions for Estimating Severity

If security is having trouble *qualifying* the severity of a vulnerability, many useful questions can be asked to improve clarity. Listed below are examples of questions which may be useful when qualifying severity levels.

1. What is the Scope after an Exploitation?
2. What is the Degree of Service Shutdown?
3. Is Exploit Using Executable Code or Arbitrary Functions?
4. Does Generated Information Help Exploit Other Systems?
5. Is There an Internal or External Impact?
6. Is the Environment Facing Unique or Aggregated Threats?

Questions for Estimating Likelihood

It is not uncommon to confuse factors that will affect the severity of the threat/vulnerability pair and the ability to estimate likelihood. If security personnel are having trouble *qualifying* the likelihood of a vulnerability, additional useful questions can be asked to improve clarity. Listed below are examples of questions which may be useful when estimating likelihood of threats.

1. What is the Size and/or Population of the Threat Universe?
2. Is There a Location Requirement for the Exposure?
3. Is There Available Information About the Exploit?
4. Is a Skill Level Required for the Exploit?
5. How Attractive is the Exploitable Target?
6. Has the Exploit Been Executed in the Past?
7. Is it Applicable in the Current Environment?
8. Is an Antivirus or IDS/IPS Signature Available?
9. Is Authentication Required for the Exploit?
10. Is the Impact on Servers and/or Endpoints?
11. Is the Vulnerability Widely Deployed?

Challenges of Quantitative Analysis

Many quantitative models have been proposed over the years with mixed success that use very complex equations for calculating risk. Although the equations may be adequate, circumstances such as those listed below pose challenges when performing an accurate quantitative analysis.

1. **Lack of Accessible Historical Data**: In some situations (such as a new process or business unit) there may not be historical data available to support an analysis.

2. **Reliance on Extremely Accurate Data**: Deficient record-keeping and/or accounting practices may not provide the extremely accurate data required for quantitative analysis.

3. **Significant Time to Analyze**: A thorough quantitative analysis requires a significant commitment of resources, time, and effort that may not be available.

4. **Reluctance to Share Vital Information**: Organizations may possess historical data beneficial to an analysis but be reluctant to share it will competitive organizations.

5. **Anonymous Surveys are Rarely Honest**: Although the purpose of anonymous surveys is to inspire honesty, those involved fear retribution and are rarely completely honest.

6. **Data Skewed to Specific Industries**: Repositories of historical data are available to the general public but may focus on specific industries that are not relevant.

Asset Value Considerations

The asset assessment must transcend line-item numbers as the assets' value can extend beyond the actual cost listed on a purchase order. Listed below are several factors that should be considered when assessing the true value of any asset.

1. The Actual Cost of the Asset
2. The Cost to Replace the Asset if Legacy
3. The Functional Value of the Asset to the Business
4. Existing Operational Dependencies
5. The Assets' Fulfillment of Compliance Requirements
6. The Criticality of the Assets' Data

Calculating SLE and ALE

Single Loss Expectancy (SLE) and *Annualized Loss Expectancy* (ALE) are used during qualitative analysis to validate expenses associated with protecting various assets.

Relevant Terms and Abbreviations

1. AV: Asset Value
2. EF: Exposure Factor
3. SLE: Single Loss Expectancy
4. ARO: Annualized Rate of Occurrence
5. ALE: Annualized Loss Expectancy

Calculating Single Loss Expectancy

AV x EF = SLE

Calculating Annualized Loss Expectancy

SLE x ARO = ALE

Annualized Rate of Occurrence (ARO)

To calculate probability over time, divide the number of years by the projected likelihood to determine the *Annualized Rate of Occurrence* (ARO).

1 Year = 1/1 = **1.0**	6 Years = 1/6 = **.17**
2 Years = 1/2 = **0.5**	7 Years = 1/7 = **.14**
3 Years = 1/3 = **.33**	8 Years = 1/8 = **.13**
4 Years = 1/4 = **.25**	9 Years = 1/9 = **.11**
5 Years = 1/5 = **0.2**	10 Years = 1/10 = **0.1**

DOMAIN 10

Risk Management Frameworks and Implementations

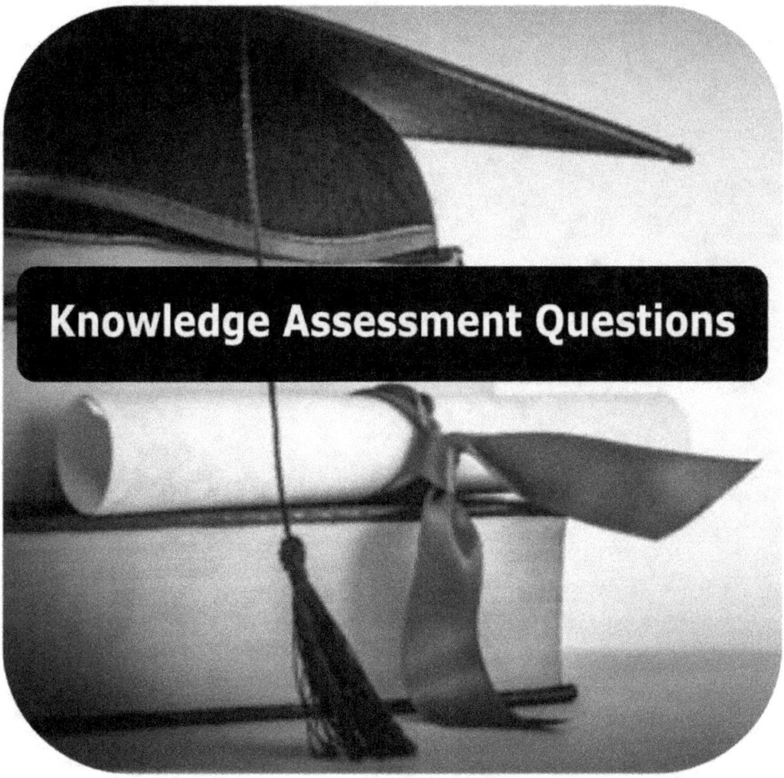

The following knowledge assessment questions are presented as true / false, multiple choice, and fill-in-the-blank. The correct answers are provided in an Answer Key at the end of this text. These questions may or may not be presented on the actual certification exam.

Domain 10: Knowledge Assessment Questions

1. Which choice below is a risk management framework utilized by security managers that is best suited for small projects and one-time assessments?

A. NIST RMF

B. FAIR

C. FRAAP

D. OCTAVE Allegro

E. None of the Above

2. The ___________ rating is meant to describe the scope of the exposure, not list all the potential consequences.

A. Risk Severity

B. Vulnerability Assessment

C. Threat Assessment

D. Threat / Vulnerability Pair

E. None of the Above

3. Select the best choice below for the following definition: "*A relative measurement of a resources' tolerance for risk exposures, independent of any threat or vulnerability.*"

A. Risk Sensitivity

B. Risk Assessment

C. Qualitative Risk

D. Risk Management

E. None of the Above

4. Most ___________ approaches use a relative scale to rate risk exposures based on a set of predefined criteria for each level.

A. Quantitative

B. Framework

C. Accepted

D. Qualitative

E. None of the Above

5. Which choice below is a risk management framework utilized by security managers that uses a detailed quantitative and probabilistic analysis method?

A. NIST RMF

B. FAIR

C. FRAAP

D. OCTAVE Allegro

E. None of the Above

6. Security managers should be involved in all phases of the SLA negotiation process and ensure supporting providers have adequate __________.

A. Budgets

B. Insurance

C. Controls

D. Training

E. None of the Above

7. Select the best choice below for the following definition: "*An event with the capacity to cause damage, disruption, liability, injury, loss, or other negative outcomes.*"

A. Risk

B. Vulnerability

C. Threat

D. Incident

E. None of the Above

8. The __________ is supporting confidential information for risk mitigation and should be documented in the asset inventory.

A. Risk Register

B. Resource Profile

C. Source Profile

D. Gantt Chart

E. None of the Above

9. Which choice below is a risk management framework utilized by security managers that is used for Certification and Accreditation?

A. NIST RMF

B. FAIR

C. FRAAP

D. OCTAVE Allegro

E. None of the Above

10. When conducting a risk assessment, ensure that risk evaluation and __________ align with business and organizational needs.

A. Mitigation

B. Documentation

C. Policies

D. Identification

E. None of the Above

11. Which choice below is an example of a manufactured risk that can cause the process of estimating costs of potential risks challenging?

A. Natural Disaster

B. Insider Threats

C. Network Outages

D. Underground Pipeline

E. None of the Above

12. A __________ tends to be a useful tool to identify system weaknesses that may be visible to potential threat sources.

A. Penetration Test

B. Vulnerability Assessment

C. Forensic Examination

D. Risk Assessment

E. None of the Above

13. Remember the influences of the attributes of threats; mentally layering threats helps to prioritize solutions.

1. True
2. False

14. The basic considerations when determining the value of a specific asset include both projected and value-added costs.

1. True
2. False

15. Information Security personnel developing risk management programs should focus on critical details and procedures of implementation.

1. True
2. False

16. The asset assessment must transcend line-item numbers as the asset value can extend well beyond the actual cost.

1. True
2. False

17. If you are having trouble quantifying the likelihood of a vulnerability, additional useful questions can be asked to improve clarity.

1. True
2. False

18. Data availability severity concerns will focus primarily on unauthorized or unintended access to create, read, update, or delete data ("CRUD").

1. True
2. False

DOMAIN 11

Vulnerability Assessment and Management

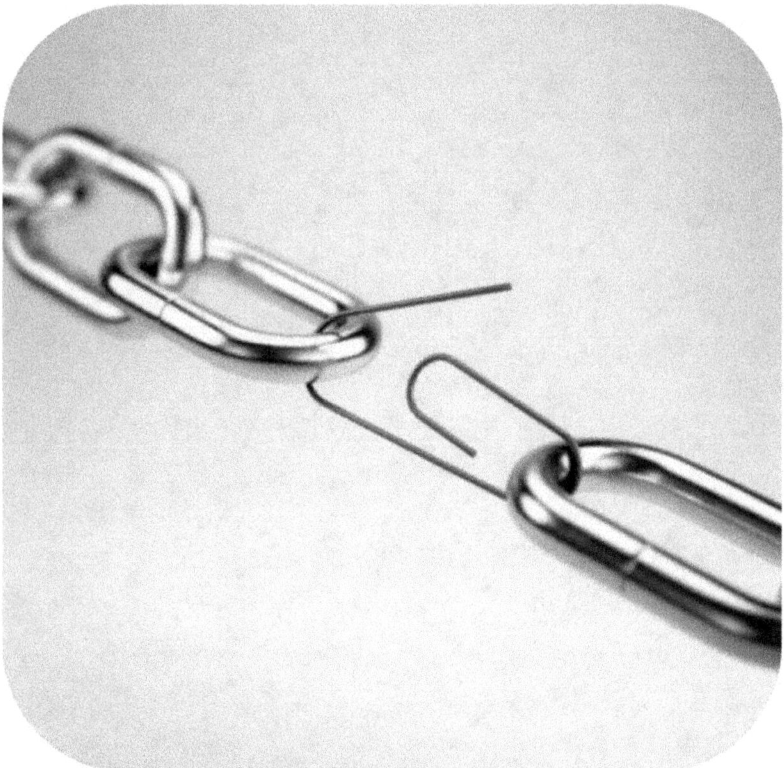

What is a Vulnerability?

Definition:

A weakness in the computational logic (e.g., code) found in software and hardware components that, when exploited, results in a negative impact to confidentiality, integrity, or availability. Mitigation of the vulnerabilities in this context typically involves coding changes but could also include specification changes or even specification deprecations (e.g., removal of affected protocols or functionality in their entirety).

NIST National Vulnerability Database
https://nvd.nist.gov/vuln

Checking for Vulnerabilities

Vulnerability assessments often use a wide variety of scans and will typically include the five high-level steps listed below in the assessment process.

1. Identify Assets and Capabilities
2. Prioritize Assets Based on Value
3. Identify Known Vulnerabilities
4. Prioritize Discovered Vulnerabilities
5. Recommend Controls for Mitigation

Vulnerability Scanning

Vulnerability scanning can identify a wide range of known weaknesses and security issues that malicious actors may be able to exploit. Scanning passively tests security controls in a manner that does not interfere with operations or attempt to exploit any of the discovered vulnerabilities. Listed below are several objectives of vulnerability scanning.

1. Identify Misconfigurations
2. Identify a Lack of Security Controls
3. Identify Known Vulnerabilities
4. Identify Systems at Risk

Identifying Vulnerabilities and Misconfigurations

Malicious actors often look for systems that are misconfigured, and vulnerability scanners can detect and identify such issues as the ones listed below.

1. Open Ports
2. Weak Passwords
3. Default Accounts and Passwords
4. Sensitive Data and *Data Loss Prevention* (DLP)
5. Security and Configuration Errors

Nmap: "Network Mapper"

Nmap runs on all major computer operating systems, and both console and graphical (Zenmap) versions are available. It is a free open-source utility that can be used to rapidly scan large networks. Listed below are examples of common uses of this tool.

1. Network Enumeration
2. Security Auditing
3. Network Inventory
4. Managing Service Upgrade Schedules
5. Monitoring Host and/or Service Uptime

Security Content Automation Protocol (SCAP)

Vulnerability scanners utilize a database or dictionary of known issues and vulnerabilities and test systems against the database. The *National Institute of Standards and Technology* (NIST) created the *National Vulnerability Database* (NVD) to provide a list of common misconfigurations and security-related software flaws. *Security Content Automation Protocol* (SCAP) is a method for using specific standards to enable automated vulnerability management, measurement, and policy compliance evaluation of systems deployed in an organization. The NIST NVD is the U.S. government content repository for SCAP. The NVD provides impact ratings (risk scores) that quantify the risk and facilitate the prioritization of vulnerabilities. It also provides risk scores for *Common Vulnerabilities and Exposures* (CVE).

Credentialed vs. Non-Credentialed Scans

Vulnerability scanners can run as a *credentialed scan* using account credentials or as a *non-credentialed scan* (as would an attacker). Scans are typically conducted in credentialed mode using administrator privileges. This allows for a deeper check of issues while having a lower impact on the system being tested. Scanning in credentialed mode tends to generate more accurate results and generate fewer false positive returns. However, there are times when administrators need to see the network from the perspective of an attacker, and non-credentialed scans provide that capability.

Offline Password Crackers

If user passwords are protected with weak methods, *password cracking tools* can discover them in a short amount of time. Breaches typically involve large amounts of data including hashed and/or encrypted passwords. These tools analyze the protected passwords and compare them to a database of known passwords. The ability to analyze passwords offline affords malicious actors an unlimited amount of time to discover the collected passwords.

Online Password Crackers

Online password crackers are one of the many tools available to security managers and network administrators for use during vulnerability assessments. Brute force attacks can be used to guess user passwords and log on to accounts remotely. Network traffic can then be collected and analyzed for passwords that may have been included by senders and receivers.

Network Scanners

A *network scanner* uses various techniques to gather information about hosts and other devices within the network. Listed below are common network scans utilized for enumeration and discovery.

1. Ping Scan

2. ARP Ping Scan
3. SYN Stealth Scan
4. Port Scan
5. Service Scan
6. Operating System Detection Scan

Wireless Scanners and Crackers

Wireless scanners typically use both active and passive scans to listen to traffic broadcast on channels in the 2.4 and 5.0 GHz frequencies. Listed below are examples of the type of information that can be obtained using wireless scanning tools.

1. SSID's
2. MAC Addresses
3. Signal Strength
4. Known Channels
5. Channel Width
6. Security Protocols

A Typical Vulnerability Management Scenario

This series of events could describe a typical day for the Vulnerability Management program when a vendor announces a new vulnerability.

1. The Vendor Announces a New Vulnerability
2. Research is Conducted via the SANS Internet Storm Center
3. Several Exploits in the Wild are Confirmed
4. The Inventory is Checked for Affected Assets
5. The Running Vulnerable Service is Confirmed
6. System Logs Confirm Several Attempted Exploits
7. A Roll-Out of the Vendor Patch is Coordinated

Vulnerability Program Essentials

The volume of vulnerability assessment and management data at any given time will always present several challenges for security teams. The best strategic approach to program development is to start small and realize perfect solutions are not required to begin the program development process. Listed below are five high-level steps to follow when strategically planning a program.

1. Prioritize the Target Environment
2. Establish an Asset Inventory
3. Profile the Environment for Sensitivity
4. Define the Criteria for Risk Scales
5. Create a Workflow for Assessment

Prioritizing Vulnerabilities and Risk

Each asset needs to be profiled to establish a risk sensitivity score before vulnerabilities can be prioritized and assessments performed. Priorities are based on the importance of the resource to the organization. Incorporating business continuity research into the planning can be beneficial as assets identified in the BCP tend to be at the top of the risk sensitivity list.

In the absence of BCP research, two approaches can be taken when creating the asset list. Security managers can focus on the most prevalent type of asset or the asset types most exposed to known threats. Once the list has been developed scales can be defined for assessing severity and a workflow can be established for processing risks.

Rating Vulnerability Levels (Part I)

It is important to know how to analyze a vulnerability report for details that affect both the likelihood and the severity of the potential threat. Listed below are several questions that are useful to rate vulnerabilities.

1. Is the Vulnerability Applicable to the Organization?
2. Does an Antivirus or IDS/IPS Signature Exist?
3. Does it Require Social Engineering?
4. Does the Exploit Require Authentication?
5. Does it Affect Desktops and/or Servers?
6. Is the Vulnerability Widely Deployed?
7. Does it Involve a Limited Scope or Arbitrary Code?

Rating Vulnerability Levels (Part II)

Sources of vulnerability data can be obtained through intelligence services, vendor announcements, published research, and scanning. Scanners provide default ratings, and high-end scanners also include confidence ratings. Use vendor-supplied default ratings when starting the program, analyze the risks of each exposure, and adjust the risk ratings accordingly to suit the needs of the organization. As this process is repeated, the analysis that is conducted will become increasingly detailed over time.

Vulnerability Severity: **LOW**

A vulnerability with a *low* severity rating typically stems from a deviation from a recommended process or an emerging standard. It may also be caused by a lack of proper security processes, management, or governance. No direct exposure to the threat results in these instances.

Vulnerability Severity: **MODERATE**

A vulnerability severity of *moderate* may contribute to unauthorized activity or service degradation, but they are limited in scope or impact. This will present a higher impact as disclosed data may aid the attackers. It may also hinder the detection and investigation of the exploit. This level of vulnerability can be mitigated by authenticating user access.

Vulnerability Severity: **HIGH**

A vulnerability severity of *high* may allow limited access and control of an application, system or any communication, including only certain data or functionality. Access is granted to sensitive functionality of the user which may allow the execution of arbitrary code at the users' level. It may allow unauthorized user access and the limited ability to modify and/or delete data. This level of vulnerability has the potential to severely degrade services and provide the attacker with system details which can be used to craft future exploits.

Vulnerability Severity: **CRITICAL**

A vulnerability severity of *critical* may allow unlimited access and control of an application, system or any communication, including all data and functionality. It has the potential to cause a complete service disruption resulting in a prolonged outage.

The attacker is able to maintain full access and escalate privileges as needed, most likely leading to the disclosure of critical information. This may also allow the attacker to modify and/or delete sensitive information.

Analyzing a Vulnerability Notification

One of the most fundamental functions in Information Security is performing risk analysis on new vulnerability advisories. Time and resources always seem to be limited, making the prioritization of vulnerability patching and mitigation important.

Risk analysis drives all decisions in this process and the analysis must be based on clear and repeatable criteria. It is important for the criteria to be based on a common set of guidelines so vulnerabilities can be analyzed and rated consistently.

Defining a Workflow

After vulnerabilities have been analyzed and categorized by severity level, a workflow must be defined to process and mitigate them. The workflow discussed in this section assumes the four-tiered risk model discussed previously (*low*, *moderate*, *high*, and *critical*). It is a best practice to focus on risks with a critical or high severity rating first, as the number of vulnerabilities with a rating of high tends to be large.

The applicability of the vulnerability must then be qualified against a comprehensive asset inventory list. This process may potentially lend itself to automated filtering as the program matures. Regardless of the process that is utilized, it is critical for it to be based on a formal risk model.

Establishing an Efficient Workflow

A viable vulnerability assessment and management workflow must be comprised of efficient and realistic processes and procedures. The advisories of trusted services should be consistently monitored and security scanning should be performed regularly. Scanning should be conducted both internally and externally to ensure the patching of critical systems is conducted.

The use of enterprise penetration testing is recommended providing the proper level of authorization is available. In addition to scanning and penetration testing, Internet reconnaissance is also recommended. Finally, it is important to document all compensating controls to better qualify identified vulnerabilities and set accurate risk severity levels.

Vulnerability Scanning Software

Vulnerability scanners are software tools that constantly monitor applications and networks to identify potential security vulnerabilities. Listed below are several examples of free and commercial tools available to security managers for vulnerability scanning. None of these tools are endorsed by Phase2 Advantage and are only listed to assist in product research efforts.

1. Nessus Professional
2. Retina CS Community
3. Qualys Cloud Suite
4. Alibaba Website Threat Inspector
5. AlienVault USM (AT&T Cybersecurity)
6. IBM Guardium Vulnerability Assessment
7. SolarWinds Network Security Toolkit

DOMAIN 11

Vulnerability Assessment and Management

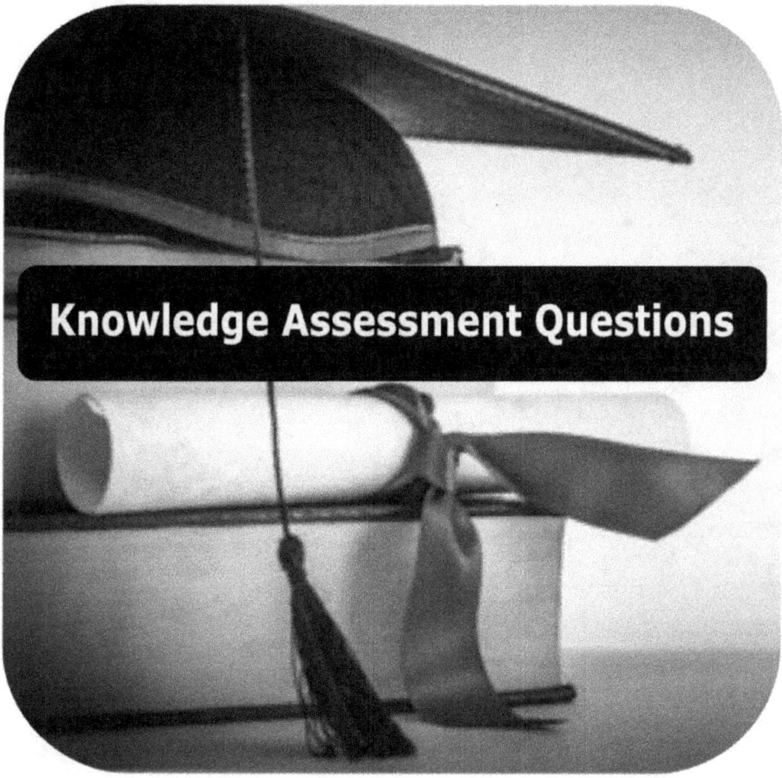

The following knowledge assessment questions are presented as true / false, multiple choice, and fill-in-the-blank. The correct answers are provided in an Answer Key at the end of this text. These questions may or may not be presented on the actual certification exam.

Domain 11: Knowledge Assessment Questions

1. Select the best choice below for the following definition: "*May allow limited access and control of an application, system or any communication, including only certain data or functionality.*"

A. Vulnerability Severity: LOW

B. Vulnerability Severity: MODERATE

C. Vulnerability Severity: HIGH

D. Vulnerability Severity: CRITICAL

E. None of the Above

2. A viable vulnerability assessment and management workflow must be comprised of efficient __________ and procedures.

A. Policies

B. Personnel

C. Planning

D. Processes

E. None of the Above

3. Which choice below is an item that should be corrected when attempting to identify potential vulnerabilities in a network?

A. Default Passwords

B. Unused Ports

C. Administrator Accounts

D. Firewall Rules

E. None of the Above

4. After vulnerabilities have been categorized by their severity level, a __________ must be defined to address them.

A. Supervisor

B. Policy

C. Workflow

D. Document

E. None of the Above

5. Select the best choice below for the following definition: "*May allow unlimited access and control of an application, system or any communication, including all data and functionality.*"

A. Vulnerability Severity: LOW

B. Vulnerability Severity: MODERATE

C. Vulnerability Severity: HIGH

D. Vulnerability Severity: CRITICAL

E. None of the Above

6. Malicious actors often look for systems that are __________, and vulnerability scanners can detect and identify these settings.

A. Wireless

B. Misconfigured

C. Older

D. Newer

E. None of the Above

7. Which choice below is a characteristic of a credentialed vulnerability scan that would be performed on a network?

A. Higher Impact on Tested System

B. Uses Guest and User Privileges

C. Generates Fewer False Positives

D. Only Conducted Annually

E. None of the Above

8. A network __________ uses various techniques to gather information about hosts and other devices within the network.

A. Scanner

B. Firewall

C. Protocol

D. Server

E. None of the Above

9. Select the best choice below for the following definition: "*May contribute to unauthorized activity or service degradation, but they are limited in scope or impact.*"

A. Vulnerability Severity: LOW

B. Vulnerability Severity: MODERATE

C. Vulnerability Severity: HIGH

D. Vulnerability Severity: CRITICAL

E. None of the Above

10. IS Managers must have the knowledge to analyze a vulnerability report for details that affect both the __________ and the severity of the potential threat.

A. Purpose

B. Origin

C. Location

D. Likelihood

E. None of the Above

11. Which choice below is an essential component to be considered when implementing a vulnerability management program?

A. Profile Environment for End-Users

B. Define Criteria for Threat Scales

C. Obtain an Organizational Chart

D. Create a Workflow for Assessment

E. None of the Above

12. The __________ of vulnerability assessment and management data at any given time will always present several challenges.

A. Quality

B. Source

C. Volume

D. Importance

E. None of the Above

13. Vulnerability assessments often use a wide variety of scans and will typically include five high-level steps in the assessment process.

1. True
2. False

14. A network scanner uses various techniques to gather information about hosts and other devices within the network.

1. True
2. False

15. Stateful firewalls typically use both active and passive scans to listen to traffic broadcast on channels in the 2.4 / 5.0 GHz frequencies.

1. True
2. False

16. The location of vulnerability assessment and management data at any given time will always present several challenges.

1. True
2. False

17. Each threat needs to be profiled to establish a risk sensitivity score before vulnerability assessments can be performed.

1. True
2. False

18. One of the most fundamental functions in Information Security is performing risk analysis on new vulnerability advisories.

1. True
2. False

DOMAIN 12

Business Continuity and Disaster Recovery

Domain 12: *Business Continuity and Disaster Recovery*

What is "Disaster Recovery"?

Definition:

A set of policies, tools, and procedures to enable the recovery and continuation of mission-critical technology infrastructure and systems following a natural or human-induced disaster.

BCP Key Definitions

Event:

Any user- or system-generated action or occurrence that can be identified by a program and has significance for system hardware or software.

Incident:

Any unlawful, unauthorized, or unacceptable action that involves a computer system, cell phone, tablet, and any other electronic device with an operating system, or that operates in a computer network.

Disaster:

Any incident that seriously disrupts mission-critical business or IT functions.

Maximum Allowable Downtime (MAD):

The absolute maximum time that systems can be unavailable without serious and/or negative impact to the organization.

Recovery Time Objective (RTO):

The targeted duration of time within which a mission-critical business process must be restored after a disaster and/or disruption in order to avoid unacceptable consequences associated with a break in business continuity.

Recovery Point Objective (RPO):

The maximum acceptable amount of data loss, measured in time, that can be incurred without serious and/or negative impact to the organization.

Quantitative Analysis:

The process of collecting and evaluating measurable and verifiable data in order to understand the condition and performance of a business.

Qualitative Analysis:

The examination and evaluation of non-measurable data using subjective judgement and non-quantifiable methods.

Map BCP to Organizational Objectives

Information Security is **not** a business objective in and of itself, but it does underlie **all** business objectives in an organization. To effectively convey the importance of a *Business Continuity Plan* (BCP) to senior leadership it should be mapped to organizational objectives such as those listed below.

1. Maintaining the Corporate Profit Margin
2. Legal and Regulatory Compliance
3. Maintaining a Competitive Advantage
4. Increasing and Protecting Brand Value
5. Delivery of Products and Services

Business Continuity Planning

The *Business Continuity Plan* (BCP) is not a monolithic or linear document. It is supported top-down, created bottom-up, and always evolving. A comprehensive BCP typically includes the components listed below.

1. Administrative BCP

2. Technical BCP
3. Work Area BCP
4. Epidemic and Pandemic BCP
5. Crisis Management Plan

Disaster Recovery Planning

The *Disaster Recovery Plan* (DRP) is not a monolithic or linear document. It has many moving parts that are executed simultaneously. A comprehensive DRP typically includes the components listed below.

1. Data Recovery Plan
2. Incident Response Plan
3. Vulnerability Assessment Plan
4. Network Forensics Plan
5. Digital Forensics Plan

Challenges to the Desired State of Security

There are many common obstacles when defining a desired security state which must be defined in both business and security terms. Listed below are examples of challenges that may be faced when presenting the concepts of BCP and DRP to leadership.

1. Overconfidence and/or Unrealistic Optimism
2. Psychological Anchoring
3. Status Quo Bias
4. Mental Accounting
5. Herd Instinct
6. False Consensus

Roles of a Business Impact Analysis

The *Business Impact Analysis* (BIA) serves many roles and functions within an organization. Listed below are six primary roles which are the most relevant to Information Security personnel.

1. **Role 01**: An analysis of the important functions that are essential to the operation of the business.

2. **Role 02**: Used to quantify the value of each function to the business.

3. **Role 03**: Used to identify the risks posed to the most valuable business functions.

4. **Role 04**: Used to suggest mitigation actions to reduce the likelihood or impact of identified risks.

5. **Role 05**: Used to indicate how much is lost per hour or per day for the length of the outage.

6. **Role 06**: Used to identify the IT systems associated with critical business functions.

Benefits of a Business Impact Analysis

A BIA provides many benefits to the organization, many of which are valuable beyond the scope of a business continuity project. Listed below are benefits that directly support the operational aspects of the organization.

1. Identify Critical Functions to Protect
2. Identify the Tangible Costs of Functions
3. Identify the Intangible Costs of Functions
4. Identify Critical Resources for Functions
5. Determine Recovery Time Objectives
6. Identify Vital Business Records
7. Prioritize the Use of Scarce Resources

BIA: Tangible Financial Costs

There are numerous ways the loss of a critical function can have a negative financial impact on the organization. Listed below are examples of tangible financial costs typically addressed in a BIA.

1. Products Cannot be Shipped
2. Services Cannot be Delivered
3. Increased Waste from Spoilage
4. Penalties Imposed by Customers

5. Legal Penalties for Non-Compliance

BIA: Intangible Financial Costs

Intangible costs due to the loss of a vital business function can be more difficult to identify than tangible costs but are no less damaging. Listed below are examples of intangible financial costs typically addressed in a BIA.

1. Loss of Customer Goodwill
2. Reduced Confidence in the Marketplace
3. Employee Turnover
4. Damage to Image and/or Brand
5. Loss of Faith in Senior Management

Selecting a BIA Project Manager

A well-run BIA will build credibility for the overall disaster recovery planning project; a poorly run BIA will be a disaster of its own making. Proper selection of a BIP Project Manager is critical as every facet of the business is exposed and trust levels must remain high. The individual must understand the true process and value of all internal functions to ensure accurate analysis is conducted. The candidate must also be comfortable moderating discussions as the communication between units has the potential to become heated.

BIA Data Collection (Part I: Overview)

An effective data collection process will help quantify the value of each function in terms of financial and legal impacts. Use the organizational chart to identify the most appropriate respondents to provide feedback and develop a targeted questionnaire for each of the business units. Ensure timely completion of the feedback by setting an expected date for completion. Once the questionnaires have been returned, review the responses for clarity and schedule review meetings. The BIA data is then summarized, compiled, and incorporated into reporting formats.

BIA Data Collection (Part II: Implementation)

Once the questionnaires have been developed and tested in a single unit, distribute them to all appropriate business units. Explain to the recipients how the BIA will help their individual units and overall mission within the organization. If possible, secure a written document confirming executive support and encouragement and use it when needed to "inspire" recipient cooperation. Provide detailed instructions with each questionnaire and consider providing examples of answer formats as well. Set a hard deadline for completion and ensure the deadline is enforced.

Questionnaire Development Considerations

Check vacation and travel schedules for all selected respondents to help ensure timely feedback and the completion of the questionnaire. The suggestions listed below will assist in streamlining the development and distribution process.

1. Select One Unit to Test the Questionnaire
2. Solicit Feedback and/or Clarifications
3. Include a Glossary of Terms for Consistency
4. Simplify Options for Answering Questions
5. Modify Questions for Individual Units

Identify Appropriate Respondents

The first step in identifying who should receive the questionnaire is to secure a current copy of the organizational chart. Select the departments and business unit to be involved with the BIA and then identify the leadership of each selected department. Leaders of the selected departments will ultimately be responsible for the completion of the questionnaires. The departments will have the responsibility of identifying vital functions and the resource requirements for those functions. Include critical suppliers at all levels whenever possible.

Often Missed Questions: Personnel

Do not overlook human costs in the questionnaire; unit managers will certainly know the answers to many of these considerations.

Listed below are examples of human topics that should be addressed with each of the department and/or unit managers.

1. Employee Morale
2. Employee Resignation
3. Cost to Hire
4. Cost to Train
5. Influence of Social Media

Often Missed Questions: Delayed Costs

Delayed costs are very real and very tangible; the crisis does not end immediately after the recovery and neither do the costs and expenses. Listed below are issues regarding delayed costs which are often overlooked in BIA questionnaires.

1. Wages Paid for no Work
2. Overtime Wages Paid for Recovery
3. Additional Cost of Organizational Credit
4. Devaluation of Stock (Public Entities)
5. Additional Cost of Insurance

Often Missed Questions: Goodwill

Ensure that the right people are asked the right questions; there are many intangible costs with tangible consequences after a disaster. Listed below are issues regarding goodwill and trust which are often overlooked in BIA questionnaires.

1. Loss of Shareholder Confidence
2. Loss of Supplier Confidence
3. Loss of Customer Confidence
4. Damage to Brand and/or Image
5. Loss of Competitive Advantage

Key Personnel Considerations

Consider creating an "Employee Skills Matrix" to anticipate and prepare for personnel issues that are unforeseen and/or unpredictable. Knowing the skills of all employees will allow for last-minute substitutions when unforeseen and/or unpredictable circumstances such as those listed below force key employees to be unavailable during a recovery process.

1. Stress Created by Traumatic Events
2. Payment, Housing, and Insurance
3. Labor and Talent Management Issues
4. Directed to Return but Refuse and/or Unable
5. National Guard, Firefighters, and EMS

Writing a Testing Strategy

To maximize the benefit to the organization while minimizing costs, develop a written testing strategy for the *Business Continuity Plan* (BCP). The written strategy should describe the type of testing, frequency of testing, and included in the Administrative BCP as approved testing plans assist in generating compliance. Individual unit plans should be created first and then expanded to include BCP groupings. The testing calendar should be planned two to three years in advance and consider department "busy seasons" and vacation times.

Developing Testing Goals

As with all things in the *Business Continuity Program* (BCP), begin setting objectives and goals for the testing plan by referring to the BIA. Specific process *Recovery Time Objectives* (RTO's) may differ. Brief RTO's require more frequent testing, longer RTO's require less frequent testing. Regardless of the RTO, critical processes must be tested more frequently, and all testing participants must fully understand their roles and objectives.

Creating the Testing Team

The best BCP testing results come from a clear explanation of the responsibilities of team members and training to show them what to do. Listed below are the categories of participants involved in BCP testing and exercises.

1. Business Continuity Manager
2. Test Sponsor
3. Exercise Recorder
4. Exercise Participants
5. Non-Organizational Participants

Leading BCP Testing Exercises

The testing scenario should be focused on the type of problem or disaster that a specific group of people are likely to face. The scenarios should reflect potential threats based on established risk analysis and risk assumptions. The expertise of the testing coordinator is essential as the individual will be responsible for the important responsibilities listed below.

1. Create a Detailed Timeline of Test Events
2. Coordinate and Stage Required Resources
3. Establish Participant Roles and Responsibilities
4. Identify Relevant Interdependencies

Benefits of BCP Testing

An untested plan is nothing more than process documentation. During times of crisis, perception (good or bad) tends to become the reality. Listed below are examples of useful information that can be discovered during BCP testing.

1. Reveal Plan Errors and/or Wrong Assumptions
2. Uncover Changes Since Writing the Plan
3. Reveal Missing and/or Unnecessary Steps
4. Identify Unknown Contingencies
5. Verify Resource and/or Asset Availability

The 5 Progressions of BCP Testing

The *five progressions of BCP testing* allow for incremental improvements over time and a wider variety of testing to be conducted more often. Listed below are the categories of BCP testing presented from the simplest to the most complex.

1. Checklist Testing
2. Table-Top Testing
3. Structured Walk-Through
4. Parallel Testing
5. Fail-Over Testing (Full Interruption)

Progression 01: Checklist Testing

The objective of *Checklist Testing* is to create and work through a BCP that is standardized and understood by all participants. It is the first level of plan error checking and required after significant changes have been made to critical systems. It tests individual IT and business processes with the objective of recovery from nothing. It is designed to make the recovery plan understandable to all participants.

Progression 02: Table-Top Testing

The objective of a *Table-Top Test* is to train specific team members, identify omissions, and raise general awareness of the BCP. It presents a simulated emergency scenario to test the decision-making process of participants. The testing coordinator will typically incorporate mid-exercise problem injections to build the participants' analysis, communication, and collaboration skills. These are typically presented as half-day exercises.

Progression 03: Structured Walk-Through

A *Structured Walk-Through* is conducted in the actual test environment and typically focuses on specific IT systems. Multiple plans are tested in logical groups to ensure efficient data exchange and communication occurs. If actual Disaster Recovery site machines and systems are used for the testing the strength of interdependencies can be tested as well. This type of test will assist in determining a realistic RTO.

Progression 04: Parallel Testing

The objective of a *Parallel Test* is to evaluate the BCP with actual systems without the risk of interrupting the business operation. It presents a realistic emergency scenario to test a logical grouping of plans using the individuals and equipment which would be involved in a real disaster. This type of exercise is typically conducted at the Disaster Recovery site and lasts several days.

Progression 05: Fail-Over Testing

The objective of a *Fail-Over Test* is to create a full interruption of the business system to definitively test the BCP. The type of exercise involves a full shutdown of the primary location and a full activation of the secondary site. It is the riskiest of all testing progressions and tends to be suited for organizations with mature Disaster Recovery capabilities, but it does generate 100% confidence in the BCP/DRP plan. This type of exercise typically lasts several days.

Potential Testing Scenarios

Realistic testing scenarios based on recent events tend to generate more "buy in" from BCP testing participants and stakeholders. Regardless of the testing scenario implemented, the objectives and goals should be relevant and achievable. Listed below are realistic BCP testing scenarios.

1. Natural Disasters
2. Civil Crisis and Unrest
3. Location and/or Proximity Threats
4. Network and/or Information Security

Planned Improvisational Exercises

Scheduled events can create opportunities to execute improvisational testing scenarios that are relevant to the business operation. Listed below are examples of scheduled events that may be conducive to improvisation BCP testing opportunities.

1. Scheduled Power Outages
2. Facility Construction Projects
3. Business Unit Relocation

4. New Facility Acquisition
5. Local Government Disaster Drills

Demonstrating RTO Capability

Recovery Time Objective (RTO) estimates are never completely accurate despite best efforts – testing measures theory against reality. The RTO is decided based on a perceived need that does not always reflect true capability. Entering actual recovery times during testing provides accurate data required to adjust implementations. Parallel options can be identified, sequences of processes can be adjusted, and non-essential tasks can be identified and eliminated.

Debriefing Exercise Participants

Whenever an incident occurs that is covered by the BCP, conduct an after-action review on the next available workday after the recovery. Listed below are questions that should be addressed after a BCP incident and response.

1. What Happened?
2. What Should Have Happened?
3. What Went Well?
4. What Did Not Go Well?
5. What Will We Do Differently?

Participant Testing Considerations

When testing exercise outcomes fall short of expectations, do not blame participants; blame and fault discourage any subsequent participation. Listed below are rules and guidelines for interacting with participants when testing has been concluded.

1. Praise in Public and Criticize in Private
2. Do Not Assign Blame to Participants
3. Discovering Gaps does not Equal Failure
4. Use Objective Observations and Not Judgment
5. Respect Dissenting Opinions

DOMAIN 12

Business Continuity and Disaster Recovery

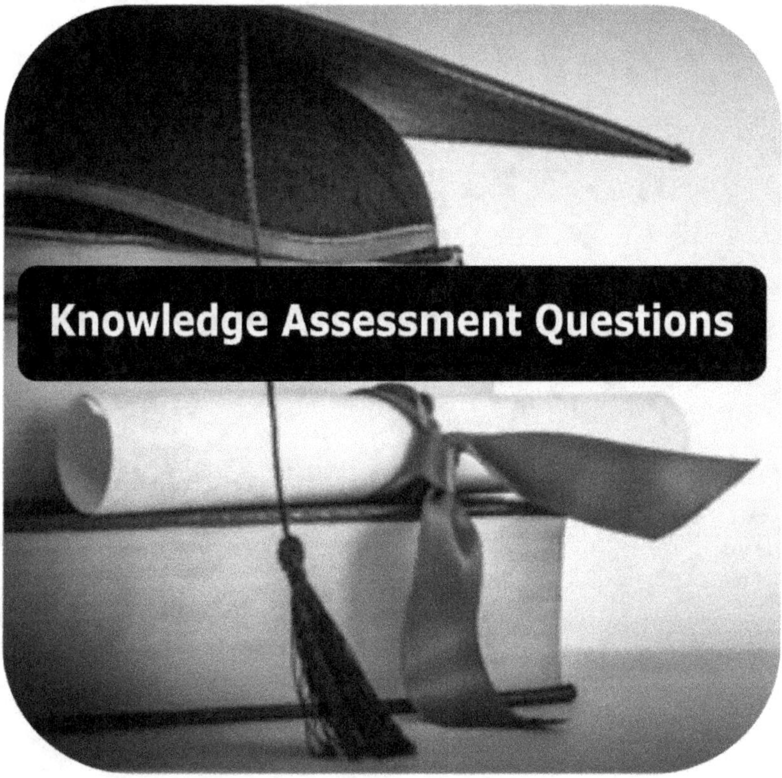

The following knowledge assessment questions are presented as true / false, multiple choice, and fill-in-the-blank. The correct answers are provided in an Answer Key at the end of this text. These questions may or may not be presented on the actual certification exam.

Domain 12: Knowledge Assessment Questions

1. Which choice below can be defined as any incident that seriously disrupts mission-critical business or IT functions?

A. Disaster

B. Event

C. Incident

D. Incursion

E. None of the Above

2. Whenever an incident occurs that is covered by the BCP, conduct a(n) __________ on the next workday after the recovery.

A. Media Briefing

B. Employee Survey

C. Board Meeting

D. After-Action Review

E. None of the Above

3. Select the best choice below for the following definition: "*The absolute maximum time that systems can be unavailable without serious and/or negative impact to the organization.*"

A. Recovery Time Objective

B. Recovery Point Objective

C. Maximum Allowable Downtime

D. Quantitative Analysis

E. None of the Above

4. As with all things in the business continuity program, begin setting goals for the testing plan by referring to the __________.

A. Mission Statement

B. Quantitative Analysis

C. Business Impact Analysis

D. Disaster Recovery Plan

E. None of the Above

5. Which choice below is a common obstacle for Information Security Managers when defining a desired security state?

A. Lack of Consensus

B. Lack of Confidence

C. Financial Accounting

D. Mental Accounting

E. None of the Above

6. An effective __________ process will help quantify the value of each function in terms of financial and legal impacts.

A. Qualitative Analysis

B. Data Collection

C. Interview

D. Policy Development

E. None of the Above

7. Select the best choice below for the following definition: "*Examination and evaluation of non-measurable data using subjective judgement and non-quantifiable methods.*"

A. Business Impact Analysis

B. Qualitative Analysis

C. Maximum Allowable Downtime

D. Quantitative Analysis

E. None of the Above

8. Which choice below is **not** a primary consideration when implementing risk management procedures?

A. Identify Information Assets and Value

B. Monitor Risk and Communicate Results

C. Scope, Charter, and Methodology

D. Accept / Reject Residual Risk

E. None of the Above

9. Which testing method listed below is designed to evaluate the BCP with actual systems without the risk of interrupting the business operation?

A. Fail-Over Test

B. Checklist Test

C. Parallel Test

D. Structured Walk-Through

E. None of the Above

10. __________ costs due to the loss of a vital business function can be difficult to identify but are no less damaging.

A. Tangible

B. Personnel

C. Technical

D. Intangible

E. None of the Above

11. Which testing method listed below is designed to train specific team members, identify omissions, and raise general awareness of the BCP?

A. Fail-Over Test

B. Checklist Test

C. Parallel Test

D. Table-Top Test

E. None of the Above

12. __________ Analysis estimates are never completely accurate despite best efforts; testing measures theory against reality.

A. Sales Projection

B. Quantitative

C. Business Impact

D. Marketing

E. None of the Above

13. An effective data collection process will help quantify the value of each function in terms of financial and legal impacts.

1. True
2. False

14. Check vacation and travel schedules for all selected respondents to help ensure timely completion of the disaster recovery.

1. True
2. False

15. Do not overlook unknowable costs in the questionnaire; unit managers will certainly know the answers to these considerations.

1. True
2. False

16. To maximize the benefit to the organization while minimizing costs, develop a written testing strategy for the BCP.

1. True
2. False

17. The best BCP testing results come from a clear explanation of the job titles of team members and incidents to show them what to do.

1. True
2. False

18. The testing scenario should be focused on the type of problem or disaster that a specific group of people are likely to enjoy.

1. True
2. False

DOMAIN 13

Threat Intelligence Collection and Analysis

Threat Intelligence

Definition:

Threat intelligence is evidence-based knowledge, including context, mechanisms, indicators, implications and actionable advice, about an existing or emerging menace or hazard to assets that can be used to inform decisions regarding the subject's response to that menace or hazard.

https://www.gartner.com/en/documents/2487216/definition-threat-intelligence

Cyber Adversaries vs. Cyber Defenders

Cyber Adversaries	Cyber Defenders
No Regard for Laws	Hack Back Prohibited
No Limits or Boundaries	Regulation and Compliance
Tax Free Funding	Limited Budgets and Personnel
Acquire Exploit Technology	Change and Version Control
Unlimited Time Frame	Prove Security Value Daily
Must be Right Once	Must be Right Always

Nation-State Actors

The role of *nation-state actors* in cyberattacks that involve hacking and data theft has gained substantial attention over the last two decades. They have the power to exert influence over citizens and compel them to act as agents—willing or unwilling—and provide indirect economic support to malicious actors to conceal official involvement in illegal activities. Listed below are three criteria that must be met to meet the definition of a nation-state actor.

1. **Sovereignty**: Possess the Authority to Rule
2. **Territoriality**: Possess Recognized Borders
3. **Abstraction**: Possess an Independent Persona that is Separate and Distinct from the Population it Governs.

Non-Nation-State Actors

Non-nation-state actors may work individually or complete attacks with a wide network of participants and then disband rapidly. The actors tend to have fewer resources, their attacks are typically less sophisticated, and they generally profit from data theft. Although they made have different targets and methods, they still have the potential to disrupt the operational capabilities of their victims and cause fear among the general population. They also benefit from a higher degree of flexibility as they are not restricted by traditional command-and-control hierarchies.

Components of the Threat Landscape

The Internet and computer technologies have dramatically reshaped the threats posed to modern society and the ways we defend against them. Listed below are crimes associated with this landscape which have either emerged or increased exponentially over the last two decades as a result of this technology.

1. Computer Hackers and Hacking
2. Economic Crimes and Identity Theft
3. Intellectual Property Theft and Piracy
4. Cyber-Stalking and Online Harassment
5. Hacktivism and Online Extremism
6. Cyber-Terror and Cyber-Warfare

Computer Hackers and Hacking

A "hack" involves the modification of technology in order to allow it to be used in unintended ways for both legal and illegal purposes. Many hackers use non-technical strategies such as social engineering, realizing that humans will always be the weak link in the security chain. The technology used is ethically neutral; the same tools used by hackers are the same as those used to attempt to prevent them from hacking. They tend to commit a significant amount of time to studying their craft and form online relationships to both assist in their studies and validate their behaviors. Hackers typically fall into one of three categories: *white hat* (good), *gray hat* (good and bad), and *black hat* (criminals).

Economic Crimes and Identity Theft

The ability to buy and sell goods at any time or location is revolutionary for both commerce and cybercrime. Email is a critical resource for attackers who target for mass exploitation. They may stress a time-sensitive problem in an effort to compel their victims to impart personally identifiable information to use for fraud and/or impersonation. The emergence of "carding markets" (credit card data on the Darknet) has increasingly fueled the demand for this information. Interestingly, many victims of these crimes report the fraud to banks to recover account funds but never report the crime to law enforcement agencies.

Intellectual Property Theft and Piracy

Ideas become *intellectual property* when they are physical and tangible works that may be accessed and viewed by others. Low-income countries are the leaders in pirating software and their changing tactics and behaviors make it difficult to prevent these types of crimes. Utilizing bit-torrent links to a multitude of "seeder servers" (severs containing pirated content) allow concurrent uploads and downloads to be executed quickly and reduces the risk and likelihood of detection. Listed below are examples of intellectual property that are common targets of digital piracy.

1. Copyrights
2. Trademarks
3. Patents
4. Trade Secrets (Strategy)
5. Trade Secrets (Processes)

Cyber-Stalking and Online Harassment

The open nature in which people can lead their lives is unparalleled—except by the access they provide to their own personal information. This crime involves constant use of email and text and has the potential to cause real-world harm. Victims of these crime report feeling anxiety, depression, and a feeling of powerlessness. Victims may reduce exposure by changing their behaviors, contributing to high levels of absenteeism from work and social gatherings. In both cyber-stalking and online harassment the offender does not need to know the person being victimized.

Hacktivism and Online Extremism

A carefully targeted attack against any critical infrastructure asset can cause serious harm to the functionality and security of the network. "Hacktivists" utilize technology to promote an activist agenda. The primary differences between hacktivism and online extremism is the motive of the actor and the number of people harmed. Online extremists tend to target larger groups of people with the intention of impacting innocent people. In addition to causing panic and fear in the general population, these actions can cause mass collateral damage on a physical level that rivals traditional terrorist attacks.

Cyber-Terror and Cyber-Warfare

The ability to communicate with others of diverse backgrounds ensures that individuals can be steadily introduced to a movements' principles. Although it is well-established that - warfare is a very real threats, there is no agreed upon definition it. Social media plays a key role in cyber-terrorism; Twitter is a key platform for the radicalization of individuals.

Group such as "Al Qaeda" use website to publish the magazine *Inspire*, a publication dedicated to providing detailed tactics for conducting terrorist activities. "eJihad" online forums such as *al-Farouq* and *al-Jinan* provide their visitors with the ability to obtain free exploit tools to compromise systems belonging to entities with opposing ideologies.

Understanding the Maneuver Warfare Mindset

Organizations must change their tactics in order to survive conflict and adapt to opponents that do not follow conventional rules. Listed below are the seven key components of the maneuver warfare mindset.

1. A High Operational Tempo
2. The OODA Loop
3. Surprise: Exploiting Opportunity
4. The Center of Gravity
5. Combined Arms and Collaboration
6. Flexibility and Adaptability
7. A Decentralized Command

A High Operational Tempo

Key Performance Indicators (KPI's) are measurable values that provide metrics to gauge how well a specific function is achieving its objectives. They are used during the resolution of incidents to accurately measure effort and progress with certainty. Uncertainty cripples the decision-making process and can lead to "paralysis by analysis." Listed below are the three KPI's used to measure progress in the majority of incidents.

1. Mean Time to Detect (MTTD)
2. Mean Time to Identify (MTTI)
3. Mean Time To Resolve (MTTR)

The OODA Loop

The organization or adversary who has the most advantage is the one who can cycle through the *OODA Loop* the fastest. The OODA Loop is a recognitional decision-making model developed by Col. John Boyd (USAF) to enhance the efficiency and speed of tactical and operational missions. Listed below are the components of Boyd's OODA Loop.

1. **O**bserve
2. **O**rient
3. **D**ecide
4. **A**ct
5. *Evaluate* (Added in Later Models)

Surprise: Exploiting Opportunity

In addition to improving decision-making and understanding strengths and weaknesses, security personnel must adapt to the unexpected. Security personnel are usually required to operate from a defensive position, but defense still allows for the element of surprise. To apply an active defense requires knowledge of four key components: the adversary's capability, the adversary's intent, the defenders' strengths, and the defenders' weaknesses. It is then possible to create path of least resistance for the adversary that is too attractive to avoid. Once the adversary is on the path the defender has an opportunity for tactical advantage.

The Center of Gravity (CoG)

Center of gravity is the concept that each organization has a focal point of strength and capability that is possessed and being utilized. The objective is to identify the adversary's CoG and deprive them of its capability without eliminating it completely. The application of strength to this relative weakness will cause the adversary the most disruption. Although security personnel are not authorized to counterattack under most conditions, they are allowed to be proactive in their defense.

Combined Arms and Collaboration

Leaders of an organizations' security program must plan to orchestrate and utilize their combined resources to complete mission objectives. The goals of this effort are *collaboration* and *synergy*. The high degree of complexity in Information Technology and a shift to remote management of resources can create silos which make collaboration challenging. These challenges can be overcome by developing proper communication channels between the collective components. An effective use of combined arms and collaboration will help to identify incidents and their subsequent solutions quickly and efficiently.

Flexibility and Adaptability

Flexibility and adaptability is achieved through understanding the capabilities within an organization and training to address different relevant scenarios. It increases the ability to react to multiple opponents and/or rapidly changing tactics. Flexibility can also enhance people, processes, and skills by providing them with the environment necessary to grow and flourish. This enhancement tends to reduce single points of failure and create a structure of redundant capabilities.

A Decentralized Command

With proper guidance, a *decentralized command* allows leaders to take initiative in the planning, training, and execution of their missions. Greater autonomy empowers teams to take more control over the outcome of their efforts. It's a system which distributes operational tasks, operational risks, and has the potential to reduce individual burdens. It also facilitates a more efficient decision-making process that may further lead to greater operational expansion.

The Threat Intelligence Cycle

To have an intelligence capability, a process must be developed to take raw information and produce a product that can be used for action. The *Threat Intelligence Cycle* provides this capability using the six phases listed below.

1. Planning and Direction
2. Intelligence Collection
3. Intelligence Processing
4. Analysis and Production
5. Dissemination of Intelligence
6. Utilization and Feedback

Planning and Direction

The *Planning and Direction* phase is composed of all activities that identify information requirements and ensure requirements are met. It manages the end-to-end intelligence cycle. Information requirements (IR's) are prioritized, collection plans are prepared, and collection capabilities are tasked. The requirements of this phase are based on leadership (the consumer of the intelligence product). The IR's are managed as the situation changes so that collection, production, and dissemination efforts are utilized in the most efficient manner.

Intelligence Collection

The *Intelligence Collection* phase acquires and provisions the information to be provided to teams in the next chain of the intelligence cycle. Individual teams are allowed to collect their specific portions of the IR's which contributes to a redundancy of information. The redundancy allows assessments to be confirmed or disproved and facilitates cross-communication between teams. Once the collected information is reconciled it can be forwarded to the next phase of the intelligence cycle.

Intelligence Processing

During the *Intelligence Processing* phase, processed information regarded as actual intelligence will be mapped to correlating points for future phases. This phase includes exploitation of the data and a conversion process which may include decryption, translation, and interpretation. The information is now regarded as actual intelligence and is organized in a format specific to the organization.

Analysis and Production

The *Analysis and Production* phase analyzes, evaluates, interprets, and integrates raw intelligence into finished intelligence products. This final product must be delivered in a timely manner and focused on the needs of the stakeholder. The stakeholder decides if the intelligence report is complete, accurate, and if additional collection efforts may be required. This report provides an overview of the subject area in a clear, concise manner that allows the stakeholder to draw conclusions.

Dissemination of Intelligence

Intelligence Dissemination portrays an accurate picture of the threat to leadership in a form that facilitates rapid understanding of the issue. Listed below are several examples of the many types of architectures utilized for intelligence dissemination.

1. *Supply-Push*: No Request Needed
2. *Demand-Pull*: As Needed by Querying
3. *Standard Channel*: Routine Intelligence
4. *Alarm Channel*: Critical Intelligence
5. *Broadcast Mode*: All Authorized Users
6. *Point-to-Point Mode*: Specific Users

Utilization and Feedback

The *Utilization and Feedback* phase ensures a dialog occurs between all parties before and after the intelligence has been received. The threat intelligence cycle is a closed-loop system in which feedback occurs fluidly between all phases. A determination is made whether IR's are adequately being met by analysts or if adjustments need to be made to the process. Determinations are also made whether revisions to the IR's are required and if more collection efforts are required. It must be noted that the consumers of the intelligence product are not required to act on it.

Challenges to Cyber Crime Investigations

The legal system, refined over centuries, was forged in the physical world for physical crimes; Internet crime is not even five decades old. While investigative best practices will withstand the test of time the academies and institutions tasked with the responsibility to train modern investigators could have never predicted the challenges posed by cybercrimes.

Investigators must now overcome anonymizing IP addresses used in conjunction with proxy servers. Anonymous networks (such as TOR) designed to obfuscate traffic provide safe haven for masked websites offering hidden services (such as the Darknet). In these instances, identification and attribution of malicious actors is very difficult, and back-tracing is very time-consuming. The challenges are compounded by a "brain drain" of cyber expertise in many organizations due to high turnover, career changes, and a lack of qualified applicants to fill vacant positions.

International Enforcement Challenges

Although most industrialized nations have criminalized various forms of computer crime, there is limited parity in the language of the statutes. No universal jurisdiction exists which would allow nations to arrest criminals abroad. Extradition treaties suffer from a lack of enforcement, and most computer-related crimes are not reported to law enforcement.

A lack of knowledge in nation-state legislative bodies has caused technology to outpace the legal system. In many cases, there is no legal violation to prosecute even though a crime has been committed.

Threat Intelligence Sources

For threat intelligence programs to have the highest probability of a successful outcome, sources must be known and tailored to the specific needs of the organization. Listed below are examples of the types of threat intelligence sources that have the potential to provide value to security mangers and investigators.

1. AlienVault's Open Threat Exchange
2. Cisco's GOSINT
3. The Malware Information Sharing Platform
4. Information Sharing and Analysis Centers
5. Rich Site Summary Feeds (RSS)
6. Social Media Platforms (Especially Twitter)

DOMAIN 13

Threat Intelligence Collection and Analysis

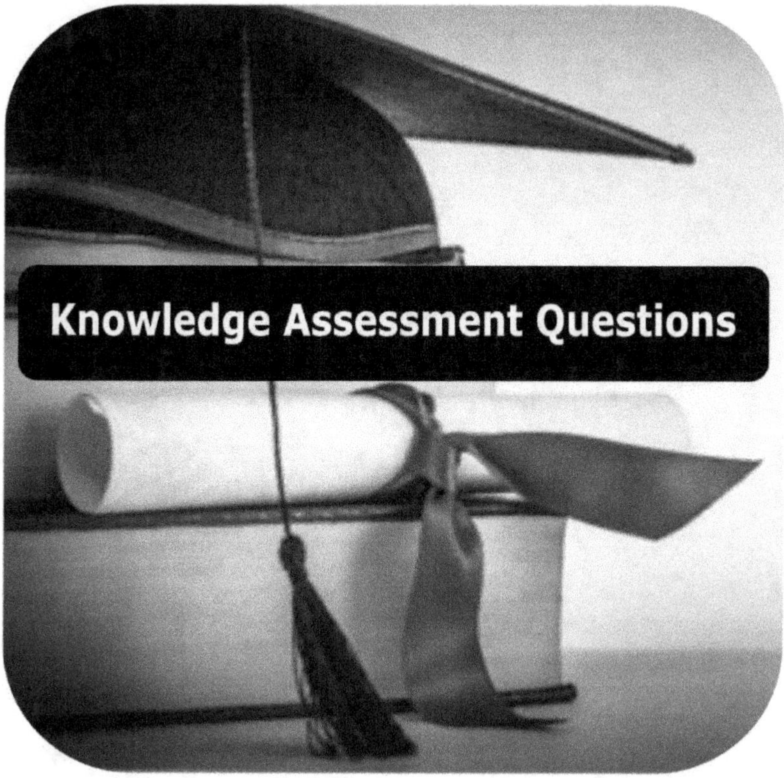

The following knowledge assessment questions are presented as true / false, multiple choice, and fill-in-the-blank. The correct answers are provided in an Answer Key at the end of this text. These questions may or may not be presented on the actual certification exam.

Domain 13: Knowledge Assessment Questions

1. What phase of the Threat Intelligence Life Cycle is composed of all activities that identify information requirements and ensure requirements are met?

A. Utilization and Feedback

B. Planning and Direction

C. Analysis and Production

D. Intelligence Collection

E. None of the Above

2. With proper guidance, a(n) __________ allows leaders to take initiative in the planning, training, and execution of their missions.

A. High Operational Tempo

B. Center of Gravity

C. Element of Surprise

D. Decentralized Command

E. None of the Above

3. Select the best choice below for the following definition: *"Measurable values that provide metrics to gauge how well a specific function is achieving its objectives."*

A. Mean Time To Resolve

B. Mean Time to Detect

C. Key Performance Indicators

D. Mean Time to Identify

E. None of the Above

4. __________ is the idea that each organization has a focal point of strength and capability that is possessed and being utilized.

A. High Operational Tempo

B. Element of Surprise

C. Center of Gravity

D. Decentralized Command

E. None of the Above

5. In what phase of the Threat Intelligence Life Cycle will processed information be regarded as actual intelligence and mapped to correlating points for future phases?

A. Intelligence Processing

B. Planning and Direction

C. Analysis and Production

D. Intelligence Collection

E. None of the Above

6. Organizations must change their __________ in order to survive conflict and adapt to opponents that do not follow conventional rules.

A. Training

B. Tactics

C. Leadership

D. Expectations

E. None of the Above

7. What phase of the Threat Intelligence Life Cycle acquires and provisions information to be handed over to the Processing and Production phases?

A. Utilization and Feedback

B. Planning and Direction

C. Analysis and Production

D. Intelligence Collection

E. None of the Above

8. __________ is achieved through understanding the capabilities within an organization and training to address different relevant scenarios.

A. Flexibility

B. Capability

C. Sustainability

D. Scalability

E. None of the Above

9. What phase of the Threat Intelligence Life Cycle analyzes, evaluates, interprets, and integrates raw intelligence into finished intelligence products?

A. Utilization and Feedback

B. Planning and Direction

C. Analysis and Production

D. Intelligence Collection

E. None of the Above

10. To have an intelligence capability, a process must be developed to take __________ and produce a product that can be used for action.

A. Risk Analysis

B. Threat Sources

C. Known Vulnerabilities

D. Raw Information

E. None of the Above

11. What phase of the Threat Intelligence Life Cycle portrays an accurate picture of the threat to leadership in a form that facilitates rapid understanding of the issue?

A. Utilization and Feedback

B. Intelligence Dissemination

C. Analysis and Production

D. Intelligence Collection

E. None of the Above

12. The role of __________ in cyberattacks that involve hacking and data theft has gained substantial attention over the last two decades.

A. Non-Nation-States

B. Advanced Technology

C. Nation-States

D. Illegal Software

E. None of the Above

13. Nation-state actors may work individually or complete attacks with a wide network of participants and then disband rapidly.

1. True
2. False

14. For threat intelligence programs to have the highest probability of a successful outcome, sources must be known and tailored to the need.

1. True
2. False

15. Virtualization involves the modification of technology in order to allow it to be used in unintended ways for both legal and illegal purposes.

1. True
2. False

16. Although most industrialized nations have criminalized various forms of trespass and fraud, there is limited parity in the language of statutes.

1. True
2. False

17. Ideas become industry standards when they are physical and tangible works that may be accessed and viewed by others.

1. True
2. False

18. The organization or adversary who has the most advantage is the one who can cycle through the *OODA Loop* the fastest.

1. True
2. False

DOMAIN 14

Cloud Computing Architecture and Security

Definition of Cloud Computing

NIST SP 800-145:

> *Cloud computing is a model for enabling ubiquitous, convenient, on-demand network access to a shared pool of configurable computing resources (e.g., networks, servers, storage, applications, and services) that can be rapidly provisioned and released with minimal management effort or service provider interaction. This cloud model is composed of five essential characteristics, three service models, and four deployment models.*

Cloud Computing Characteristics

Despite many functions and configurations, the five characteristics listed below are accepted as part of the cloud computing definition.

1. On-Demand Self-Service
2. Broad Network Access
3. Resource Pooling
4. Rapid Elasticity
5. Measured Service (Metering)

Cloud Computing Service Models

Cloud services are typically offered in three standard models based on the providers' capability and the customers' needs. Listed below are the standard models and examples of services they support.

1. **Infrastructure as a Service** (IaaS): Hardware and Connectivity

2. **Platform as a Service** (PaaS): Operating Systems

3. **Software as a Service** (SaaS): Applications, CRM, and Email

Infrastructure as a Service (IaaS)

In the *IaaS* model, the cloud service provider contracts access to its infrastructure and is fully responsible for administration. The customer installs the operating systems and applications; the provider controls the hardware. Control of the operating system affords the client more security for data stored on the hardware. This arrangement is typically utilized when the client requires cloud services for limited needs such as data archiving, disaster recovery planning, or business continuity planning.

Platform as a Service (PaaS)

In the *PaaS* model, the cloud service provider offers not only the IaaS capability but provides the customer with operating systems as well. The client can choose from multiple operating systems which are then maintained by the provider. This arrangement is useful for software development when testing must occur in isolated environments and compatibility testing is needed involving multiple operating systems. Additionally, the operating systems provided to the client are usually hardened.

Software as a Service (SaaS)

In the *SaaS* model, the customer receives all the underlying IaaS and PaaS capabilities, as well as end user applications. In this arrangement, the provider maintains all hardware, operating systems and applications. This hosted full production environment only requires the customer to upload and process data as needed. Examples of applications used in the service include Google Docs, Microsoft Office 365, CRM applications, and accounting software.

Public Cloud

When discussing cloud service providers and cloud capabilities, the *public cloud* tends to be the solution to which is being referred. The cloud resources are owned by the provider, offered to the general public, and rented or leaded to clients based on their needs. The companies listed below are well-known providers of public cloud services.

1. Microsoft Azure
2. Amazon Web Services (AWS)
3. Rackspace Managed Cloud

Private Cloud

Private clouds are owned and operated by individual organizations for the specific use of their staff, customers, and vendors. This is a traditional legacy environment which was formerly referred to as an "intranet." Connections are made through the Web for remote access capabilities and users share internal resources and storage.

Community Cloud

Community clouds provide infrastructure and functionality that is owned and operated by affinity groups and similar organizations. Segments are owned by different organizations that perform joint tasks and functions. Listed below is an example of how an affinity group—in this case the gaming community—may use this service.

1. *PlayStation Network*: The Umbrella Unit
2. *Sony*: Hosts the Network IAM Functions
3. *Game Vendors*: Host the DRM Servers
4. *Game Users*: Conduct Processing and Testing

Hybrid Cloud

Hybrid clouds contain elements of public, private, and community cloud models to varying degrees based on customer needs. Private cloud resources are retained in legacy production environments which allow users remote access to resources. Additionally, public cloud resources are leased for specific needs—such as PaaS services for software development—which serves to protect the legacy production environment. In this arrangement, there is less risk of harming systems in both environments.

Cloud Data Security: Encryption

Like its legacy environment counterpart, cloud computing solutions have a significant level of dependency on encryption to operate. Encryption is used to protect data at rest, in use, in motion, and to maintain secure remote connections. It allows the enterprise to protect data while simultaneously allowing the cloud provider to isolate the enterprise data. The dependency on encryption is so significant that without, cloud services could not exist.

Cloud Data Security: Key Management

The methods and locations chosen to manage encrypted keys impacts the overall risk to cloud customer data in several ways. The level of protection is determined by the key life and the criticality of the data being protected. Listed below are four critical components of key management that must be addressed when handled in-house or through a third-party key management provider such as a *Cloud Access Security Broker* (CASB).

1. Key Recovery
2. Key Distribution
3. Key Revocation
4. Key Escrow

Obfuscation, Masking, and Anonymization

In certain instances, customers using cloud provider solutions may find it necessary to obscure data and use a representation of data instead. This is accomplished by implementing obfuscation, masking, and anonymization techniques instead of encryption. Popular uses of these approaches include test environments (sandboxing), least privilege enforcement, and secure remote access. Listed below are four methods commonly used to obscure data when encryption is not an optimal solution.

1. Randomization (Replacement of Data Characters)
2. Hashing (A One-Way Function)
3. Masking (Hiding Data with Data)
4. Shuffling (Reordering Production Data)

Security Information and Event Management

To better collect, manage, analyze, and display log data, a set of *Security Information and Event Management* (SIEM) tools have been developed and deployed specifically for that purpose. They centralize the collection of log data and provide enhanced log analysis capabilities. The risk if this efficiency is all log data is stored in one location. SIEM solutions also provide the capability of trend detection in large datasets, automated response capabilities, and dashboarding (management displays).

These tools compensate for human inefficiencies in long-term log analysis. If personnel spend too much time analyzing log data, they tend to become complacent, bored, and fatigued. If personnel spend too little time analyzing log data, they lack the experience to effectively interpret the data they are analyzing.

Data Loss Prevention: Egress Monitoring

An *egress monitoring* solution—also referred to as *Data Loss Prevention* (DLP)—will examine data leaving the production environment and react based on preestablished rules and parameters. It is viewed as an enhanced layer of security and a policy enforcement mechanism to detect sensitive data that has been inadvertently or maliciously disclosed. The three primary benefits provided by DLP are enhanced monitoring capabilities, enhanced regulatory compliance, and data dissemination control.

Cloud Platform Risks (Part I)

Because the cloud customer and provider will each process data, they will share responsibilities and risks associated with the data. In the event of unauthorized disclosure and/or use of *Personally Identifiable Information* (PII), the service provider will only be financially liable if those terms are codified in an agreement. The client will be able to seek and recover damages from the provider, but that process may take years in large cases. Even when those terms are codified, the customer is civilly and criminally liable for the breach. The government and regulatory agencies will target the customer as the owner of all associated liabilities.

Cloud Platform Risks (Part II)

If the customer is protected by the providers' acceptance of fiscal responsibility, legal repercussions are still not the only negative impact the customer will experience. Listed below are negative impacts which extend beyond financial considerations.

1. Negative Publicity
2. Loss of Clientele Faith
3. Decrease in Market Share
4. Decrease in Share Value (Public)
5. Increase in Insurance Costs

Private Cloud Risks

A *private cloud* configuration is a legacy configuration of a datacenter with distributed computing capabilities. Organizations retain complete control over their assets. The risks listed below are not unique to private cloud configurations, but they are present.

1. Internal Threats
2. Natural Disasters
3. External Threats
4. Regulatory and Compliance Risks
5. Malware Risks (Internal and External)

Community Cloud Risks

In a *community cloud* configuration, resources are allocated, shared, and dispersed among affinity groups. Shared ownership does enhance resiliency but creates multiple potential nodes of entry as well. This model provides the benefit of shared and distributed costs but that comes with the risk of shared access and control. Overhead is reduced as centralized administration is not required but this leads to a lack of reliable centralized standards.

Public Cloud Risks

In a *public cloud* configuration, a company offers cloud services to any entity wanting to become a cloud customer. This model shares all the risks associated with private clouds but also introduces several unique risks such as those listed below.

1. Customer Loses Control
2. Customer Loses Oversight
3. Customer Loses Audit Ability
4. Customer Loses Enforcement Ability
5. Potential of Vendor Lock-In
6. Potential of Vendor Lock-Out

Vendor Lock-Out

Vendor lock-out can be caused when the provider goes out of business, is acquired by another interest, or ceases operation for any reason. The factors listed below should be considered when choosing a cloud service provider.

1. Provider Longevity
2. Core Competency
3. Jurisdictional Suitability
4. Supply Chain Dependencies
5. Legislative Environment

Risks: IaaS (Infrastructure as a Service)

In the IaaS (*Infrastructure as a Service*) public cloud model, the customer will have the most control over its resources. This model shares many risks common to other models but also presents several unique risks that are listed below.

1. Internal Threats
2. External Threats
3. All Access via Remote Connection
4. Lack of Required Skillsets
5. Operational and Security Functions
6. Lack of Sufficient Personnel

Risks: PaaS (Platform as a Service)

In the PaaS (*Platform as a Service*) public cloud model, the customer will have all IaaS risks as well as a few unique to this model. The operating systems used by the client are administered by the provider which may cause interoperability issues with client applications after patches or upgrades have been applied. If the clients' developers use persistent backdoors in their applications that are overlooked when transferred to a production environment, they may be creating the next zero-day exploit. If the client is utilizing virtualization to share resources between clients, mistakes and mismanagement my lead to information bleed and side-channel attacks.

Risks: SaaS (Software as a Service)

In the SaaS (*Software as a Service*) public cloud model, the customer will have all IaaS and PaaS risks as a few unique to this model. The service provider may use proprietary formats for data storage and applications, making it difficult to transfer information between systems when required. The provider must be entrusted to contain and control all risks associated with virtualization. Web application security issues may exist if the clients' customers must access data via web browsers and the providers' API's have weaknesses which have not been addressed.

Virtualization Risks

Many potential threats posed by virtualization require attenuation via the use of controls that can only be implemented by the provider. Listed below are risks associated with virtualization services offered by public cloud providers.

1. Attacks on the Hypervisor (Primarily Type II)
2. Guest Escape
3. Host Escape
4. Information Bleed
5. Process-Specific Information Discovery
6. Data Seizure by Law Enforcement

Private Cloud Threats

Although many threats to cloud computing are the same faced in legacy operations, they may manifest in novel ways and present new risks in private cloud environments. Listed below are several threats associated with private cloud computing.

1. Internal Threats (External Contractors)
2. External Attackers
3. Man-in-the-Middle Attacks
4. Increased Remote Access Capability
5. Social Engineering
6. Theft or Loss of Devices (BYOD)
7. Regulatory and Compliance Violations

Public Cloud Threats

The public cloud not only includes all threats associated with private clouds but also includes threats totally outside the customers' control. Rogue administrators have the potential to cause more damage than in legacy environments, especially when they can escalate privileges.

They tend to operate under two sets of governance—the clients' and the providers'—and external pressures may cause them to make client governance secondary. There is also the possibility of a complete contractual failure on the part of the provider. Although this unlikely it must still be considered as a potential threat.

Provider: Physical Plant

The *physical plant* of the datacenter will include the facility campus, all physical components, and the services that support them. Listed below are several components of the physical plant for which the service provider has total responsibility.

1. Secure Hardware Components
2. TPM Standards for BIOS Firmware
3. Managed Hardware Configurations
4. Logging Events and Incidents
5. Incidents, Forensics, and Attribution
6. Components for Customer Needs
7. Configuration of Secure Remote Access

Provider: Secure Logical Framework

In addition to securing the hardware components, the cloud service provider must ensure that the logical elements required to secure client accounts are equally protected. Listed below are several components of the secure logical framework for which the service provider has total responsibility.

1. Virtual Operating System(s) Installation
2. Virtualization Management Tools
3. Configuration Policy Enforcement
4. Configuration of Secure VM Elements
5. Attenuation of Potential Risks
6. Data Leakage and/or Malicious Aggregation

Provider: Secure Networking

Secure networking often involves the same tactics, methods and solutions used in legacy environments, but with cloud-specific permutations. Listed below are several components of secure networking for which the service provider has total responsibility.

1. Firewalls, Routers, and Segmentation
2. IDS, IPS, and SIEM Solutions
3. Honeypots and Sandboxing
4. Vulnerability Assessments
5. Penetration Testing
6. Ensuring Secure Communication
7. Encryption and Strong Authentication
8. *Virtual Private Networks* (VPN's)

Provider: Mapping and Selection of Controls

The cloud provider must apply the proper security controls according to a customers' relevant regulatory frameworks and planned usage. The cloud service providers publish governance documents will guide the selection of the most appropriate controls and the security policies associated with those controls.

The selected controls must be justified by established standards—such as industry best-practices and accepted frameworks—and have direct applicability to the needs and requirements of both the service providers' datacenter and the client. *The Cloud Security Alliance Cloud Controls Matrix* (CSA CCM) is an excellent resource for security personnel seeking additional detailed information on this topic.

Cloud Security Alliance Cloud Controls Matrix

The Cloud Security Alliance Cloud Controls Matrix (CSA CCM) is specifically designed to provide fundamental security principles to guide cloud vendors and to assist prospective cloud customers in assessing the overall security risk of a cloud provider. The CSA CCM provides a controls framework that gives detailed understanding of security concepts and principles that are aligned to the Cloud Security Alliance guidance in 13 domains. The foundations of the Cloud Security Alliance Controls Matrix rest on its customized relationship to other industry-accepted security standards, regulations, and controls frameworks such as the ISO 27001/27002, ISACA COBIT, PCI, NIST, Jericho Forum and NERC CIP and will augment or provide internal control direction for service organization control reports attestations provided by cloud providers.

https://cloudsecurityalliance.org

Lack of Physical Access

The cloud provider will not have any reason to allow the customer any physical access to the facility containing the customers' data. In fact, the provider has every reason to always prevent access. It provides services to a wide variety of customers with varying degrees of trust which in most cases is unknown. The more knowledge customers have regarding the internal structure and process of the providers' physical plant, the more risk exists that a client will a low trust level may exploit that knowledge.

This presents the client with a situation that is simultaneously beneficial and challenging. The benefit exists in that this standard is applied to every client which, in turn, tends to increase the clients' trust in the provider. The challenge presented by the lack of access is the client is forced to rely on the security assertions of the provider that cannot be verified or validated.

Lack of Auditing Ability

The cloud providers' unwillingness to allow client access to the facility applies to the client's auditors as well. Clients may have regulatory requirements that must be demonstrated to governing organizations. In some cases, the clients' stakeholders require audit results based on organizational policy.

The cloud service providers address these issues by commissioning licensed and chartered auditing services which are trusted by the industry to conduct the required audits and publish the results.

Listed below are the three categories of *Service Organization Controls* (SOC) reports that are typically generated by chartered audit firms. The *SOC 3* report is the document most likely to be encountered by Information Security personnel.

1. **SOC 1**: Financial Reporting
2. **SOC 2**: Security Control Audits
3. **SOC 3**: Published Audit Assertion

DOMAIN 14

Cloud Computing Architecture and Security

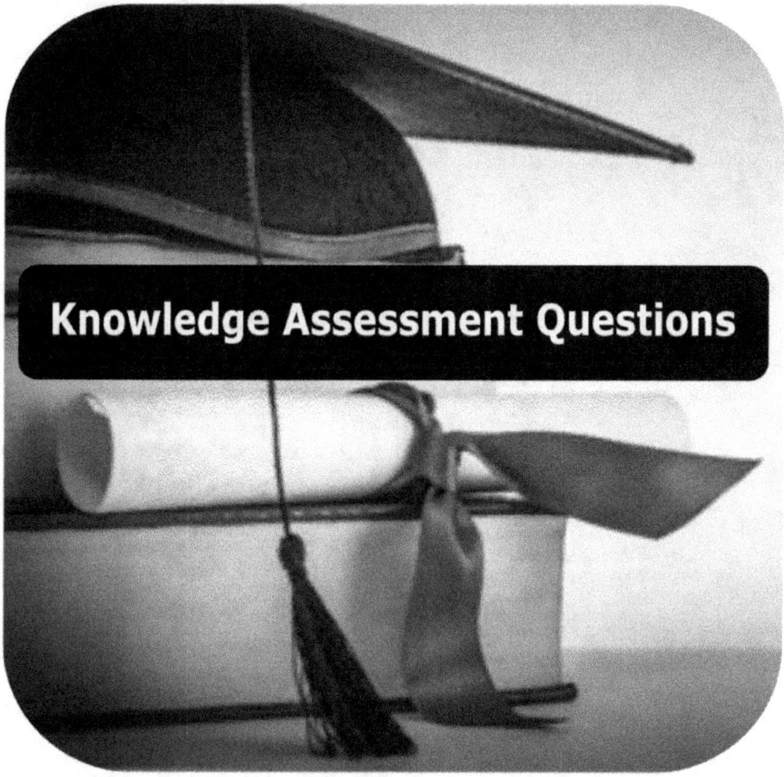

The following knowledge assessment questions are presented as true / false, multiple choice, and fill-in-the-blank. The correct answers are provided in an Answer Key at the end of this text. These questions may or may not be presented on the actual certification exam.

Domain 14: Knowledge Assessment Questions

1. Which component of the datacenter will include the facility campus, all physical components, and the services that support them?

A. Headquarters

B. Physical Plant

C. Off-Site Location

D. Secure Storage

E. None of the Above

2. In the __________ model, the cloud service provider contracts access to its infrastructure and is fully responsible for administration.

A. Security as a Service

B. Software as a Service

C. Platform as a Service

D. Infrastructure as a Service

E. None of the Above

3. Which choice below is a cloud configuration in which resources are allocated, shared, and dispersed among affinity groups?

A. Hybrid

B. Private

C. Community

D. Public

E. None of the Above

4. __________ clouds are owned and operated by individual organizations for the specific use of their staff, customers, and vendors.

A. Public

B. Hybrid

C. Private

D. Community

E. None of the Above

5. Which choice below is a cloud model that not only includes all threats associated with private clouds but includes threats totally outside the customers' control?

A. Hybrid

B. Community

C. Distributed

D. Public

E. None of the Above

6. Like its legacy environment counterpart, cloud computing solutions have a significant dependency on __________ to operate.

A. Maintenance

B. Encryption

C. Functionality

D. Performance

E. None of the Above

7. Which choice below is an example of obfuscation, masking, and anonymization a customer may choose to implement in a cloud environment?

A. Randomization

B. Symmetric Encryption

C. Cipher Block-Chaining

D. Asymmetric Encryption

E. None of the Above

8. A(n) __________ monitoring solution will examine data leaving the production environment and react based on preestablished rules and parameters.

A. Egress

B. Managed

C. Proprietary

D. Ingress

E. None of the Above

9. Which choice below is a model in which the cloud provider offers customers the IaaS capability and provides the operating systems as well?

A. Security as a Service

B. Platform as a Service

C. Software as a Service

D. Infrastructure as a Service

E. None of the Above

10. In a __________ cloud configuration, a company offers cloud services to any entity wanting to become a cloud customer.

A. Private

B. Hybrid

C. Community

D. Public

E. None of the Above

11. Which choice below is a characteristic of all cloud computing models that is required to meet the cloud computing definition?

A. Budgetary Pooling

B. Broad Facility Access

C. Measured Service

D. Deferred Elasticity

E. None of the Above

12. __________ clouds contain elements of public, private, and community cloud models to varying degrees based on customer needs.

A. Private

B. Community

C. Hybrid

D. Public

E. None of the Above

13. Cloud services are typically offered in three standard models based on the providers' capability and the customers' needs.

1. True
2. False

14. The cloud provider must apply the proper security controls according to a customers' relevant operational capacity and available budget.

1. True
2. False

15. When discussing cloud serve providers and cloud capabilities, the private cloud tends to be the solution to which is being referred.

1. True
2. False

16. Many potential threats posed by virtualization require attenuation via the use of controls that can only be implemented by the provider.

1. True
2. False

17. Private clouds are owned and operated by individual organizations for the specific use of their staff, customers, and vendors.

1. True
2. False

18. Vendor lock-in can be caused when the provider goes out of business, is acquired by another interest, or ceases operation for any reason.

1. True
2. False

DOMAIN 15

Service Level Agreements and Legal Contracts

*** Legal Advice Disclaimer ***

The information provided in this domain does not, and is not intended to, constitute legal advice; all information is for general informational purposes only. Always consult legal counsel and technological experts for guidance with organizational initiatives. Google is an outstanding source of information but it did **not** pass any states' bar exam. The content presented in this domain is for general understanding, and general understanding is not the equivalent of subject matter expertise.

Good Fences Make Good Neighbors

The best way to avoid arguments in a business relationship is to write down the parties' expectations ahead of time in a formal agreement. Contracts are not created due to a lack of trust, nor are they created to win lawsuits at a later date. The contract is simply a boundary marker—like a fence—which explains the responsibilities of all parties involved. Good contracts actually prevent disputes and attempt to keep the involved parties out of court by uncovering mismatched expectations in advance.

"Legalese" Does Not Exist

One may feel uncomfortable because of the unfamiliar language used, but most well-written contracts are easily understood by all involved. There is no such thing as "legalese;" lawyers use special legal shorthand in the same way technical specialists use special technical shorthand (such as "bot," "bug," or "sandbox"). While some contracts still use formal stilted language, they are slowly being phased out. The three tips listed below will provide benefit when experiencing difficulty reading contracts.

1. Reference *Black's Law Dictionary*
2. Ask Someone with Legal Expertise for Help
3. Relax and Read the Sentences Slowly

Seek Best Options Over Fairness

Each party has a choice about whether to enter into a contract; neither side owes the other any special considerations or terms. It is impossible to define the work "fair" within the context of law. A strict focus on "fairness" may cause a person to reject economic common sense or accept ridiculous offers. Furthermore, accepting bad terms is not unfair, and if the majority accepts those terms can they be considered unfair at all? The best guiding principle is leverage and focusing on securing the best options available.

General Contract Structures

Information Technology contracts are typically organized into three subset components: *prime clauses*, *general clauses*, and *boilerplate clauses*. Listed below is the basic structure of most legal contracts:

1. Introduction and Recitals
2. Definitions
3. Prime Clauses
4. General Clauses
5. Boilerplate Clauses

Prime Clauses

Prime clauses address the terms of the agreement with the highest priority and the most significant outcomes. Clients should protect themselves against unclear descriptions and ensure all promises address the expectations of services and terms. Listed below are examples of high priority items that tend to be included in this section of the legal agreement.

1. Defining the Professional Service
2. Statements of Work (Separate Attachments)
3. Change Order Procedures
4. Customer Fees
5. Distributor and Reseller Fees
6. Due Dates and Invoices

General Causes

The term General Clauses is a catch-all category that refers to issues not addressed in either the primary or boilerplate clauses.

Although they do not rise to the priority level of prime clauses, they are still important supporting components of the contract. The one characteristic shared by all elements of general clauses is that they typically generate the most disagreement, debate, and compromise. Listed below are examples of high priority items that tend to be included in this section of the legal agreement.

1. Technical Specifications
2. Service Level Agreements
3. Response, Repair, and Remedy
4. Maintenance, Upgrades, and Updates
5. Schedules and Milestones
6. Delivery, Acceptance, and Rejection
7. Data Management and Security
8. General and Specific Indemnity
9. Limitation of Liability
10. Non-Compete and Non-Solicit
11. Financial Stability and Reporting
12. Alternative Dispute Resolution
13. Term and Termination

Boilerplate Clauses

Boilerplate clauses include a set of standard terms usually placed at the end of a contract and used for introductory material as well. You cannot predict what issues may arise in a business relationship, so you cannot know when boilerplate clauses will become vital in providing clarification and/or settling disputes. Listed below are examples of high priority items that tend to be included in this section of the legal agreement.

1. Introductions and Recitals
2. Definitions (Terms Used Often)
3. Time is of the Essence (Critical Deadlines)
4. Independent Contractors
5. Choice of Law and Courts
6. Government Restricted Rights
7. Technology Export (International Regulations)
8. Force Majeure (List of Specific Events)
9. Severability (Limits Unknown Impact)
10. Bankruptcy Rights
11. Conflicts Among Attachments

12. Construction (Unclear Terms in Courts)
13. Entire Agreement (No Prior Documents)
14. Amendments (Typical and Unilateral)

Service Level Agreement (SLA) and Contract Review Process

Most lawsuits arise from contracts that are not clear, complete, and that do not express the agreement as it was understood by the parties. To avoid the potential for conflict, it is important for all parties to agree on the definitions listed in the beginning of the agreement. Resist the urge to make assumptions; it is perfectly acceptable to question everything and receive clarification when needed. Identify any missing items (omissions) and be comfortable changing the boilerplate clauses when necessary. If in doubt, always seek a second opinion from a qualified professional.

General Contract Review Checklist

When reviewing contracts and service level agreements, consider the use of checklists to help ensure a consistent approach. Every contract reviewed will always have unique issues to be considered. The checklists presented below are not meant to be all-inclusive and are only offered as an example of components and topics typically encountered in legal documents.

1. Verify all Parties are Properly Identified
2. Verify all Capitalized Terms are Defined
3. Verify all Signature and/or Initial Blocks are Correct
4. Confirm all Exhibits are Correct and Attached
5. Confirm all Boilerplate is Relevant (Cut and Paste Mistakes)
6. Ensure Performance Obligations are Accurate
7. Ensure Payment Terms are Accurate
8. Ensure Payment Dates and Methods are Accurate
9. Confirm the Service Term and Termination are Correct
10. Confirm the Law, Jurisdiction, and Venue are Correct

Provisions of an Enforceable Contract

A contract or service level agreement cannot violate the law in any manner and can become void if either party acts in an illegal fashion. Contracts must meet certain standards to be considered legal and enforceable. List below are seven provisions which must be present in a contract for it to be legally enforceable.

1. Capacity (Authorized Parties)
2. Offer
3. Acceptance
4. Competent Parties
5. Mutuality of Obligation
6. Consideration (Time to Review)
7. Agreement

Common Myths and Misunderstandings

There are many commonly-held myths and misunderstandings regarding contracts and service level agreements. Be aware and prepared. Listed below are four areas deserving of special review and consideration which tend to be overlooked in the process.

1. **Guaranteed Uptime = Guaranteed Uptime**: The term "uptime" is easily understood, but the term "downtime" can mean much more than being inaccessible. Degradation of performance can cause a service to become unreliable and unusable even though it is still technically "up." Service providers do not consider scheduled maintenance as downtime and will rarely address the topic unless broached by the client. If scheduled maintenance plans are excluded attempt to negotiate an iterative maintenance schedule that will minimize negative impacts on operations. It is also important to note that although contracts may stipulate "downtime refunds," the losses incurred by the organization during those periods can significantly exceed the refunds.

2. **Contracts Scale with the Business**: A contract is structured to meet the needs of an organization at the time it is written. The size of an organization can change dramatically—expanding or reducing—in a short amount of time. Contract review intervals should be outlined during the negotiation process to include notifications when the organization is close to a breach (over-utilization) or when services are being under-utilized. The contract should also state that new negotiations will begin as soon as the change

in scale is recognized. Attempt to guarantee these meetings will occur "off paper" (in person) if and when it is practical for both parties to do so.

3. **Changing Service Providers is Easy**: A transition clause (moving from one provider to another) should be included in all contracts that activates at the time any breach occurs. This clause should also ensure there are no overlapping costs for the client during the period of transition. If a 12-month contract which allows "X" amount of data transfer per month is terminated by a breach in month 11, the client will be required to transfer "11 x X" amount of data to change providers. If the client is required to pay "11 x X" it may be cost prohibitive to change providers and enforce the penalty for the breach. Confirming a transition clause in the contract will address this issue and reduce the potential of a lawsuit in the event a breach occurs.

4. **Providers Should Choose Measurements**: Many clients allow providers to choose the metrics used to measure performance in service contracts based on the assumption that the provider is best qualified to make this decision. It is the organizations' responsibility to decide the metrics best suited for its own use. Providers are not likely to reveal shortcomings and choose metrics based solely on their strengths. Establish measurable and specific benchmarks as performance standards and avoid using ambiguous numbers and language in the agreement. Require specific monitoring tools and reporting standards to validate service standards which simultaneously demanding and enforcing penalties for performance deficiencies.

Contract Negotiation Strategies

Negotiators understand the importance of reaching a win-win solution; when both sides are satisfied, better partnerships are the result. Listed below are five strategies that can be incorporated into any contract or service level agreement negotiation.

1. Make Multiple Offers Simultaneously
2. Include a Matching Right

3. Attempt a Contingency Agreement
4. Negotiate Damages Early in the Process
5. Search for Post-Settlement Settlements

Make Multiple Offers Simultaneously

In negotiations involving many issues, a great amount of value can be created by making *multiple equivalent simultaneous offers* (MESO). Identify several proposals related to the primary proposal being negotiated and be prepared to present the proposals as multiple offers during the negotiation. The proposals should be valued equally by all parties involved. It gives the appearance of flexibility and provides a deeper understanding of the oppositions' preferences which can then be used to craft future proposals. If presented correctly, this tactic increases the odds of agreement.

Include a Matching Right

In negotiation, include a *matching right* in the contract—a guarantee that one side can match any offer that the other side later receives. This tactic is gaining popularity in legal contracts used at all levels in many industries. In this arrangement, the grantor provides a contracted right to the holder with the power to match third-party offers later received by the grantor.

For example, a landlord may grant a tenant this type of right in a 12-month lease. During that period, the landlord decides to increase the rent. When the tenants' lease come to term, the tenant will be offered the right to accept or reject the new lease terms before any third party. This arrangement is referred to as "first right of refusal." This tactic can preserve mutual flexibility during the negotiation process.

Attempt a Contingent Agreement

In negotiation, parties often reach impasse because they have different beliefs about the likelihood of future events. If one party believes the proposal is realistic and the opposing party believes the proposal will never work, the negotiation may not continue.

This tactic creates flexible contingent agreements based on "if, then" challenges. This allows the discussion to continue despite disagreements between the parties. This tactic is most commonly utilized for agreements regarding incentives and penalties.

Negotiate Damages Early in Process

When formulating the initial contract, both sides can—and should—specify what will happen if the other side violates the contract terms. This discussion should clearly stipulate the cost associated with the breach. Lawsuits cause all involved to lose focus on important daily operational issues which can have severe negative impacts on the organization.

The parties may consider *Alternative Dispute Resolution* (ADR) and alternative means of compensation in the event of a breach as opposed to the use of courts. Another benefit of discussing damages early in the process is the addition of new bargaining issues which can be used during the negotiation.

Search for Post-Settlement Settlements

According to conventional doctrine, the conversation should end once a contract is negotiated for fear of derailing the agreement. That traditional thought may not be entirely accurate. Once the contract has been negotiated and signed there is no harm in asking the involved parties to review it further to determine if it can be improved.

The proposed revisions must benefit all parties equally, and all parties involved have the right to reject the revised proposal if they choose. If this tactic is implemented successfully, it can create new sources of value and increase trust levels between the parties involved in the process.

DOMAIN 15

Service Level Agreements and Legal Contracts

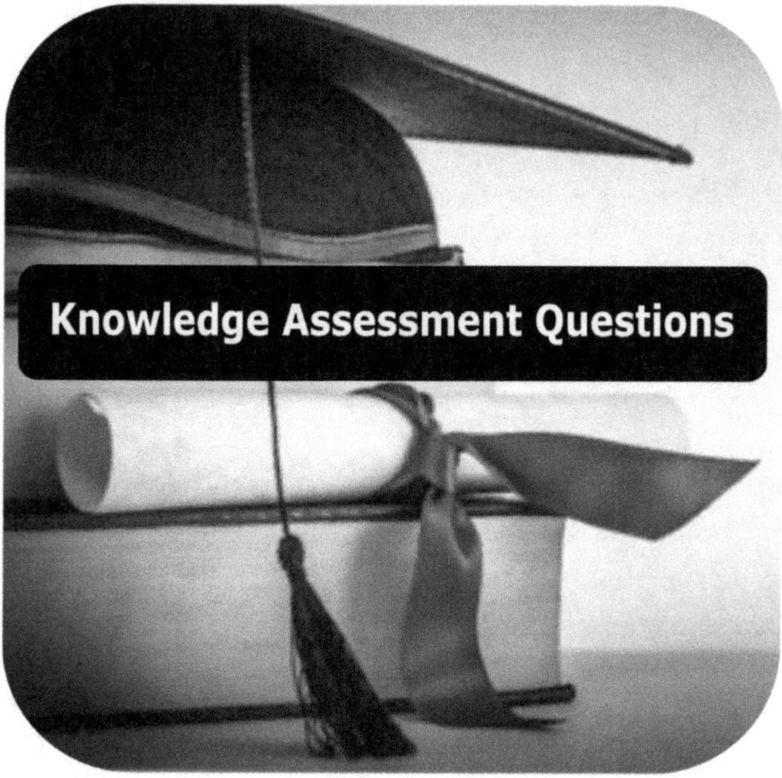

The following knowledge assessment questions are presented as true / false, multiple choice, and fill-in-the-blank. The correct answers are provided in an Answer Key at the end of this text. These questions may or may not be presented on the actual certification exam.

Domain 15: Knowledge Assessment Questions

1. Which choice below is a potential benefit from achieving post-settlement settlements during the contract negotiation process?

A. Identify Contract Loopholes

B. Elevate Negotiating Position

C. Less Potential for Lawsuits

D. Increase Mutual Trust

E. None of the Above

2. In negotiation, include a __________ in your contract—a guarantee that one side can match any offer that the other side later receives.

A. Simultaneous Offer

B. Matching Right

C. Contingent Agreement

D. Post-Settlement

E. None of the Above

3. Which choice below is a reason to have a legal contract between all parties in any type of business relationship?

A. Uncover Mismatched Expectations

B. Win Lawsuits Later

C. Stronger Negotiating Position

D. Lack of Mutual Trust

E. None of the Above

4. Most __________ arise from contracts that are not clear, complete, and that do not express the agreement as it was understood by the parties.

A. Solutions

B. Questions

C. Lawsuits

D. Expectations

E. None of the Above

5. Which choice below is a reason to seek the best option instead of fairness when parties negotiate any type of business contract?

A. "Fair" is Clearly Defined in Law

B. Guiding Principle is Leverage

C. Special Considerations are Due

D. Special Terms are Expected

E. None of the Above

6. ___________ include a set of terms usually placed at the end of a contract and used for introductory material as well.

A. Prime Clauses

B. Specific Clauses

C. General Clauses

D. Boilerplate Clauses

E. None of the Above

7. Which choice below is an example of a topic that may be covered in the *Prime Clauses* section of a legal contract between parties?

A. Technical Specifications

B. Response, Repair, and Remedy

C. Change Order Procedures

D. Choice of Law and Courts

E. None of the Above

8. Customers should protect themselves against ___________ and ensure that all promises address the expectation of help needed.

A. Unclear Descriptions

B. Unfair Contracts

C. Statements of Work

D. Distributor Fees

E. None of the Above

9. Which choice below is an example of a topic that may be covered in the *General Clauses* section of a legal contract between parties?

A. Distributor and Reseller Fees

B. Defining the Professional Service

C. Government Restricted Rights

D. Delivery, Acceptance, and Rejection

E. None of the Above

10. The best way to avoid arguments in a business relationship is To ___________ the expectations of the parties' ahead of time.

A. Negotiate

B. Write Down

C. Reject

D. Lessen

E. None of the Above

11. Which choice below is an example of a topic that may be covered in the *Boilerplate Clauses* section of a legal contract between parties?

A. Introductions and Recitals

B. Alternative Dispute Resolution

C. Non-Compete and Non-Solicit

D. Due Dates and Invoices

E. None of the Above

12. When formulating the ___________ contract you can, and should, specify what will happen if one of the parties violates the contract.

A. Business

B. Technical

C. Initial

D. Operational

E. None of the Above

13. Information Technology contracts can be organized into three groups: *capacity*, *mutuality of obligation*, and *acceptance*.

1. True
2. False

14. The term "General Clauses" is a catch-all category that refers to issues not addressed in a *Primary* or *Boilerplate Clause*.

1. True
2. False

15. In negotiation, parties often reach impasse because they have different beliefs about the likelihood of winning the case.

1. True
2. False

16. When reviewing contracts and service level agreements, consider the use of checklists to help ensure a consistent approach.

1. True
2. False

17. You cannot predict what issues may arise in a business relationship, so you cannot know when *Primary Clauses* will become vital.

1. True
2. False

18. The one characteristic shared by all elements of *General Clauses* is that they generate the most disagreement, debate, and compromise.

1. True
2. False

DOMAIN 16

Creating Playbooks and Testing Scenarios

Response Playbook Components

An *Incident Response Playbook* is a set of rules, describing at least one action to be executed with data and triggered by one or more events. The typical components included in a response playbook are listed below.

1. Initiating Condition
2. Process Steps
3. Best Practices
4. Local Policies
5. End State Goals
6. Regulatory and Compliance Requirements

Response Playbook Characteristics

Review the playbook quarterly, making updates and adjustments accordingly, and schedule annual tests to identify any existing gaps. Playbooks should have the characteristics listed below. In order to be as effective as possible.

1. Highly Detailed but Very Flexible
2. Effective Communication is Addressed
3. Presented in an Understandable Format
4. Inclusive of all Stakeholders
5. Tested and Validated Consistently
6. Always Accessible to Stakeholders

Building a Response Playbook

Many organizations never evaluate or test response capabilities to determine if the processes will satisfy the desired end state outcomes. The following steps are required to build the playbook but will have little value if it's never tested.

1. Identify the Initiating Condition
2. List All Potential Resulting Outcomes
3. List Required and Optional Actions
4. Build the Playbook with Required Actions First
5. Insert the Optional Actions if Needed

6. Identify the End State Goals of the Response
7. List the Regulatory Issues Satisfied by the Playbook

Common Playbook Response Scenarios

Organizations test response capabilities to determine the effectiveness of the processes and to identify potential weaknesses or deficiencies. The examples provided below will assist the team in the creation of practical testing scenarios.

1. Phishing Emails
2. Malware Outbreaks
3. Data Theft
4. Denial of Service
5. Unauthorized Access
6. Escalation of Privilege
7. Improper System Usage

Planning Table-Top Exercises

Table-Top Exercises generally take the form of a discussion-based exercise and reviews roles, responsibilities, and response efforts. The scope and breadth of the exercises will be determined by the incident in question and the needs of the organization.

The Incident Response Team should take the time and effort to thoroughly prepare for the exercise. Ensuring that the test scenarios are relevant will help to provide more engagement from the exercise participants.

Involving multiple functional units within the organization will add depth to the exercise, provide a higher level of expertise and scrutiny, and more closely resemble the composition of a team during an actual incident.

Ensure the exercise rules and guidelines are known by all the participants, observers, and the members of senior leadership involved. Not knowing the rules and guidelines—or having various groups operating with different rules and standards—will cause frustration for the participants and undermine the validity of the test outcome.

Leverage existing industry resources if possible—such as alerting, analysis, and logging reports—if the organization will utilize the functionality during an actual event. In addition to adding a sense of realism to the exercise this will also allow participants to become familiar with these types of reports.

Once the exercises and the subsequent evaluations have been completed, review the playbook for any gaps that are discovered. It is recommended that participants be asked to evaluate the exercise itself to ensure the testing and real-world outcomes will be aligned as closely as possible.

Planning Simulated Attacks

A *simulated attack* is the most effective way of testing the response processes as it uses real, controlled attacks to measure testing outcomes. It is the most resource-intensive method as it involves all the components of the team and the systems that will be supporting their incident response initiatives.

The exercises is typically conducted from an actual command center using all of the protocols—such as command and control, communications, and status reporting—that will be used during a real-world event.

The simulated attack exercise should be designed to test and evaluate the teams' incident response procedures and the effective implementation of the procedures as well. If the simulated attack exercise results in a successful outcome, the test will validate the playbook in its current form.

If the exercise does not yield successful results, the test will definitively reveal the gaps that must be addressed prior to an actual incident. The planners of this type of exercise should consider the benefits of incorporating Response Orchestration Platforms into the testing scenario.

Benefits of Implementing SOAR

Security Orchestration, Automation, and Response (SOAR) platforms allow an organization to collect data about threats—and in many circumstances—respond without the need for human assistance. The ability to augment the process with automated threat intelligence reporting further allows the Incident Response Team to resolve security alters proactively.

The SOAR platforms are designed to generate automatic metrics and reporting, enhancing the standardization of incident response process within all components of the team. Additionally, the use of automation to power the teams' event orchestration can increase the overall incident response capability significantly.

DOMAIN 16

Creating Playbooks and Testing Scenarios

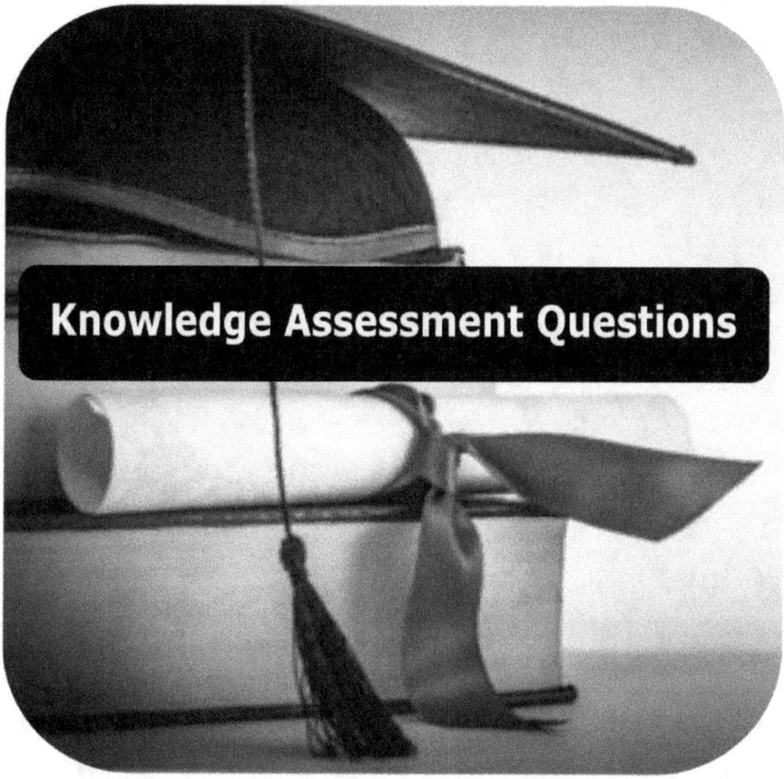

The following knowledge assessment questions are presented as true / false, multiple choice, and fill-in-the-blank. The correct answers are provided in an Answer Key at the end of this text. These questions may or may not be presented on the actual certification exam.

Domain 16: Knowledge Assessment Questions

1. Which choice below is a potential benefit for Incident Response Teams when implementing a SOAR solution?

A. Enhanced Response with Threat Intelligence

B. Resolve Security Alerts Reactively

C. Manual Metrics and Reporting

D. Enhanced Response with Unique Processes

E. None of the Above

2. A(n) __________ is a set of rules, describing at least one action to be executed with data and triggered by one or more events.

A. Corporate Security Policy

B. Acceptable Use Policy

C. Malware Analysis Plan

D. Incident Response Playbook

E. None of the Above

3. Which choice below is **not** a characteristic of simulated attack exercises that should be considered when creating testing scenarios?

A. Conducted from Command Center

B. Testing of Teams' Procedures

C. Testing of Teams' Implementation

D. Least Resource-Intensive Method

E. None of the Above

4. Organizations __________ incident response capabilities to determine the effectiveness of the processes and to identify potential weaknesses or deficiencies.

A. Create

B. Implement

C. Test

D. Document

E. None of the Above

5. Which choice below is a likely scenario that an Incident Response Team should consider including in the response playbook?

A. Proper System Usage

B. Biological Attacks

C. Unauthorized Access

D. Chemical Hazards

E. None of the Above

6. Review the response playbook __________, make required updates and adjustments accordingly, and schedule annual tests to identify any existing gaps.

A. Monthly

B. Quarterly

C. Annually

D. Occasionally

E. None of the Above

7. Which choice below is **not** a characteristic that should be considered when creating an incident response playbook?

A. Effective Communication is Addressed

B. Highly Detailed but Very Structured

C. Presented in Understandable Format

D. Tested and Validated Consistently

E. None of the Above

8. __________ exercises will generally take the form of a discussion-based exercise and reviews roles, responsibilities, and response efforts.

A. Table-Top

B. Walk-Through

C. Parallel

D. Simulated Attack

E. None of the Above

9. Which choice below is an important component of an incident response playbook that should be included in all scenarios?

A. Process Steps

B. Terminating Condition

C. National Policies

D. Initiating State Goals

E. None of the Above

10. A __________ exercise is the most effective way of testing the response processes as it uses real, controlled attacks to measure outcomes.

A. Table-Top

B. Walk-Through

C. Parallel

D. Simulated Attack

E. None of the Above

11. Which choice below is a characteristic of table-top exercises that should be considered when creating testing scenarios?

A. Tests and Validates the Playbook

B. Involves all Components of the Team

C. Conducted from Command Center

D. Least Resource-Intensive Method

E. None of the Above

12. __________ allows an organizations' Incident Response Team to collect data about threats and respond without human assistance.

A. Security Information and Event Management

B. Automated Dynamic Malware Analysis

C. Security Orchestration, Automation, and Response

D. Indicator of Compromise Generation

E. None of the Above

13. A simulated attack is the most effective way of testing the response processes as it uses real, controlled attacks to measure outcomes.

1. True
2. False

14. Table-Top exercises generally take the form of an event-based exercise and assigns roles, responsibilities, and response efforts.

1. True
2. False

15. Organizations test response capabilities to determine the effectiveness of the processes and to identify potential weaknesses or deficiencies.

1. True
2. False

16. The majority of organizations frequently evaluate or test response capabilities to determine if the processes will satisfy the desired end state outcomes.

1. True
2. False

17. Review the response playbook annually, making updates and adjustments accordingly, and schedule monthly tests to identify any existing gaps.

1. True
2. False

18. An Incident Response Playbook is a set of rules, describing at least one action to be executed with data and triggered by one or more events.

1. True
2. False

Certified Cyber Security Operations Manager

Knowledge Assessment Questions ANSWER KEY

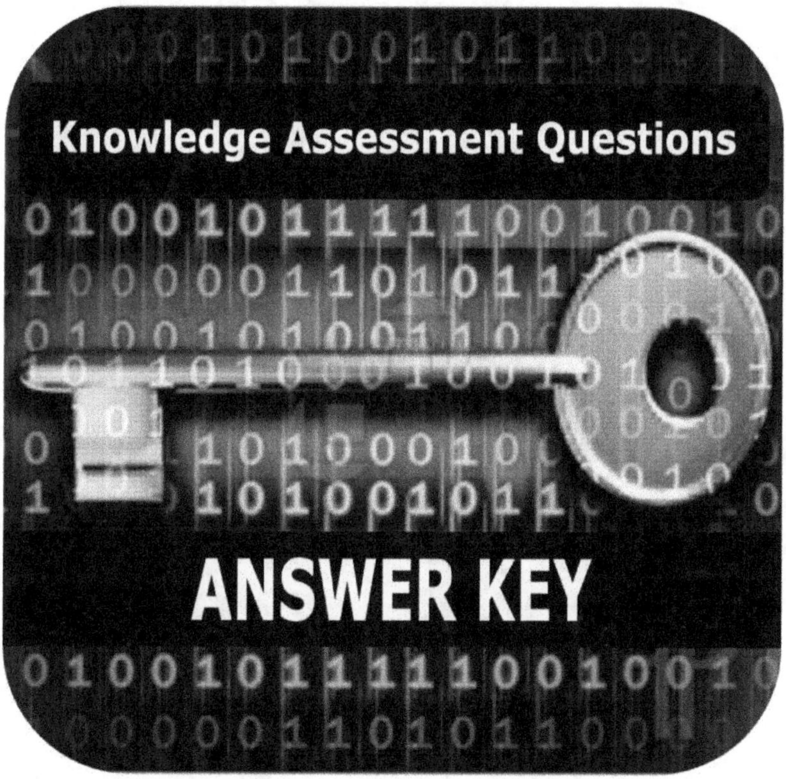

Domain 01: Knowledge Assessment Answer Key

1. Which of the choices listed below presents a day-to-day challenge for organizations implementing the NICE Framework?

C. Bottom-Up Implementation

Bottom-up implementation presents a day-to-day challenge for organizations implementing the NICE Framework.

2. Each __________ represents an area of concentrated work, or function, within cybersecurity and related work.

B. Specialty Area

Each Specialty Area represents an area of concentrated work, or function, within cybersecurity and related work.

3. Select the best choice below for the following definition: *"A specific defined piece of work that, combined with other identified Tasks, composes the work in a specific specialty area or work role."*

D. Task

A task is a specific defined piece of work that, combined with other identified Tasks, composes the work in a specific specialty area or work role.

4. The __________ Category identifies, analyzes, and mitigates threats to internal information technology (IT) systems and/or networks.

C. Protect and Defend

The Protect and Defend Category identifies, analyzes, and mitigates threats to internal information technology (IT) systems and/or networks.

5. Which choice listed below is one of the first six knowledge points common to all work roles in the NICE Framework?

D. Impacts of Cyber Security Lapses

Domain 01: *The NICE Cybersecurity Workforce Framework*

The impact of cyber security lapses is one of the first six knowledge points common to all work roles in the NICE Framework

6. __________ are the attributes required to perform work roles and are generally demonstrated through relevant experience, education, or training.

C. Knowledge, Skills, and Abilities

Knowledge, skills, and abilities are the attributes required to perform work roles and are generally demonstrated through relevant experience, education, or training.

7. Select the best choice below for the following definition: "*Identifies, analyzes, and mitigates threats to internal information technology (IT) systems and/or networks*."

C. Protect and Defend

The Protect and Defend Category identifies, analyzes, and mitigates threats to internal information technology (IT) systems and/or networks.

8. The __________ Category provides leadership, management, direction, or development and advocacy so the organization may effectively conduct cybersecurity work.

D. Oversee and Govern

The Oversee and Govern Category provides leadership, management, direction, or development and advocacy so the organization may effectively conduct cybersecurity work.

9. Which choice listed below is one of the six critical observable competencies listed as skill points in the NICE Framework?

A. Analyzing Network Traffic Capacity

Analyzing network traffic capacity is one of the six critical observable competencies listed as skill points in the NICE Framework.

10. A __________ is a specific defined piece of work that, combined with other identified Tasks, composes the work in a specific specialty area or work role.

D. Task

A task is a specific defined piece of work that, combined with other identified Tasks, composes the work in a specific specialty area or work role.

11. Select the best choice below for the following definition: "*Competence to perform an observable behavior or a behavior that results in an observable product*."

B. Ability

Ability is the competence to perform an observable behavior or a behavior that results in an observable product.

12. The __________ Category performs highly-specialized review and evaluation of incoming cybersecurity information to determine its usefulness for intelligence.

A. Analyze

The Analyze Category performs highly-specialized review and evaluation of incoming cybersecurity information to determine its usefulness for intelligence.

13. NICE is committed to cultivating an integrated cybersecurity workforce that is globally competitive from "hire to retire."

1. True

14. An integrated cyber workforce consists of only technical roles that are staffed with knowledgeable and experienced people.

2. False

An integrated cyber workforce includes technical and nontechnical roles that are staffed with knowledgeable and experienced people.

15. NICE promotes national initiatives that increase the number of people with the knowledge, skills, and abilities to perform required tasks.

1. True

16. An integrated workforce can address challenges by preparing organizations to implement their policies and vision statements.

1. True

17. The NICE Framework will strengthen an organizations' ability to communicate consistently and clearly about its cybersecurity workforce.

1. True

18. The NICE Framework organizes business processes and related work and defines its profit potential in support of those areas.

2. False

The NICE Framework organizes cybersecurity and related work and defines its core components in support of those areas.

Domain 02: Knowledge Assessment Answer Key

1. Which choice below is a function and/or characteristic typically associated with physical tokens used for two-factor authentication?

C. Synchronized with Server

Synchronization with a server is a characteristic typically associated with physical tokens used for two-factor authentication.

2. __________ is a suite of protocols that provides authentication, integrity, and confidentiality within Windows systems.

D. New Technology LAN Manager

New Technology LAN Manager is a suite of protocols that provides authentication, integrity, and confidentiality within Windows systems.

3. Select the best choice below for the following definition: "*An authentication protocol that uses tickets to allow communication over a network to prove identity in a secure manner.*"

D. Kerberos

Kerberos is an authentication protocol that uses tickets to allow communication over a network to prove identity in a secure manner.

4. __________ is a directory service for Windows domain networks that is included in most Windows Server operating systems.

C. Active Directory

Active Directory is a directory service for Windows domain networks that is included in most Windows Server operating systems.

5. Which choice below is a message used by Microsoft New Technology LAN Manager in its challenge / response process of authentication?

A. NEGOTIATE_MESSAGE

NEGOTIATE_MESSAGE is a message used by Microsoft New Technology LAN Manager in its challenge / response process of authentication.

6. __________ specifies formats and methods to query a directories (databases of objects).

B. Lightweight Directory Access Protocol

Lightweight Directory Access Protocol specifies formats and methods to query a directories (databases of objects).

7. Select the best choice below for the following definition: "*Uses object labels to determine access levels and is the strictest of all control models."*

B. Mandatory Access Control

Mandatory Access Control uses object labels to determine access levels and is the strictest of all control models.

8. __________ refers to the ability of a user to log on or access multiple systems by providing credentials only once.

A. Single Sign-On

Single Sign-On is the ability of a user to log on or access multiple systems by providing credentials only once.

9. Which choice below is a function and/or characteristic typically associated with geolocation technologies used to identify users?

C. Uses IP and/or MAC Addresses

The use of IP and/or MAC addresses is a function and/or characteristic typically associated with geolocation technologies used to identify users.

10. __________ serves as an authentication layer positioned on top of the OAuth 2 authorization framework.

B. OpenID Connect

OpenID Connect serves as an authentication layer positioned on top of the OAuth 2 authorization framework.

11. Select the best choice below for the following definition: *"Ensures only authenticated and authorized individuals with proper permissions can access system resources."*

D. Access Control Model

An Access Control Model ensures only authenticated and authorized individuals with proper permissions can access system resources.

12. __________ ensures access is allowed or denied to resources based on a set of rules defined by a system administrator.

C. Rule-Based Access Control

Rule-based access control ensures access is allowed or denied to resources based on a set of rules defined by a system administrator.

13. Authentication, authorization, and accounting (AAA) work together with prioritization to provide a comprehensive access management system.

2. False

Authentication, authorization, and accounting (AAA) work together with identification to provide a comprehensive access management system.

14. Multiple factors may be implemented for basic authentication, two factors for more security, and one factor for maximum security.

2. False

One factor may be implemented for basic authentication, two factors for more security, and multiple factors for maximum security.

15. A strong password has enough length, does not include words found in a dictionary or name, and combines four types of characters.

1. True

16. It is important to provide adequate training to users on password security if they use passwords within the organizations.

1. True

17. Password policies typically start as a verbal directive that identifies the organizations' security goals related to passwords.

2. False

Password policies typically start as a written document that identifies the organizations' security goals related to passwords.

18. A Time-Based One-Time Password (TOTP) is a persistent passcode that uses the current time of day as one of its identification factors.

2. False

A Time-Based One-Time Password (TOTP) is a temporary passcode that uses the current time of day as one of its authentication factors.

Domain 03: Knowledge Assessment Answer Key

1. Which choice below is a factor to be considered when selecting a specific biometric technology with a specific application?

B. Accepted by the Public

Acceptance by the public is a factor to be considered when selecting a specific biometric technology with a specific application.

2. Technologies used to store and process voice prints typically include frequency estimation, pattern-matching algorithms, and ___________.

D. Neural Networks

Technologies used to store and process voice prints typically include frequency estimation, pattern-matching algorithms, and neural networks.

3. Select the best choice below for the following definition: "*The traces of an impression from the friction ridges of any part of a human hand.*"

C. Fingerprints

Fingerprints are the traces of an impression from the friction ridges of any part of a human hand.

4. Iris recognition is a relatively new technology and is incompatible with the substantial investments made in ___________ recognition systems.

C. Fingerprint

Iris recognition is a relatively new technology and is incompatible with the substantial investments made in fingerprint recognition systems.

5. Which choice below is a system of manual fingerprint classification that was created in India and based on three basic fingerprint patterns?

D. Henry

The Henry System of manual fingerprint classification was created in India and based on three basic fingerprint patterns.

6. A(n) __________ recognition system is an application capable of identifying or verifying a person from a digital image or video frame image.

B. Facial

A facial recognition system is an application capable of identifying or verifying a person from a digital image or video frame image.

7. Select the best choice below for the following definition: "*A biometric scanning technique that uses the unique patterns of a persons' blood vessels in the retina.*"

A. Retinal Imaging

Retinal imaging is a biometric scanning technique that uses the unique patterns of a persons' blood vessels in the retina.

8. __________ is the ability of electrical conductors and insulators to store an electric charge when a potential difference in voltage exists.

A. Capacitance

Capacitance is the ability of electrical conductors and insulators to store an electric charge when a potential difference in voltage exists.

9. Which choice below is a reason the iris of the eye has been described as the ideal part of the human body for biometric identification?

B. Well-Protected Internal Organ

The iris of the eye has been described as the ideal part of the human body for biometric identification because it is a well-protected internal organ.

10. __________ classification systems are based on the general friction ridge patterns of several (or all) fingers.

D. Manual

Manual classification systems are based on the general friction ridge patterns of several (or all) fingers.

11. Select the best choice below for the following definition: "*The ability of an electronic security device to recognize the voice (as unique as a fingerprint) of an individual.*"

C. Voice Recognition

The ability of an electronic security device to recognize the voice of an individual is called voice recognition.

12. Soft biometric traits are defined as __________, behavioral, or adhered characteristics that are derived from the way humans distinguish their peers.

C. Physical

Soft biometric traits are defined as physical, behavioral, or adhered characteristics that are derived from the way humans distinguish their peers.

13. The first time a person uses a biometric system is called registration, at which time biometric information is captured and stored.

2. False

The first time a person uses a biometric system is called enrollment, at which time biometric information is captured and stored.

14. Unimodal biometric systems use multiple sensors or biometrics to overcome the limitations of multimodal biometric systems.

2. False

Multimodal biometric systems use multiple sensors or biometrics to overcome the limitations of unimodal biometric systems.

15. Soft biometric traits are physical, behavioral, or adhered characteristics that are derived from the way humans distinguish their peers.

1. True

16. Ultrasonic fingerprint imaging involves using specialized electronic devices to capture a digital image of the print using visible light.

2. False

Optical fingerprint imaging involves using specialized electronic devices to capture a digital image of the print using visible light.

17. A facial recognition system is an application capable of identifying or verifying a person from a digital image or video frame image.

1. True

18. Keystroke dynamics is the detailed timing information which describes when each key was pressed and when it was released.

1. True

Domain 04: Knowledge Assessment Answer Key

1. Which choice below is one of the several key management issues associated with symmetric key encryption that can make implementation impractical?

D. Does not Scale Well

One of the several key management issues associated with symmetric key encryption that can make implementation impractical is its inability to scale well.

2. Hexadecimal characters are composed of __________ bits and use the numbers "0-9" and the characters "a-f."

B. Four

Hexadecimal characters are composed of four bits and use the numbers "0-9" and the characters "a-f."

3. Select the best choice below for the following definition: "*The required components for encryption and decryption operations (software, protocols, algorithms, keys).*"

C. Cryptosystem

The required components for encryption and decryption operations (software, protocols, algorithms, keys) is called a cryptosystem.

4. A(n) __________ is a fixed-length string of bits like other hashing algorithms such as MD5 and SHA-1 (HMAC-MD5 and HMAC-SHA1).

C. Hash-Base Message Authentication Code

A Hash-Based Message Authentication Code is a fixed-length string of bits like other hashing algorithms such as MD5 and SHA-1 (HMAC-MD5 and HMAC-SHA1).

5. Which choice below is one of the advantages associated with asymmetric encryption that cannot be provided by symmetric encryption?

B. No "Out-of-Band" Key Exchange

One of the advantages associated with asymmetric encryption that cannot be provided by symmetric encryption is that no out-of-band key exchange is required.

6. __________ is an encryption methodology that uses a single key to encrypt (encode) and decrypt (decode) data.

D. Symmetric Encryption

Symmetric encryption is an encryption methodology that uses a single key to encrypt (encode) and decrypt (decode) data.

7. Select the best choice below for the following definition: "*An attacker can perform both encryption queries and decryption queries for accessed plaintext and ciphertext messages.*"

A. Chosen-Ciphertext Attack

In a Chosen-Ciphertext attack, an attacker can perform both encryption queries and decryption queries for accessed plaintext and ciphertext messages.

8. The two methods used for encryption and decryption, regardless of the degree of algorithmic complexity, are __________ and transposition.

A. Substitution

The two methods used for encryption and decryption, regardless of the degree of algorithmic complexity, are substitution and transposition.

9. Which choice below is one of the advantages associated with the symmetric encryption method known as "Diffie-Hellman Key Exchange"?

D. No Prior Relationship Required

One of the advantages associated with the symmetric encryption method known as "Diffie-Hellman Key Exchange" is no prior relationship between the parties is required.

10. A __________ encrypts data as a stream of bits or bytes rather than dividing the data into blocks of specific sizes.
B. Stream Cipher

A stream cipher encrypts data as a stream of bits or bytes rather than dividing the data into blocks of specific sizes.

11. Select the best choice below for the following definition: "*An authentication process that verifies a message was sent from a legitimate user of an email address.*"
C. DomainKeys Identified Mail

DomainKeys Identified Mail is an authentication process that verifies a message was sent from a legitimate user of an email address.

12. __________ is an authentication system designed to prevent email spoofing by verifying that domain IP addresses are valid.
C. Sender Policy Framework

Sender Policy Framework is an authentication system designed to prevent email spoofing by verifying that domain IP addresses are valid.

13. A Chosen-Ciphertext Attack forces a target system to downgrade its security and allow an attacker to exploit the lesser level of security control.
2. False

A Downgrade Attack forces a target system to downgrade its security and allow an attacker to exploit the lesser level of security control.

14. Hashing is an algorithm performed on data to produce a number called a hash (also referred to as a checksum).
1. True

15. The Certificate Directory is a function of the Certificate Authority that is responsible for storing and safeguarding issued certificates.

1. True

16. The *Inclusive AND* operation is used extensively because it can be used to encrypt or decrypt easily and quickly.

2. False

The Exclusive OR operation is used extensively because it can be used to encrypt or decrypt easily and quickly.

17. A Known-Plaintext attacker has access to both ciphertext and plaintext forms of a message and employs analysis to determine the key.

1. True

18. Key Stretching (or the length of the key) represents all possible values that can be used to generate a cryptographic key.

2. False

The Key Space (or the length of the key) represents all possible values that can be used to generate a cryptographic key.

Domain 05: Knowledge Assessment Answer Key

1. Which choice below is a characteristic of *The Open Group Architecture Framework* that provides an approach for developing enterprise architecture?

D. Defines System Components

The defining of system components is a characteristic of *The Open Group Architecture Framework* that provides an approach for developing enterprise architecture.

2. Modern networks and usage patterns no longer resemble those that made traditional __________ a practical solution years ago.

A. Perimeter Defense

Modern networks and usage patterns no longer resemble those that made traditional perimeter defense a practical solution years ago.

3. Select the best choice below for the following definition: "*An enterprise ontology that provides a fundamental and formalized structure for enterprise architecture.*"

C. Zachman Framework

The Zachman Framework is an enterprise ontology that provides a fundamental and formalized structure for enterprise architecture.

4. The ___________ identifies and defines the organizations' strategy, governance, structure, goals, and key business processes.

B. Business Architecture

The business architecture identifies and defines the organizations' strategy, governance, structure, goals, and key business processes.

5. Which choice below is a potential risk and/or attack vector associated with Zero Trust Networks that can undermine its utility?

B. Control Plane Security

Control plane security is a potential risk and/or attack vector associated with Zero Trust Networks that can undermine its utility.

6. __________ is/are complex technological components of security architecture that are crucial for the protection of information assets.

C. Cryptographic Services

Cryptographic services are complex technological components of security architecture that are crucial for the protection of information assets.

7. Select the best choice below for the following definition: *"Describes the hardware, software, and network infrastructure needed to support the deployment of a solution."*

A. Technology Architecture

The technology architecture describes the hardware, software, and network infrastructure needed to support the deployment of a solution.

8. The __________ is where most vulnerabilities are presented and the greatest effort in reducing vulnerabilities is expended.

D. Application Layer

The Application layer is where most vulnerabilities are presented and the greatest effort in reducing vulnerabilities is expended.

9. Which choice below is one of the six phases comprising the Software Development Life Cycle (SDLC)?

D. Planning

Planning is one of the six phases comprising the Software Development Life Cycle (SDLC).

10. A(n) __________ is a document which provides recommended integrations of products and services to form a solution.

A. Reference Security Architecture

A Reference Security Architecture is a document which provides recommended integrations of products and services to form a solution.

11. Select the best choice below for the following definition: *"Complex technological components of security architecture that are crucial for the protection of information assets."*

C. Cryptographic Services

Cryptographic services are complex technological components of security architecture that are crucial for the protection of information assets.

12. The __________ documents solution deployments, system interactions, and their relationships to core business processes.

D. Application Architecture

The application architecture documents solution deployments, system interactions, and their relationships to core business processes.

13. The TOGAF Framework is an enterprise ontology that provides a fundamental and formalized structure for enterprise architecture.

2. False

The Zachman Framework is an enterprise ontology that provides a fundamental and formalized structure for enterprise architecture.

14. The granularity of data stored within a trust agent can vary based on the needs of the organization and maturity of the system.

1. True

15. Border protection is typically thought of as the component technological devices that provide security at the transport layer.

2. False

Border protection is typically thought of as the component technological devices that provide security at the network layer.

16. Technology architecture describes the hardware, software, and network infrastructure needed to support the deployment of a solution.

1. True

17. Identity management is implemented to ensure that a solution remains in the configuration for which is was originally intended.

2. False

Configuration management is implemented to ensure that a solution remains in the configuration for which is was originally intended.

18. The perimeter model attempts to build a wall between trusted and untrusted sources; zero trust assumes all actors are malicious.

1. True

Domain 06: Knowledge Assessment Answer Key

1. Which choice below is an issue that must be taken into consideration when measuring network baselines?

A. Business Cycles

Business cycles is an issue that must be taken into consideration when measuring network baselines.

2. Teams interested in ___________ IOC's should consider *YARA*, Mitre's *CybOX*, and FireEye's *OpenIOC* solutions as options.

A. Host-Based

Teams interested in host-based IOC's should consider *YARA*, Mitre's *CybOX*, and FireEye's *OpenIOC* solutions as options.

3. Which choice below must be considered due to the affect it may have on the placement of network monitoring sensors?

B. Network Bandwidth

Network bandwidth must be considered due to the affect it may have on the placement of network monitoring sensors.

4. ___________ focuses on the high-level view of what flows, or connections, are traversing the network.

D. Statistical Monitoring

Statistical monitoring focuses on the high-level view of what flows, or connections, are traversing the network.

5. Which choice below is a condition which makes statistical monitoring an optimal approach for incident investigators?

C. Characteristics of Beaconing

Characteristics of beaconing is a condition which makes statistical monitoring an optimal approach for incident investigators.

6. The placement of the network ___________ is possibly the most important factor in setting up an effective monitoring system.

B. Sensor

The placement of the network sensor is possibly the most important factor in setting up an effective monitoring system.

7. Which choice below is **not** an objective to be considered when establishing network baseline measurement objectives?

D. Business Capacity

Business capacity does not represent an objective to be considered when establishing network baseline measurement objectives.

8. ___________ alerting is the form of monitoring to which most Incident Response and IT personnel are accustomed.

A. Event-Based

Event-based alerting is the form of monitoring to which most Incident Response and IT personnel are accustomed.

9. Which tool listed below is uniquely useful to Incident Response Teams conducting full packet captures on a network?

C. Wireshark Analyzer

The Wireshark network analyzer is uniquely useful to Incident Response Teams conducting full packet captures on a network.

10. Indicator generation is a(n) ___________ process with a goal of creating robust, sustainable signatures to generate reliable information.

C. Iterative

Indicator generation is an iterative process with a goal of creating robust, sustainable signatures to generate reliable information.

11. Which choice below considered to be the last phase of the Indicator Generation Life Cycle?

A. Publish

Publishing the IOC is considered to be the last phase of the Indicator Generation Life Cycle.

12. __________ rules help in differentiating between normal internet activities and malicious activities in real time.

D. Snort

Snort rules help in differentiating between normal internet activities and malicious activities in real time.

13. Baselining is the practice of establishing performance, usage, and behavioral norms for systems and networks.

1. True

14. Event-based monitoring relies on alerts (or warnings) matched against traffic observed by the network sensor.

2. False

Event-based monitoring relies on indicators (or signatures) matched against traffic observed by the network sensor.

15. Network maintenance typically includes configuration management, fault management, performance, security, and account management.

1. True

16. Ensure that the properties of a new indicator can identify the malware or activity solely at a specific point in the life cycle.

2. False

Ensure that the properties of a new indicator do not identify the malware or activity solely at a specific point in the life cycle.

17. Intrusion Detection System platforms cannot reliably perform both intrusion detection services and network surveillance duties simultaneously.

1. True

18. Prioritization during IOC investigations is based on two specific factors: the criticality of data and the business processes affected.

2. False

Prioritization during IOC investigations is based on numerous factors, not just the criticality of data and/or the business processes affected.

Domain 07: Knowledge Assessment Answer Key

1. Which choice below is a tactic an attacker may choose to use in Stage 01 of the Attack Life Cycle to execute the initial compromise?

D. Social Engineering

Social engineering is a tactic an attacker may choose to use in Stage 01 of the Attack Life Cycle to execute the initial compromise.

2. Effective Incident Response requires a two-pronged approach: incident __________ and incident remediation.

D. Investigation

Effective Incident Response requires a two-pronged approach: incident investigation and incident remediation.

3. Which choice below is a tactic an attacker may choose to use in Stage 05 of the Attack Life Cycle to move laterally in the network?

C. Access Windows Task Scheduler

Accessing the Windows Task Scheduler is a tactic an attacker may choose to use in Stage 05 of the Attack Life Cycle to move laterally in the network.

4. Regardless of the type of incident encountered, there are typically __________ common factors specific to each incident that must be considered.

C. Seven

Regardless of the type of incident encountered, there are typically seven common factors specific to each incident that must be considered.

5. Which choice below is a tactic an attacker may choose to use in Stage 03 of the Attack Life Cycle to escalate acquired privileges?

A. Keystroke / Credential Logging

Keystroke and credential logging are tactics an attacker may choose to use in Stage 03 of the Attack Life Cycle to escalate acquired privileges.

6. ___________ actions are taken during an ongoing incident and are designed to be implemented with minimum impact on the attacker.

B. Posturing

Posturing actions are taken during an ongoing incident and are designed to be implemented with minimum impact on the attacker.

7. Which choice below is a tactic an attacker may choose to use in Stage 06 of the Attack Life Cycle to maintain a presence?

B. Access Virtual Private Networks

Accessing Virtual Private Networks is a tactic an attacker may choose to use in Stage 06 of the Attack Life Cycle to maintain a presence.

8. ___________ actions are implemented during a short period of time to remove the attacker from the environment.

A. Eradication

Eradication actions are implemented during a short period of time to remove the attacker from the environment.

9. Which choice below is a tactic an attacker may choose to use in Stage 02 of the Attack Life Cycle to establish a foothold?

C. Install a Persistent Backdoor

Installation of a persistent backdoor is a tactic an attacker may choose to use in Stage 02 of the Attack Life Cycle to establish a foothold.

10. An ideal time to execute the eradication event is when the team has properly __________ the compromise and has implemented posturing actions.

D. Scoped

An ideal time to execute the eradication event is when the team has properly scoped the compromise and has implemented posturing actions.

11. Which choice below is a tactic an attacker may choose to use in Stage 04 of the Attack Life Cycle to conduct internal reconnaissance?

D. Identify Key Responsibilities

Identifying key responsibilities of system users is a tactic an attacker may choose to use in Stage 04 of the Attack Life Cycle to conduct internal reconnaissance.

12. Once the networking actions have been completed, the system and application administrators can start __________ compromised systems.

C. Remediating

Once the networking actions have been completed, the system and application administrators can start remediating compromised systems.

13. Incident Response is a linear, sequential system whose processes are initiated in parallel execution and iterate occasionally.

2. False

Incident Response is a non-linear, cyclical system whose processes are initiated in parallel execution and iterate continuously.

14. Although it may be tempting to make wide, sweeping changes to improve the organizations' security posture, is not advisable to do so.

1. True

15. Incident Response is a coordinated and structured approach to manage incidents from detection to resolution.

1. True

16. The remediation owner delegates responsibility for the remediation effort and interacts exclusively with technical personnel.

2. False

The remediation owner accepts responsibility for the remediation effort and interacts with both technical and non-technical personnel.

17. The planning process for the eradication event should start as soon as executive management has decided upon a remediation approach.

2. False

The planning process for the eradication event should start as soon as the incident owner has decided upon a remediation approach.

18. Taking actions that alert attackers that they have been discovered is usually considered detrimental to the investigation.

1. True

Domain 08: Knowledge Assessment Answer Key

1. Which choice below presents a challenge to system and network administrators attempting to access data that has been collected?
D. Data may be Encoded

Encoded data presents a challenge to system and network administrators attempting to access data that has been collected.

2. It is important to note that operating system settings can greatly affect the __________, leaving questions unanswered.
C. Available Evidence

It is important to note that operating system settings can greatly affect the available evidence, leaving questions unanswered.

3. Select the best choice below for the following definition: *"Leftover storage that can be found on a hard drive when the system does not need all the space being allocated for the file."*
A. Slack Space

Slack space is leftover storage that can be found on a hard drive when the system does not need all the space being allocated for the file.

4. Maintaining the __________ of the device being secured is critical for capturing all available data and not modifying the device itself.
B. Power State

Maintaining the power state of the device being secured is critical for capturing all available data and not modifying the device itself.

5. Which choice below is a location of potentially volatile data that should be collected as quickly as possible during an investigation?
B. Process Register

Domain 08: *Network and Host Data Collection Methods*

The Process Register is a location of potentially volatile data that should be collected as quickly as possible during an investigation.

6. From an investigative standpoint, the file system is the place where the __________ of the system users will be found.

A. "Fingerprints"

From an investigative standpoint, the file system is the place where the "fingerprints" of the system users will be found.

7. Which choice below is a component of the Windows Registry that should be considered as a potential source of digital evidence?

C. HKEY_CLASSES_ROOT

HKEY_CLASSES_ROOT is a component of the Windows Registry that should be considered as a potential source of digital evidence.

8. A(n) __________ copy of the original endpoint hard drive is needed prior to investigating any data in the file system.

D. Bit-Level

A bit-level copy of the original endpoint hard drive is needed prior to investigating any data in the file system.

9. Which choice below is a characteristic of Microsoft's New Technology File System (NTFS) that presents evidence collection challenges?

D. Reduces Slack Space

The significant reduction of slack space is a characteristic of Microsoft's New Technology File System (NTFS) that presents evidence collection challenges.

10. Many IoT companies are new to networking and tend to focus on the production of products versus dealing with __________.

C. Vulnerabilities

Domain 08: *Network and Host Data Collection Methods*

Many IoT companies are new to networking and tend to focus on the production of products versus dealing with vulnerabilities.

11. What is the first action that should be taken prior to analyzing artifacts, identifying malicious behavior, or looking for indicators of compromise?

A. Copy all System Data

All system data should be copied prior to analyzing artifacts, identifying malicious behavior, or looking for indicators of compromise.

12. Forensic copies of __________ consider all system data, including areas the operating system does not recognize but can still be used.

D. Hard Drives

Forensic copies of hard drives consider all system data, including areas the operating system does not recognize but can still be used.

13. Before analysis can be performed, the team needs to explore possible sources of data and understand how to use them.

1. True

14. The Domain Controller is essentially a database that records virtually every action and activity performed in the operating system.

2. False

The Windows Registry is essentially a database that records virtually every action and activity performed in the operating system.

15. From a technical viewpoint, the Recycle Bin works by moving deleted files into two special directories: RECYCLE and RECYCLE2.

2. False

From a technical viewpoint, the Recycle Bin works by moving deleted files into two special directories: INFO and INFO2.

16. Once data has been obtained to analyze, one of the first challenges likely to be encountered is determining how to access it.

1. True

17. Persistent data is potentially valuable to the incident investigation and can be lost when the device being secured is powered off.

2. False

Volatile data is potentially valuable to the incident investigation and can be lost when the device being secured is powered off.

18. Although every operating system has unique and proprietary sources of evidence, many areas of commonality exist between all of them.

1. True

Domain 09: Knowledge Assessment Answer Key

1. Select the best choice below for the following definition: "*A factual document of findings, with any opinions clearly identified and supported by facts included in the report.*"

A. Investigative Report

An investigative report is a factual document of findings, with any opinions clearly identified and supported by facts included in the report.

2. ___________ define(s) the elements of a claim and are typically driven by the primary consumer of the investigative report.

C. Elements of Proof

Elements of proof define the elements of a claim and are typically driven by the primary consumer of the investigative report.

3. Which choice below refers to any influence that changes, obscures, adds, contaminates, or obliterates evidence regardless of intent?

C. Evidence Dynamics

Evidence dynamics refers to any influence that changes, obscures, adds, contaminates, or obliterates evidence regardless of intent.

4. A(n) ___________ is a systematic inquiry and/or examination, typically conducted for the purpose of identifying and/or verifying facts.

D. Investigation

An investigation is a systematic inquiry and/or examination, typically conducted for the purpose of identifying and/or verifying facts.

5. The non-verbal cue referred to as ___________ can be defined as, "*A pattern in which the sender gives conflicting messages on verbal and nonverbal levels.*"

B. Incongruent Communication

The non-verbal cue referred to as incongruent communication can be defined as, *"A pattern in which the sender gives conflicting messages on verbal and nonverbal levels."*

6. Which choice below refers to the documentation of acquisition, control, analysis, and disposition of physical and digital evidence?

D. Chain of Custody

Chain of custody is the documentation of acquisition, control, analysis, and disposition of physical and digital evidence.

7. The __________ protects people from self-incrimination, meaning giving a statement that might expose oneself to a crime.

A. Fifth Amendment

The Fifth Amendment protects people from self-incrimination, meaning giving a statement that might expose oneself to a crime.

8. Select the best choice below for the following definition: *"A systematic inquiry and/or examination, typically conducted for the purpose of identifying and/or verifying facts."*

B. Investigation

An investigation is a systematic inquiry and/or examination, typically conducted for the purpose of identifying and/or verifying facts.

9. Select the best choice below for the following definition: *"When a person or object comes into contact with another person or object, a cross-transfer of materials occurs."*

C. Locard's Principle of Exchange

Locard's Principle of Exchange states *"when a person or object comes into contact with another person or object, a cross-transfer of materials occurs."*

10. Regardless of the type of investigation being conducted—physical or digital—__________ items should be a part of the investigative toolkit.

C. Standard

Regardless of the type of investigation being conducted—physical or digital—standard items should be a part of the investigative toolkit.

11. What choice below best is the primary purpose and importance of evidence dynamics in incident response investigations?

A. Reconstruction of the Incident

Reconstruction of the incident is the primary purpose of evidence dynamics in incident response investigations.

12. The non-verbal cue referred to as __________ can be defined as, *"The non-lexical component of communication such as intonation, pitch and speed of speaking."*

A. Paralanguage

The non-verbal cue referred to as paralanguage can be defined as, *"The non-lexical component of communication such as intonation, pitch and speed of speaking."*

13. All case types and investigations have the same considerations—whether the goal is litigation or developing a stronger security posture.

2. False

Every case type and investigation has its own considerations—whether the goal is litigation or developing a stronger security posture.

14. Regardless of the type of investigation being conducted—physical or digital—standard items should be a part of the investigative toolkit.

1. True

15. In most investigations, interviews are the primary tool investigators use to find out what happened and/or verify physical and technical evidence.

1. True

16. We respond to thousands of verbal cues and behaviors including postures, facial expression, eye gaze, gestures, and tone of voice.

2. False

We respond to thousands of nonverbal cues and behaviors including postures, facial expression, eye gaze, gestures, and tone of voice.

17. *Nulla poena sine lege* is a universal legal principle, requiring that one cannot be punished for doing something that is not prohibited by law.

1. True

18. An investigation is a systematic inquiry and/or examination, typically conducted for the purpose of identifying and/or verifying assumptions.

2. False

An investigation is a systematic inquiry and/or examination, typically conducted for the purpose of identifying and/or verifying facts.

Domain 10: Knowledge Assessment Answer Key

1. Which choice below is a risk management framework utilized by security managers that is best suited for small projects and one-time assessments?

D. OCTAVE Allegro

OCTAVE Allegro is a risk management framework utilized by security managers that is best suited for small projects and one-time assessments.

2. The __________ rating is meant to describe the scope of the exposure, not list all the potential consequences.

A. Risk Severity

The risk severity rating is meant to describe the scope of the exposure, not list all the potential consequences.

3. Select the best choice below for the following definition: "*A relative measurement of a resources' tolerance for risk exposures, independent of any threat or vulnerability.*"

A. Risk Sensitivity

Risk sensitivity is a relative measurement of a resources' tolerance for risk exposures, independent of any threat or vulnerability.

4. Most __________ approaches use a relative scale to rate risk exposures based on a set of predefined criteria for each level.

D. Qualitative

Most qualitative approaches use a relative scale to rate risk exposures based on a set of predefined criteria for each level.

5. Which choice below is a risk management framework utilized by security managers that uses a detailed quantitative and probabilistic analysis method?

B. FAIR

FAIR is a risk management framework utilized by security managers that uses a detailed quantitative and probabilistic analysis method.

6. Security managers should be involved in all phases of the SLA negotiation process and ensure supporting providers have adequate __________.

C. Controls

Security managers should be involved in all phases of the SLA negotiation process and ensure supporting providers have adequate controls.

7. Select the best choice below for the following definition: "*An event with the capacity to cause damage, disruption, liability, injury, loss, or other negative outcomes.*"

C. Threat

A threat is an event with the capacity to cause damage, disruption, liability, injury, loss, or other negative outcomes.

8. The __________ is supporting confidential information for risk mitigation and should be documented in the asset inventory.

B. Resource Profile

The resource profile is supporting confidential information for risk mitigation and should be documented in the asset inventory.

9. Which choice below is a risk management framework utilized by security managers that is used for Certification and Accreditation?

A. NIST RMF

The NIST RMF is a risk management framework utilized by security managers that is used for Certification and Accreditation.

10. When conducting a risk assessment, ensure that risk evaluation and __________ align with business and organizational needs.

A. Mitigation

When conducting a risk assessment, ensure that risk evaluation and mitigation align with business and organizational needs.

11. Which choice below is an example of a manufactured risk that can cause the process of estimating costs of potential risks challenging?

D. Underground Pipeline

Underground pipelines are an example of a manufactured risk that can cause the process of estimating costs of potential risks challenging.

12. A(n) __________ tends to be a useful tool to identify system weaknesses that may be visible to potential threat sources.

B. Vulnerability Assessment

A vulnerability assessment tends to be a useful tool to identify system weaknesses that may be visible to potential threat sources.

13. Remember the influences of the attributes of threats; mentally layering threats helps to prioritize solutions.

2. False

Remember the influences of the attributes of risk; mentally layering risk helps to prioritize solutions.

14. The basic considerations when determining the value of a specific asset include both projected and value-added costs.

2. False

The basic considerations when determining the value of a specific asset include both tangible and intangible costs.

15. The asset assessment must transcend line-item numbers as the asset value can extend well beyond the actual cost.

1. True

16. Information Security personnel developing risk management programs should focus on critical details and procedures of implementation.

1. True

17. If you are having trouble quantifying the likelihood of a vulnerability, additional useful questions can be asked to improve clarity.

2. False

If you are having trouble qualifying the likelihood of a vulnerability, additional useful questions can be asked to improve clarity.

18. Data availability severity concerns will focus primarily on unauthorized or unintended access to create, read, update, or delete data ("CRUD").

2. False

Integrity severity concerns will focus primarily on unauthorized or unintended access to create, read, update, or delete data ("CRUD").

Domain 11: Knowledge Assessment Answer Key

1. Select the best choice below for the following definition: "*May allow limited access and control of an application, system or any communication, including only certain data or functionality.*"

C. Vulnerability Severity: HIGH

A vulnerability severity level of HIGH may allow limited access and control of an application, system or any communication, including only certain data or functionality.

2. A viable vulnerability assessment and management workflow must be comprised of efficient ___________ and procedures.

D. Processes

A viable vulnerability assessment and management workflow must be comprised of efficient process and procedures.

3. Which choice below is an item that should be corrected when attempting to identify potential vulnerabilities in a network?

A. Default Passwords

A default password is an item that should be corrected when attempting to identify potential vulnerabilities in a network.

4. After vulnerabilities have been categorized by their severity level, a ___________ must be defined to address them.

C. Workflow

After vulnerabilities have been categorized by their severity level, a workflow must be defined to address them.

5. Select the best choice below for the following definition: "*May allow unlimited access and control of an application, system or any communication, including all data and functionality.*"

D. Vulnerability Severity: CRITICAL

A vulnerability level of CRITICAL may allow unlimited access and control of an application, system or any communication, including all data and functionality.

6. Malicious actors often look for systems that are __________, and vulnerability scanners can detect and identify these settings.

B. Misconfigured

Malicious actors often look for systems that are misconfigured, and vulnerability scanners can detect and identify these settings.

7. Which choice below is a characteristic of a credentialed vulnerability scan that would be performed on a network?

C. Generates Fewer False Positives

A characteristic of a credentialed vulnerability scan that would be performed on a network is the generation of fewer false positives.

8. A network __________ uses various techniques to gather information about hosts and other devices within the network.

A. Scanner

A network scanner uses various techniques to gather information about hosts and other devices within the network.

9. Select the best choice below for the following definition: "*May contribute to unauthorized activity or service degradation, but they are limited in scope or impact.*"

B. Vulnerability Severity: MODERATE

A vulnerability severity level of MODERATE may contribute to unauthorized activity or service degradation, but they are limited in scope or impact.

10. IS Managers must have the knowledge to analyze a vulnerability report for details that affect both the __________ and the severity of the potential threat.

D. Likelihood

IS Managers must have the knowledge to analyze a vulnerability report for details that affect both the likelihood and the severity of the potential threat.

11. Which choice below is an essential component to be considered when implementing a vulnerability management program?

D. Create a Workflow for Assessment

An essential component to be considered when implementing a vulnerability management program is creating a workflow for assessment.

12. The __________ of vulnerability assessment and management data at any given time will always present several challenges.

C. Volume

The volume of vulnerability assessment and management data at any given time will always present several challenges.

13. Vulnerability assessments often use a wide variety of scans and will typically include five high-level steps in the assessment process.

1. True

14. A network scanner uses various techniques to gather information about hosts and other devices within the network.

1. True

15. Stateful firewalls typically use both active and passive scans to listen to traffic broadcast on channels in the 2.4 / 5.0 GHz frequencies.

2. False

Wireless scanners typically use both active and passive scans to listen to traffic broadcast on channels in the 2.4 / 5.0 GHz frequencies.

16. The location of vulnerability assessment and management data at any given time will always present several challenges.

2. False

The volume of vulnerability assessment and management data at any given time will always present several challenges.

17. Each threat needs to be profiled to establish a risk sensitivity score before vulnerability assessments can be performed.

2. False

Each asset needs to be profiled to establish a risk sensitivity score before vulnerability assessments can be performed.

18. One of the most fundamental functions in Information Security is performing risk analysis on new vulnerability advisories.

1. True

Domain 12: Knowledge Assessment Answer Key

1. Which choice below can be defined as any incident that seriously disrupts mission-critical business or IT functions?

A. Disaster

A disaster can be defined as any incident that seriously disrupts mission-critical business or IT functions.

2. Whenever an incident occurs that is covered by the BCP, conduct an __________ on the next workday after the recovery.

D. After-Action Review

Whenever an incident occurs that is covered by the BCP, conduct an after-action review on the next workday after the recovery.

3. Select the best choice below for the following definition: "*The absolute maximum time that systems can be unavailable without serious and/or negative impact to the organization.*"

C. Maximum Allowable Downtime

The absolute maximum time that systems can be unavailable without serious and/or negative impact to the organization is called Maximum Allowable Downtime (MAD).

4. As with all things in the business continuity program, begin setting goals for the testing plan by referring to the __________.

C. Business Impact Analysis

As with all things in the business continuity program, begin setting goals for the testing plan by referring to the Business Impact Analysis.

5. Which choice below is a common obstacle for Information Security Managers when defining a desired security state?

D. Mental Accounting

Mental accounting is a common obstacle for Information Security Managers when defining a desired security state.

6. An effective ___________ process will help quantify the value of each function in terms of financial and legal impacts.

B. Data Collection

An effective data collection process will help quantify the value of each function in terms of financial and legal impacts.

7. Select the best choice below for the following definition: *"Examination and evaluation of non-measurable data using subjective judgement and non-quantifiable methods."*

B. Qualitative Analysis

A qualitative analysis is an examination and evaluation of non-measurable data using subjective judgement and non-quantifiable methods.

8. Which choice below is **not** a primary consideration when implementing risk management procedures?

C. Scope, Charter, and Methodology

The scope, charter, and methodology are considerations when initially developing a risk management program and occur in advance of any implementation of procedures.

9. Which testing method listed below is designed to evaluate the BCP with actual systems without the risk of interrupting the business operation?

C. Parallel Test

A parallel test is designed to evaluate the BCP with actual systems without the risk of interrupting the business operation.

10. __________ costs due to the loss of a vital business function can be difficult to identify but are no less damaging.

D. Intangible

Intangible costs due to the loss of a vital business function can be difficult to identify but are no less damaging.

11. Which testing method listed below is designed to train specific team members, identify omissions, and raise general awareness of the BCP?

D. Table-Top Test

A table-top test is designed to train specific team members, identify omissions, and raise general awareness of the BCP.

12. __________ Analysis estimates are never completely accurate despite best efforts; testing measures theory against reality.

C. Business Impact

Business Impact Analysis estimates are never completely accurate despite best efforts; testing measures theory against reality.

13. An effective data collection process will help quantify the value of each function in terms of financial and legal impacts.

1. True

14. Check vacation and travel schedules for all selected respondents to help ensure timely completion of the disaster recovery.

2. False

Check vacation and travel schedules for all selected respondents to help ensure timely completion of the questionnaire.

15. Do not overlook unknowable costs in the questionnaire; unit managers will certainly know the answers to these considerations.

2. False

Do not overlook human costs in the questionnaire; unit managers will certainly know the answers to these considerations.

16. To maximize the benefit to the organization while minimizing costs, develop a written testing strategy for the BCP.

1. True

17. The best BCP testing results come from a clear explanation of the job titles of team members and incidents to show them what to do.

2. False

The best BCP testing results come from a clear explanation of the responsibilities of team members and training to show them what to do.

18. The testing scenario should be focused on the type of problem or disaster that a specific group of people are likely to enjoy.

2. False

The testing scenario should be focused on the type of problem or disaster that a specific group of people are likely to experience.

Domain 13: Knowledge Assessment Answer Key

1. What phase of the Threat Intelligence Life Cycle is composed of all activities that identify information requirements and ensure requirements are met?

B. Planning and Direction

The Planning and Direction phase of the Threat Intelligence Life Cycle is composed of all activities that identify information requirements and ensure requirements are met.

2. With proper guidance, a(n) ___________ allows leaders to take initiative in the planning, training, and execution of their missions.

D. Decentralized Command

With proper guidance, a Decentralized Command allows leaders to take initiative in the planning, training, and execution of their missions.

3. Select the best choice below for the following definition: *"Measurable values that provide metrics to gauge how well a specific function is achieving its objectives."*

C. Key Performance Indicators

Key Performance Indicators are measurable values that provide metrics to gauge how well a specific function is achieving its objectives.

4. ___________ is the idea that each organization has a focal point of strength and capability that is possessed and being utilized.

C. Center of Gravity

Center of Gravity is the idea that each organization has a focal point of strength and capability that is possessed and being utilized.

5. In what phase of the Threat Intelligence Life Cycle will processed information be regarded as actual intelligence and mapped to correlating points for future phases?

A. Intelligence Processing

In the Intelligence Processing phase of the Threat Intelligence Life Cycle, processed information will be regarded as actual intelligence and mapped to correlating points for future phases.

6. Organizations must change their __________ in order to survive conflict and adapt to opponents that do not follow conventional rules.

B. Tactics

Organizations must change their tactics in order to survive conflict and adapt to opponents that do not follow conventional rules.

7. What phase of the Threat Intelligence Life Cycle acquires and provisions information to be handed over to the Processing and Production phases?

D. Intelligence Collection

The Intelligence Collection phase of the Threat Intelligence Life Cycle acquires and provisions information to be handed over to the Processing and Production phases.

8. __________ is achieved through understanding the capabilities within an organization and training to address different relevant scenarios.

A. Flexibility

Flexibility is achieved through understanding the capabilities within an organization and training to address different relevant scenarios.

9. What phase of the Threat Intelligence Life Cycle analyzes, evaluates, interprets, and integrates raw intelligence into finished intelligence products?

C. Analysis and Production

The Analysis and Production phase of the Threat Intelligence Life Cycle analyzes, evaluates, interprets, and integrates raw intelligence into finished intelligence products.

10. To have an intelligence capability, a process must be developed to take ___________ and produce a product that can be used for action.

D. Raw Information

To have an intelligence capability, a process must be developed to take raw information and produce a product that can be used for action.

11. What phase of the Threat Intelligence Life Cycle portrays an accurate picture of the threat to leadership in a form that facilitates rapid understanding of the issue?

B. Intelligence Dissemination

The Intelligence Dissemination phase of the Threat Intelligence Life Cycle portrays an accurate picture of the threat to leadership in a form that facilitates rapid understanding of the issue.

12. The role of ___________ in cyberattacks that involve hacking and data theft has gained substantial attention over the last two decades.

C. Nation-States

The role of nation-states in cyberattacks that involve hacking and data theft has gained substantial attention over the last two decades.

13. Nation-state actors may work individually or complete attacks with a wide network of participants and then disband rapidly.

2. False

Non-nation-state actors may work individually or complete attacks with a wide network of participants and then disband rapidly.

14. For threat intelligence programs to have the highest probability of a successful outcome, sources must be known and tailored to the need.

1. True

15. Virtualization involves the modification of technology in order to allow it to be used in unintended ways for both legal and illegal purposes.

2. False

Hacking involves the modification of technology in order to allow it to be used in unintended ways for both legal and illegal purposes.

16. Although most industrialized nations have criminalized various forms of trespass and fraud, there is limited parity in the language of statutes.

1. True

17. Ideas become industry standards when they are physical and tangible works that may be accessed and viewed by others.

2. False

Ideas become Intellectual Property when they are physical and tangible works that may be accessed and viewed by others.

18. The organization or adversary who has the most advantage is the one who can cycle through the *OODA Loop* the fastest.

1. True

Domain 14: Knowledge Assessment Answer Key

1. Which component of the datacenter will include the facility campus, all physical components, and the services that support them?

B. Physical Plant

The physical plant will include the facility campus, all physical components, and the services that support them.

2. In the __________ model, the cloud service provider contracts access to its infrastructure and is fully responsible for administration.

D. Infrastructure as a Service

In the infrastructure as a Service model, the cloud service provider contracts access to its infrastructure and is fully responsible for administration.

3. Which choice below is a cloud configuration in which resources are allocated, shared, and dispersed among affinity groups?

C. Community

A community cloud is a configuration in which resources are allocated, shared, and dispersed among affinity groups.

4. __________ clouds are owned and operated by individual organizations for the specific use of their staff, customers, and vendors.

C. Private

Private clouds are owned and operated by individual organizations for the specific use of their staff, customers, and vendors.

5. Like its legacy environment counterpart, cloud computing solutions have a significant dependency on __________ to operate.

B. Encryption

Like its legacy environment counterpart, cloud computing solutions have a significant dependency on encryption to operate.

6. Which choice below is a cloud model that not only includes all threats associated with private clouds but includes threats totally outside the customers' control?

D. Public

The public cloud is a model that not only includes all threats associated with private clouds but includes threats totally outside the customers' control.

7. Which choice below is an example of obfuscation, masking, and anonymization a customer may choose to implement in a cloud environment?

A. Randomization

Randomization is an example of obfuscation, masking, and anonymization a customer may choose to implement in a cloud environment.

8. A(n) ___________ monitoring solution will examine data leaving the production environment and react based on preestablished rules and parameters.

A. Egress

An egress monitoring solution will examine data leaving the production environment and react based on preestablished rules and parameters.

9. Which choice below is a model in which the cloud provider offers customers the IaaS capability and provides the operating systems as well?

B. Platform as a Service

Platform as a Service is a model in which the cloud provider offers customers the IaaS capability and provides the operating systems as well.

10. In a __________ cloud configuration, a company offers cloud services to any entity wanting to become a cloud customer.

D. Public

In a public cloud configuration, a company offers cloud services to any entity wanting to become a cloud customer.

11. Which choice below is a characteristic of all cloud computing models that is required to meet the cloud computing definition?

C. Measured Service

Measured service is a characteristic of all cloud computing models that is required to meet the cloud computing definition.

12. __________ clouds contain elements of public, private, and community cloud models to varying degrees based on customer needs.

C. Hybrid

Hybrid clouds contain elements of public, private, and community cloud models to varying degrees based on customer needs.

13. Cloud services are typically offered in three standard models based on the providers' capability and the customers' needs.

1. True

14. The cloud provider must apply the proper security controls according to a customers' relevant operational capacity and available budget.

2. False

The cloud provider must apply the proper security controls according to a customers' relevant regulatory frameworks and planned usage.

15. When discussing cloud serve providers and cloud capabilities, the private cloud tends to be the solution to which is being referred.

2. False

When discussing cloud serve providers and cloud capabilities, the public cloud tends to be the solution to which is being referred.

16. Many potential threats posed by virtualization require attenuation via the use of controls that can only be implemented by the provider.

1. True

17. Private clouds are owned and operated by individual organizations for the specific use of their staff, customers, and vendors.

1. True

18. Vendor lock-in can be caused when the provider goes out of business, is acquired by another interest, or ceases operation for any reason.

2. False

Vendor lock-out can be caused when the provider goes out of business, is acquired by another interest, or ceases operation for any reason.

Domain 15: Knowledge Assessment Answer Key

1. Which choice below is a potential benefit from achieving post-settlement settlements during the contract negotiation process?

D. Increase Mutual Trust

Increased mutual trust is a potential benefit from achieving post-settlement settlements during the contract negotiation process.

2. In negotiation, include a __________ in your contract—a guarantee that one side can match any offer that the other side later receives.

B. Matching Right

In negotiation, include a matching right in your contract—a guarantee that one side can match any offer that the other side later receives.

3. Which choice below is a reason to have a legal contract between all parties in any type of business relationship?

A. Uncover Mismatched Expectations

A legal contract will uncover mismatched expectations in any type of business relationship.

4. Most __________ arise from contracts that are not clear, complete, and that do not express the agreement as it was understood by the parties.

C. Lawsuits

Most lawsuits arise from contracts that are not clear, complete, and that do not express the agreement as it was understood by the parties.

5. Which choice below is a reason to seek the best option instead of fairness when parties negotiate any type of business contract?

B. Guiding Principle is Leverage

Seeking the best options in a legal contract is based on the guiding principle of leverage, not fairness.

6. __________ include a set of terms usually placed at the end of a contract and used for introductory material as well.

D. Boilerplate Clauses

The Boilerplate Clauses include a set of terms usually placed at the end of a contract and used for introductory material as well.

7. Which choice below is an example of a topic that may be covered in the *Prime Clauses* section of a legal contract between parties?

C. Change Order Procedures

A change order procedure is an example of a topic that may be covered in the Prime Clauses section of a legal contract between parties.

8. Customers should protect themselves against __________ and ensure that all promises address the expectation of help needed.

A. Unclear Descriptions

Customers should protect themselves against unclear descriptions and ensure that all promises address the expectation of help needed.

9. Which choice below is an example of a topic that may be covered in the *General Clauses* section of a legal contract between parties?

D. Delivery, Acceptance, and Rejection

Delivery, acceptance, and rejection are examples of topics that may be covered in the *General Clauses* section of a legal contract between parties.

10. The best way to avoid arguments in a business relationship is to __________ the expectations of the parties ahead of time.

B. Write Down

The best way to avoid arguments in a business relationship is to write down the expectations of the parties' ahead of time.

11. Which choice below is an example of a topic that may be covered in the *Boilerplate Clauses* section of a legal contract between parties?

A. Introductions and Recitals

Introductions and Recitals are examples of topics that may be covered in the *Boilerplate Clauses* section of a legal contract between parties.

12. When formulating the __________ contract you can, and should, specify what will happen if one of the parties violates the contract.

C. Initial

When formulating the initial contract you can, and should, specify what will happen if one of the parties violates the contract.

13. Information Technology contracts can be organized into three groups: *capacity*, *mutuality of obligation*, and *acceptance*.

2. False

Information Technology contracts can be organized into three groups: *prime clauses*, *general clauses*, and *boilerplate clauses*.

14. The term "General Clauses" is a catch-all category that refers to issues not addressed in a primary or boilerplate clause.

1. True

15. In negotiation, parties often reach impasse because they have different beliefs about the likelihood of winning the case.

2. False

In negotiation, parties often reach impasse because they have different beliefs about the likelihood of future events.

16. When reviewing contracts and service level agreements, consider the use of checklists to help ensure a consistent approach.

1. True

17. You cannot predict what issues may arise in a business relationship, so you cannot know when *Primary Clauses* will become vital.

2. False

You cannot predict what issues may arise in a business relationship, so you cannot know when *Boilerplate Clauses* will become vital.

18. The one characteristic shared by all elements of *General Clauses* is that they generate the most disagreement, debate, and compromise.

1. True

Domain 16: Knowledge Assessment Answer Key

1. Which choice below is a potential benefit for Incident Response Teams when implementing a SOAR solution?

A. Enhanced Response with Threat Intelligence

One of the potential benefits for Incident Response Teams when implementing a SOAR solution is the ability to enhance their response using threat intelligence.

2. A(n) __________ is a set of rules, describing at least one action to be executed with data and triggered by one or more events.

D. Incident Response Playbook

An Incident Response Playbook is a set of rules, describing at least one action to be executed with data and triggered by one or more events.

3. Which choice below is **not** a characteristic of simulated attack exercises that should be considered when creating testing scenarios?

D. Least Resource-Intensive Method

A characteristic of simulated attack exercises that should be considered when creating testing scenarios is that they are the most resource-intensive method of testing.

4. Organizations __________ incident response capabilities to determine the effectiveness of the processes and to identify potential weaknesses or deficiencies.

C. Test

Organizations test incident response capabilities to determine the effectiveness of the processes and to identify potential weaknesses or deficiencies.

5. Which choice below is a likely scenario that an Incident Response Team should consider including in the response playbook?

C. Unauthorized Access

Unauthorized access is a likely scenario that an Incident Response Team should consider including in the response playbook.

6. Review the response playbook __________, make required updates and adjustments accordingly, and schedule annual tests to identify any existing gaps.

B. Quarterly

Review the response playbook quarterly, make required updates and adjustments accordingly, and schedule annual tests to identify any existing gaps.

7. Which choice below is **not** a characteristic that should be considered when creating an incident response playbook?

B. Highly Detailed but Very Structured

A characteristic that should be considered when creating an incident response playbook is that while they are highly detailed they must also be very flexible.

8. __________ exercises will generally take the form of a discussion-based exercise and reviews roles, responsibilities, and response efforts.

A. Table-Top

Table-top exercises will generally take the form of a discussion-based exercise and reviews roles, responsibilities, and response efforts.

9. Which choice below is an important component of an incident response playbook that should be included in all scenarios?

A. Process Steps

Process steps are an important component of an incident response playbook that should be included in all scenarios.

10. A __________ exercise is the most effective way of testing the response processes as it uses real, controlled attacks to measure outcomes.

D. Simulated Attack

A simulated attack exercise is the most effective way of testing the response processes as it uses real, controlled attacks to measure outcomes.

11. Which choice below is a characteristic of table-top exercises that should be considered when creating testing scenarios?

D. Least Resource-Intensive Method

A characteristic of table-top exercises that should be considered when creating testing scenarios is that it is the least resource-intensive method of testing.

12. __________ allows an organizations' Incident Response Team to collect data about threats and respond without human assistance.

C. Security Orchestration, Automation, and Response

Security Orchestration, Automation and Response (SOAR) allows an organizations' Incident Response Team to collect data about threats and respond without human assistance.

13. A simulated attack is the most effective way of testing the response processes as it uses real, controlled attacks to measure outcomes.

1. True

outcomes.

14. Table-Top Exercises generally take the form of an event-based exercise and assigns roles, responsibilities, and response efforts.

2. False

Table-Top Exercises generally take the form of a discussion-based exercise and reviews roles, responsibilities, and response efforts.

15. Organizations test response capabilities to determine the effectiveness of the processes and to identify potential weaknesses or deficiencies.

1. True

16. The majority of organizations frequently evaluate or test response capabilities to determine if the processes will satisfy the desired end state outcomes.

2. False

Many organizations never evaluate or test response capabilities to determine if the processes will satisfy the desired end state outcomes.

17. Review the response playbook annually, making updates and adjustments accordingly, and schedule monthly tests to identify any existing gaps.

2. False

Review the response playbook quarterly, making updates and adjustments accordingly, and schedule annual tests to identify any existing gaps.

18. An Incident Response Playbook is a set of rules, describing at least one action to be executed with data and triggered by one or more events.

1. True

C)CSOM Certification Exam Voucher

For more information regarding the purchase of exam vouchers and scheduling your exam in the Technical College System of Georgia LMS, please contact our office by phone or email.

OFFICE:

912.335.2217

EMAIL:

michael.kaplan@phase2advantage.com

PHASE2

ADVANTAGE

The Future of Immersive Cybersecurity Education

www.phase2advantage.com

C)CSOM Certification Exam Voucher

For more information regarding the purchase of exam vouchers and scheduling your exam in the Technical College System of Georgia LMS, please contact our office by phone or email.

OFFICE:

912.335.2217

EMAIL:

michael.kaplan@phase2advantage.com

PHASE2 ADVANTAGE

The Future of Immersive Cybersecurity Education

www.phase2advantage.com

www.ingramcontent.com/pod-product-compliance
Lightning Source LLC
LaVergne TN
LVHW052225200926
848481LV00001B/213

* 9 7 8 1 7 3 4 0 6 4 0 5 6 *